KNIT
FOLD
PLEAT
REPEAT

# KNIT FOLD PLEAT REPEAT

## Simple Knits, Gorgeous Garments

### NORAH GAUGHAN

Abrams, New York

# CONTENTS

6
Introduction

CHAPTER 1
## Concepts

**The Chapters** 10
**General Philosophies** 11

CHAPTER 2
## Square Up

Garments and accessories made
from squares and rectangles

**Kerchief I** 15

**Kerchief II** 19

**Weave** 23

**Eitherway** 27

**Rib Jacket** 33

**Trio** 39

**Impatiens** 43

**Blouse** 47

## CHAPTER 3
# Manipulate

Flat surfaces are magically transformed with repetitive stitchwork

**Folded Headband** 55

**Floret** 59

**Multiflora** 63

**Smocked** 67

**Hussar** 71

**Pinion** 77

**Longitude** 81

## CHAPTER 4
# Multiply

Multiple squares, rectangles, or folded shapes joined to create unique surfaces

**Patch** 87

**Kite** 95

**Forty-Five°** 101

**Pyramid** 107

**Polly** 111

**Facet** 117

**Octagram** 123

## CHAPTER 5
# Hone

The addition of shaping refines the fit

**Dickey** 129

**Centrale** 133

**Lotus** 139

**Afloat** 145

**Tilt** 153

**Outward** 159

**Ladder** 167

## CHAPTER 6
# Hybrid

Folds, tucks, and rectangular inserts enhance traditional shapes

**Skyward** 175

**Anne²** 181

**Ruche** 187

**Waterfall** 193

**Georgia** 201

**Jabot** 209

**Squash** 215

220
Abbreviations

221
Special Techniques

222
Resources

223
Acknowledgments

Introduction

**AFTER A FEW DECADES** of designing primarily traditionally shaped garments—pullovers with a front, a back, and a pair of sleeves, or cardigans with two fronts, a back, and a pair of sleeves—I found myself becoming increasingly interested in building garments in other ways. While still covering the body, and needing to accommodate the head and arms, a sweater can be shaped from a single rectangle, or folded from a few simple shapes, or composed of multiple geometric shapes joined together.

Have you ever had the experience of becoming aware of an idea and immediately starting to see similar ideas everywhere you looked? Almost the minute I became interested in alternative constructions, I noticed many fashion designers were exploring similar concepts. I began taking note of those who were on a like-minded journey, as well as those who had designed such garments centuries earlier. These were not just knitwear designers: Many of the folks I admired were sewing dresses, jackets, or even skirts. Still, the concepts applied. As always, I collected magazine clippings and saved ideas digitally. Each had the potential to seed a new design idea. Garments from museums and those seen on the runway were of equal interest. I realized that the basics of designing with folded fabric began when garment making first began, and seemed to resurface in fashion every few years, starting in the 1920s.

When exploring garments made out of basic shapes like squares and rectangles, naturally, the idea of origami as inspiration came to mind. I ruminated on this book idea for a while.

Would the designs be made from rectangles alone? Over time the scope and parameters began to expand. Not only can rectangles make interesting and useful sweaters, the surfaces of knit rectangles can be manipulated. Woven fabric can be transformed with pleats, tucks, and smocking—why not knit fabric? Loosening the grip on my original "rectangles only" concept, I let in the idea of working with polygonal shapes like pentagons, hexagons, and octagons. When paper is being prepared for its final folding in traditional Japanese origami, the surface becomes adorned with interesting and beautiful fold lines. The polygon and fold line ideas seemed to intersect naturally: Repeating patterns on a hexagon looked very much like the lines left on paper after folding and unfolding. Why not include fold lines in the book also? Studying the photos I had gathered, there were many that applied folds and pleats to otherwise conventional garments. Eventually, I knew that I would want to introduce some conventional shaping in the later chapters, which led to applying folded elements to more typical sweater shapes and constructions.

As I obsessively collected inspirations over a decade or so, I grew some of the seeds of thought into designs for magazines and yarn companies. As I explored and learned, more new ideas sprang up, and I learned a lot about how to make these ideas easier to knit and easier to design. For those who wonder if it is possible to run out of ideas, I believe that the answer is no. The more you explore, the more notions spring to mind.

# CHAPTER 1

# CONCEPTS

## THE CHAPTERS

The designs in this book begin with the simplest and, as the chapters progress, build in complexity, transitioning from basic geometric shapes to conventionally constructed garments with folded features and adornments.

### Square Up

Every garment and accessory in Square Up is composed of rectangles. Our exploration begins with a simple square, worked on the bias and transformed into an oversized kerchief with a simple slit for fastening. The complexity of the projects grows as rectangles are joined and knit onto each other to create easy-to-wear garments. Ribs and textural patterns are a joy to knit, with no worry about keeping in pattern while shaping, since there *is* no shaping. Accessories—built from rectangles and tubes—have fun with touches of color and with sections knit in their own shade. For adventurous knitters, I've included a cable challenge. While the techniques might seem daunting at first glance, you can indulge in mastering two-sided cables while knitting a shifting rectangular cowl, which can be worn in multiple ways. The final item, a pullover, is knit in one big piece with only cast-ons and bind-offs to create the sleeves and neck opening. A few pleats add beauty and shaping to the center front and sleeves, foreshadowing the surface treatments introduced in the next chapter.

### Manipulate

Items in Manipulate are also constructed entirely of rectangles. Here, the focus shifts to creating interesting sculptural surfaces, while the basic construction remains simple. Cowls, scarves, and even a pillow and headband are made more ornate with repetitive surface manipulations like smocking and pleating. These techniques are infinitely easier with the addition of knit-in guide stitches and guidelines. For instance, strategically placed purls make smocking a breeze—it's easy to know where to thread the smocking yarn without any fussy measuring. Rows of garter stitch show where to place the running stitch needed to

hold down pleats, so even the sewing-averse need not fear, while vertical folds are aided by columns of reverse stockinette, which both mark the fold and make it turn more precisely. This section features mostly accessories, with one cardigan, again rectangular, knit sideways, center to cuff. Its scarf-like collar is adorned with bias tucks, knit as you go, creating a dramatic facade, while the rest of the knitting is easy and meditative.

### Multiply

Keeping to the theme of knitting with geometric shapes only, Multiply piles numerous squares upon each other with polygons added to the mix. Knit one onto the next for clearly defined building blocks that either create the final piece or are joined into otherwise plain rectangular garments. I've included a different take on the theme of folding: a collection of polygons (pentagons, hexagons and octagons) echoing the look of origami patterns that were folded, then unfolded, leaving radiating and crisscrossing fold lines. Further developing the theme of multiples is an unusual and versatile scarf constructed with a matrix of mitered squares. I added dimension by working extra rows in each mitered square, transforming them into pyramids.

### Hone

The design philosophy starts to shift in Hone, with rectangular constructions refined using traditional sweater shaping. Decreases creating the shoulder slope produce a more precise fit in an otherwise rectangular dickey. A yoke is shaped with short rows, transforming a very large rectangle into a sophisticated skirt. A few sloped bind-offs create angles that open up the neckline of a folded garment, and the addition of standard raglan sleeves to garments constructed of folded shapes and rectangles makes them more understandable and more wearable when the drama of the folds is the major focus. For the adventurous, a long rectangle is tilted to form an asymmetrical poncho, the with extraneous corners removed with increases and decreases.

## Hybrid

Hybrid flips the story. In the previous chapters, ideas for garments and accessories all began as rectangles. Shaping and adornments were added only as refinements. Conversely, each piece in Hybrid begins as a garment with traditional shaping and, later, rectangular and folded elements are added to the conventional base. A single fold transforms one simple tank into a striking top with dramatic cascades at the hem. A 1940s-inspired Queen Anne neckline is created by adding a slit and pleats to a dolman cap-sleeved silhouette. Extra length and a special method of picking up stitches create ruching, making the sleeves a focal point. Perhaps my favorite additions, rectangular and square inserts magically transform ordinary shapes to powerful ones, whether inserted into the center front of a pullover or added to a sleeve opening. Veering from the square theme a bit, semicircular flounces flood down the front of a triangular poncho in amazing folds.

## Design Your Own

Each pattern is followed by Design Your Own, which has two sub-sections: One describes how I set about designing that garment or accessory, and the other provides general design principles or techniques. Many of the stories about my design processes for individual garments contain confessions about how I went wrong. Who gets things right the first time? Not me. Some of the information will undoubtedly be intuitively obvious to seasoned designers and may be more helpful to newbies. My hope is that everyone will pick up a little something they hadn't thought about previously. My intent in both of these sections is to give you a peek into my brain, a glimpse of my thoughts as I designed these garments. Different people's brains work differently, and everyone approaches designing from different angles, according to their own knowledge and experience. My method is far from being the only way or the "right" way to approach the given design puzzle. It's just the way I went about it (this time). These musings are not meant to be a detailed how-to textbook. Instead, my goal is to get you thinking in new ways. Some methods may suit you and some may not, but I do hope you enjoy the glimpse into my thought process.

# General Philosophies

### KEEP IT EASY

Despite rarely knitting in the round, I chose techniques and constructions that greatly reduced sewn seams. Pieces are often knit onto each other instead of being sewn. Three-needle bind-off is used to join pieces at the shoulder or center collar. In an effort to keep the designs accessible to knitting without extensive experience, I avoided the use of techniques that I thought to be knitting gymnastics, such as attaching pieces to one another at the end of rows. While I did use that very technique for the Octagram pillow (page 123), I deemed it too complicated for the cardigan built from multiple squares, Patch (page 87). The knitting stitches are mostly basic—a lot of stockinette and easy textures such as garter, moss, and rib. A few more interesting texture stitches are thrown in the mix (but no shaping is involved), and I couldn't resist adding a few cables, because I am me.

### CHARTS

I am a chart person. Others prefer to follow the written word. In this book there are only a few patterns with charts, and those patterns includes both written-out instructions and charts.

### SIZES

Wanting my patterns to be knit, worn, and enjoyed by the widest audience possible, I have ensured that almost every garment in this book is sized to fit chest circumferences from 30 to 60 inches (76 to 152 cm). In a very few cases, the odd geometry of the design meant that the garment wouldn't work in the smallest and largest sizes. Take care to look at the schematic for your size before knitting a garment to make sure the proportions will work for you.

CHAPTER 2

# SQUARE UP

Sometimes a square or other rectangle is all you need.
These pieces have no shaping—only a slit or two made
by binding off and casting on again on the next row,
to make a handy opening or create a simple lapel.
Attach a few odd rectangles to each other and three-
dimensional forms might just begin to appear.

# Kerchief I

Shown as a folded, shoulder-warming shawl, Kerchief I is a simple arter stitch square, knit on the diagonal. Unabashedly, the pattern is an oversized version of a time-honored dishcloth pattern familiar to many, with one major addition: The small slit a few inches from one corner means that, once folded, you can insert the opposite corner though the opening and the piece will stay on your shoulders. A small snap on the outer edge near the slit helps keep everything at the desired angle. Opened up, the shawl becomes a square lap blanket, perfect for travel or for nursing a wee one (and you don't have to carry it in your bag).

## FINISHED MEASUREMENTS
30¼" (77 cm) square

## YARN
Fingering weight yarn [approximately 438 yards (400 m)/3½ ounces (100 g)]: approximately 4 skeins/1,600 yards (1,465 m) in one or more color(s) that work well together

*Note: Since sock yarn colorways are introduced and discontinued very quickly, you are unlikely to find the exact colorways shown here. I used an unidentified skein from my stash along with some skeins I picked up in my travels. One yarn is from Australia, while the one with Stellina is something I couldn't resist buying online. If you prefer more consistent color, consider using only one color or alternating between two colorways instead of three.*

Shown in:

Unidentified merino wool sock yarn from my stash: 1 skein mostly cream with streaks of green, wine, and pink

Augustbird Fantail White Gum Wool Sock [80% merino wool/20% nylon; 516 yards (472 m)/3½ ounces (100 g)]: 1 skein color Baby Fairy Wren

Dandelions & Daisies Fiber Arts Firefly Stellina Sock [75% merino/20% nylon/5% Stellina; 463 yards (423 m)/3½ ounces (100 g)]: 2 skeins color Degas

## NEEDLES
One 24" (60 cm) or longer circular needle size US 2 (2.75 mm)

Change needle size if necessary to obtain correct gauge.

## NOTIONS
One clear snap, ⁷⁄₁₆" (1.11 cm) diameter

## GAUGE
28 sts and 56 rows = 4" (10 cm) in garter stitch (knit every row), after blocking

## PATTERN NOTES

Kerchief is worked from corner to corner. A slit worked in the side corner holds the piece together when worn, and the single snap helps the kerchief maintain its shape. Unsnapped, the kerchief transforms into a small blanket, perfect for travel.

## KERCHIEF

Using color of choice and Long-Tail Cast-On (see Special Techniques, page 221), CO 2 sts.
Knit 1 row.

## INCREASE SECTION

**Row 1 (RS):** Change to second color of choice. K1, yo, k1—3 sts.
**Row 2:** K1, k1-tbl, k1.
Continue alternating colors every 2 rows, knitting the first st of every color change row with both colors held together.
**Row 3:** K1, [yo, k1] twice—5 sts.
**Row 4:** K1, [k1-tbl, k1] twice.
**Row 5:** K2, yo, k1, yo, k2—7 sts.
**Row 6:** K2, k1-tbl, k1, k1-tbl, k2.
**Row 7:** K3, yo, k1, yo, k3—9 sts.
**Row 8:** K3, knit to end.
**Row 9:** K3, [yo, k3] twice—11 sts.
**Row 10:** K3, knit to end.
**Row 11:** K3, yo, knit to last 3 sts, yo, k3—2 sts increased.
**Row 12:** Knit.
**Rows 13–298:** Repeat Rows 11 and 12, 143 more times—299 sts.

*Note: Join another skein of yarn in color of your choice, as desired. You will have 146 open yos along each side; do not count the yos that were knit tbl.*

## CENTER SECTION

**Rows 299 (RS) and 300:** Knit.

**Row 301:** Knit to last 58 sts, BO next 16 sts, knit to end.

**Row 302:** Knit to BO sts; using Cable Cast-On (see Special Techniques, page 221), CO 16 sts, knit to end.

## DECREASE SECTION

**Row 303 (RS):** K3, yo, [k2tog] twice, knit to last 7 sts, [ssk] twice, yo, k3—2 sts decreased.

**Row 304:** Knit.

**Rows 305–588:** Repeat Rows 303 and 304, 142 more times—13 sts remain.

**Row 589:** K3, yo, k2tog, s2kp2, ssk, yo, k3—11 sts remain.

**Row 590:** Knit.

**Row 591:** K3, yo, s3k2p3, yo, k3—9 sts remain.

**Row 592:** Knit.

**Row 593:** K3, s2kp2, k3—7 sts remain.

**Row 594:** Knit.

**Row 595:** K2, s2kp2, k2—5 sts remain.

**Row 596:** Knit.

**Row 597:** K1, s2kp2, k1—3 sts remain.

**Row 598:** Knit.

**Row 599:** S2kp2—1 st remains. Fasten off.

## FINISHING

Steam or wet-block to measurements. Sew both halves of snap to corner with slit, each approximately 5" (12.5 cm) in from point, and ½" (12 mm) in from each side edge.

# DESIGN YOUR OWN

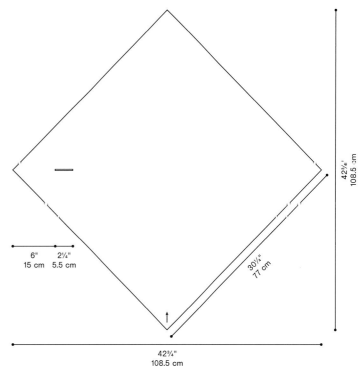

6" / 15 cm   2¼" / 5.5 cm

30¼" / 77 cm

42¾" / 108.5 cm

42¾" / 108.5 cm

## DESIGNING KERCHIEF I

As is sometimes the case, an existing ready-to-wear garment provided the seed of this design. The one I saw in a picture was cut and sewn and I couldn't see the detail, but I loved how the piece sat up on the model's shoulders in sculptural stiffness. I suspected that two layers of fabric might achieve the effect I wanted. Folding the backs of a few sweaters in half showed me that the fabric seemed about right.

Now I knew I would fold a square in half to become a triangle. The least intuitive part, the question that remained, was deciding on the size of the triangle (and square).This is where a fleece model came in handy. I found a piece of fleece that roughly represented the drape I thought I would achieve by knitting. Taking my best guess, I cut a square of

fleece and folded in into a triangle and tried it on. A few tries later and I had it right.

Note: start larger rather than smaller, because it's easy to reduce the size of the piece and much harder to add on. In a later chapter (see page 151), I talk more about making fleece models to test more complicated ideas.

## ALL SQUARES ARE RECTANGLES

Why has the phrase stuck so firmly in my head all these years? In elementary school I was taught that squares are rectangles, but not all rectangles are squares. A square is a rectangle with four equal sides. So what about these squares and other rectangles, which are so easy to knit? What else can they do for us?

Start by thinking of some rectangles so ubiquitous we take them for granted: scarves, stoles, and blankets come to mind. What happens when the ends of these rectangles are joined? The resulting cylinders become cowls, headbands, shoulder warmers, gauntlets, bandeaus, and maybe even skirts. What if you twist the rectangle before the ends are joined? Then we have a mobius strip, which also can be a lovely cowl, shoulder warmer, or headband, plus a thousand things I haven't thought of—but maybe you will.

# Kerchief II

I so enjoyed knitting the first kerchief (page 15) and using the resulting blanket/shoulder wrap that I couldn't resist designing a second version. Kerchief II is knit in a heavier gauge and uses moss stitch as the body while the edges remain knit in garter and eyelet stitches.

**FINISHED MEASUREMENTS**
33½" (85 cm) square

**YARN**
Brooklyn Tweed Shelter [100% American Targhee-Columbia wool; 140 yards (128 m)/1¾ ounces (50 g)]: 6 skeins Pentgord

*Note: Cowl uses nearly all of the sixth skein; you may wish to purchase an additional skein due to variations in individual gauge.*

**NEEDLES**
One 24" (60 cm) or longer circular needle, size US 8 (5 mm)

Change needle size if necessary to obtain correct gauge.

**NOTIONS**
One clear snap, ⁷⁄₁₆" (1.11 cm) diameter

**GAUGE**
16 sts and 30 rows = 4" (10 cm) in Moss Stitch, after blocking

## PATTERN STITCH

### MOSS STITCH
(odd number of sts; 4-row repeat)
**Row 1 (RS):** *K1, p1; repeat from * to last st, k1.
**Row 2:** Purl the knit sts and knit the purl sts as they face you.
**Row 3:** Knit the knit sts and purl the purl sts as they face you.
**Row 4:** Repeat Row 2.
Repeat Rows 1–4 for pattern.

## PATTERN NOTES

Kerchief is worked from corner to corner. A slit worked in one of the side corners holds the piece together when worn, and a single snap helps the kerchief maintain its shape. Unsnapped, the kerchief transforms into a small blanket, perfect for travel.

## KERCHIEF

Using Long-Tail Cast-On (see Special Techniques, page 221), CO 2 sts.
Knit 1 row.

## INCREASE SECTION

**Row 1 (RS):** K1, yo, k1–3 sts.
**Row 2:** K1, k1-tbl, k1.
**Row 3:** K1, [yo, k1] twice–5 sts.
**Row 4:** K1, [k1-tbl, k1] twice.
**Row 5:** K2, yo, k1, yo, k2–7 sts.
**Row 6:** K2, k1-tbl, k1, k1-tbl, k2.
**Row 7:** K3, yo, k1, yo, k3–9 sts.
**Row 8:** K3, p1, k1, p1, k3.
**Row 9:** K3, yo, k1, p1, k1, yo, k3–11 sts.
**Row 10:** K3, [p1, k1] twice, p1, k3.
**Row 11:** K3, yo, work Row 1 of Moss Stitch to last 3 sts, yo, k3–2 sts increased.
**Row 12:** K3, work Row 2 of Moss Stitch to last 3 sts, k3.
Continue working first and last 3 sts in garter st (knit every row), and remaining sts in four-row Moss Stitch patt as established.
**Rows 13–176:** Repeat Rows 11 and 12, 82 more times–177 sts.
*Note: You will have 85 open yos along each side; do not count the yos that were knit tbl.*

## CENTER SECTION

**Rows 177 (RS) and 178:** K3, work in Moss Stitch as established to last 3 sts, k3.
**Row 179:** K3, work to last 34 sts, BO next 10 sts in pattern, work to last 3 sts, k3.
**Row 180:** K3, work to BO sts; using Cable Cast-On (see Special Techniques, page 000), CO 10 sts, work to last 3 sts, k3.

## DECREASE SECTION

**Row 181 (RS):** K3, yo, k3tog, work in Moss Stitch as established to last 6 sts, sssk, yo, k3–175 sts remain.
**Row 182:** K3, work to last 3 sts, k3.
**Rows 183–344:** Repeat Rows 181 and 182, 81 more times–13 sts remain.
**Row 345:** K3, yo, k3tog, p1, sssk, yo, k3–11 sts remain.
**Row 346:** K3, work to last 3 sts, k3.
**Row 347:** K3, yo, s3k2p3, yo, k3–9 sts remain.
**Row 348:** K3, p1, k1, p1, k3.
**Row 349:** K3, s2kp2, k3–7 sts remain.
**Row 350:** Knit.
**Row 351:** K2, s2kp2, k2–5 sts remain.
**Row 352:** Knit.
**Row 353:** K1, s2kp2, k1–3 sts remain.
**Row 354:** Knit.
**Row 355:** S2kp2–1 st remains. Fasten off.

## FINISHING

Soak in lukewarm water for 30 minutes, allowing fabric to become completely saturated. Remove from water and carefully squeeze out water; do not wring fabric. Roll up in bath towel and press firmly to remove more moisture, changing towels a few times if necessary.
Unroll piece and pin to measurements on a blocking board; allow to air-dry completely.
Sew both halves of snap to corner with slit, each approximately 5" (12.5 cm) in from point, and ½" (12 mm) in from each side edge.

# DESIGN YOUR OWN

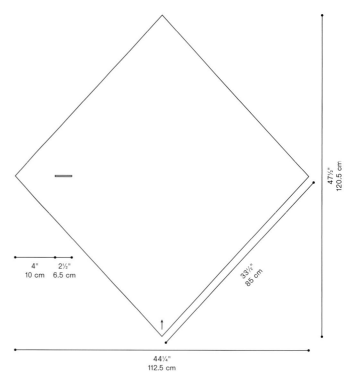

4" — 10 cm  
2½" — 6.5 cm  
47½" — 120.5 cm  
33½" — 85 cm  
44¼" — 112.5 cm

## DESIGNING KERCHIEF II

Kerchief I (page 15) was the basis for this variation, so I knew what size the square should be and where the slash needed to be placed. Next, a little playing around with the pattern stitch was in order. As simple as moss stitch sounds, I discovered, after a few false starts, that keeping in pattern and easily keeping the yarn overs a consistent size was much easier if the first row of moss was set up on a wrong-side row. Normally, I would start moss stitch on a right-side row, as I would almost every pattern stitch, to make it easy to remember. However, here, starting the moss stitch on a wrong-side row means that at each end, the increasing yarn overs are both followed by a knit stitch, keeping them a consistent size. More importantly, these yarn overs are more easily worked in moss stitch if they are followed by a knit stitch.

## THE TRANSFORMING SLASH

I don't believe I've given much thought to slashes before. However, now that I am considering them, and now that I am wondering how much a square can do, I see how slashes can be very useful. I'm talking about the kind of slash that makes a hole, most easily made by binding off on one row and replacing those stitches by casting on over the bound-off stitches as the next row is worked. Alternatively, you can make a vertical slash by adding a new ball of yarn, working with both balls for the length of the slit, and then rejoining the sides to form a solid fabric again.

1. Hold it together: Adding a slash can help hold a piece together, like in the Kerchiefs. An unruly scarf becomes a scarf that stays on. A slash or two can also make room for a belt. Have you tried belts that go under a garment in the back and on top in front? For some of us, this makes belt wearing a viable option.

2. Open up possibilities: A square or rectangle becomes a poncho when you add a slash for your head. Add slashes to accommodate arms and you have a sweater or, at least, a vest. Keep thinking about what a simple slash might accomplish for you.

# Weave

When you are new to knitting and just learning to make texture stitches, the thought of adding shaping into the pattern can be no less than terrifying. That's when a cardigan made entirely out of rectangles comes to the rescue. There is no decreasing—or worse, increasing—while keeping in pattern in this cardigan. You'll get the hang of the knit/purl pattern while working the fronts and by the time they are joined to make the back, it will be your old friend. While this cardigan is worked flat, there are no shoulder seams; the sleeves are picked up and worked downward and the only seams are the two side/sleeve seams. Garter edges worked into the pattern stitch mean the pieces are what we call "self-finishing." No additional edgings are needed.

## FINISHED MEASUREMENTS
36½ (41½, 46½, 52) (57, 62, 67, 72)" [92.5 (105.5, 118, 132) (145, 157.5, 170, 183) cm] chest, with fronts overlapping ½–¾" (1.5–2 cm)

*Note: This piece is intended to be worn with approximately 7–10" (18–25.5 cm) positive ease.*

## YARN
Seacolors Yarnery [100% wool; 270 yards (247 m)/4 ounces (113 g)]: 5 (6, 7, 7) (8, 9, 9, 10) skeins Seacolors

## NEEDLES
One 24" (60 cm) or longer circular needle, size US 7 (4.5 mm)

One spare needle in any style, size US 7 (4.5 mm)

One double-pointed needle, size US 6 or 7 (4 or 4.5 mm)

Change needle size if necessary to obtain correct gauge.

## NOTIONS
Stitch markers

Removable stitch markers

## GAUGE
19 sts and 34 rows = 4" (10 cm) in Woven Pattern

## PATTERN STITCH

### WOVEN PATTERN (SEE CHART)

(multiple of 6 sts + 9; 8-row repeat)
**Row 1 (RS):** P7, *k1, p5; repeat from * to last 2 sts, p2.
**Row 2:** Purl.
**Row 3:** Repeat Row 1.
**Row 4:** Purl.
**Row 5:** P3, *k3, p3; repeat from * to end.
**Row 6:** P6, *k3, p3; repeat from * to last 3 sts, p3.
**Row 7:** Repeat Row 5.
**Row 8:** Purl.
Repeat Rows 1–8 for pattern.

## PATTERN NOTES

The Fronts of this cardigan are worked separately, from the bottom to the base of the Back neck, then the pieces are joined and the Back is worked to the bottom edge. The Sleeves are picked up from the armhole edges and worked back and forth in rows to the cuffs. The length for all pieces can be adjusted by adding or subtracting one or more 8-row pattern repeats; each 8-row repeat is approximately 1" (2.5 cm) long.

## RIGHT FRONT

Using Cable Cast-On (see Special Techniques, page 221), CO 45 (51, 57, 63) (69, 75, 81, 87) sts.
Begin Woven Pattern, working pattern from text or chart; work even until piece measures approximately 24" (61 cm) from the beginning, or to desired Front length; place removable marker at shoulder edge for end of Front. Work approximately 3" (7.5 cm) even from marker, ending with Row 8 of pattern. Cut yarn and place sts on spare needle, with needle tip at beginning of RS row; set aside.

## LEFT FRONT

Work as for Right Front. Do not cut yarn; leave sts on needle.

## BACK

**Joining Row (RS):** Using yarn attached to Left Front, work Row 1 of Woven Pattern to last 3 Left Front sts; place these 3 sts on a dpn; holding sts for Right Front in front of sts on dpn, [p2tog (1 st from dpn together with 1 st from Right Front)] 3 times; working across Right Front sts, p4, *k1, p5; repeat from * to last 2 sts, k2—87 (99, 111, 123) (135, 147, 159, 171) sts. Work even in Woven Pattern as established across all sts until piece measures approximately 21" (53.5 cm) from Joining Row [24" (61 cm) from shoulder markers] or to same length as Fronts, ending with Row 2 of pattern. BO all sts in pattern.

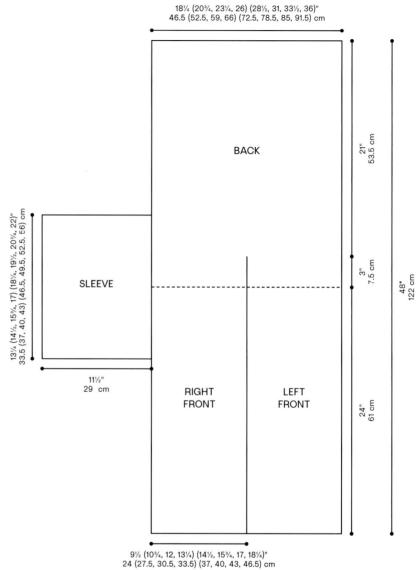

18¼ (20¾, 23¼, 26) (28½, 31, 33½, 36)"
46.5 (52.5, 59, 66) (72.5, 78.5, 85, 91.5) cm

BACK

21"
53.5 cm

3"
7.5 cm

48"
122 cm

13¼ (14½, 15¾, 17) (18¼, 19½, 20¾, 22)"
33.5 (37, 40, 43) (46.5, 49.5, 52.5, 56) cm

SLEEVE

11½"
29 cm

RIGHT
FRONT

LEFT
FRONT

24"
61 cm

9½ (10¾, 12, 13¼) (14½, 15¾, 17, 18¼)"
24 (27.5, 30.5, 33.5) (37, 40, 43, 46.5) cm

## SLEEVES

Place removable markers 7¼ (7¾, 8½,
9) (9¾, 10¼, 11, 11½)" [18.5 (19.5, 21.5, 23)
(25, 26, 28, 29) cm] down from each
shoulder marker on Fronts and Back.
*Note: The distance between the markers
is approximately 1" (2.5 cm) wider than
the top of the sleeve. This makes the
sleeve lie flat and keeps it from bulging
at the top.*
With RS facing, pick up and knit 63 (69,
75, 81) (87, 93, 99, 105) sts between
markers. Do not join; work back and forth
in rows. Purl 1 row.
Begin Woven Pattern; work even until
piece measures approximately 11½"
(29 cm) from pick-up row, or to desired
sleeve length, ending with Row 7 of
pattern. BO all sts in pattern.

## FINISHING

Block as desired.
Sew side and sleeve seams.

Woven Pattern

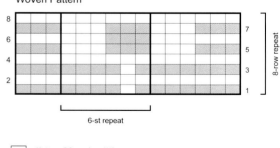

6-st repeat

8-row repeat

☐ Knit on RS, purl on WS.

▨ Purl on RS, knit on WS.

# DESIGN YOUR OWN

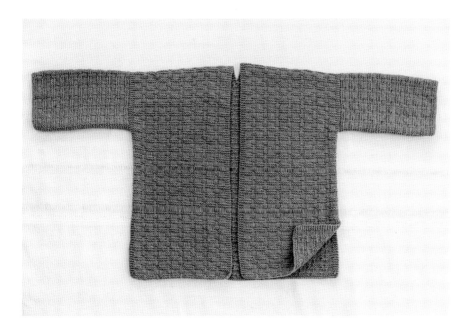

## DESIGNING WEAVE

The basic shape I wanted to work with was super simple. Two fronts, each about half the width of the back, meet a few inches past the shoulder line, which leaves room for the wearer's neck. Once joined, the piece continues straight to the bottom edge. Rectangle sleeves and a pair of seams make it a jacket or cardigan.

The number of possible proportions are endless. How wide, how fitted, how long, how short are the front and back? Are they the same? How narrow are the sleeves—how wide, long, or short? How did I decide?

Confession: I originally bought this yarn at a knitting event and I cut it close. I hadn't purchased any extra yarn for safety. I needed to calculate how much yarn the cardigan would take before I decided on the proportions. To do that, I knit up a fair-sized swatch (about 8 by 10"/20 by 25 cm) in the pattern stitch. After blocking and drying, I carefully weighed the swatch on an accurate scale, measured it carefully, and calculated the area in square inches. Dividing the square inches by the weight gave me how many grams I needed per square inch, and from there it was easy to figure out how many square inches my yarn would take me.

Now, take a deep breath. It's important to learn how to do this next part, but it is not hard. While designing, I always make a schematic, to scale, on a grid, with one square representing one inch. I like being able to see the exact proportions of the garment in the planning stages. Based on other sweaters I like, I drew out the schematic and calculated the square inches, which was simple, since every piece is a rectangle. I had to keep paring down the size of the sweater until it was clear that the sweater would take less yarn than I had. Cutting it this close made me nervous, but the fact that there is no finishing (and that the sleeves are worked last) meant I could weigh the yarn before I worked the sleeves and make sure I used half—or less—for the first sleeve.

## WEAVING TRADITIONS

The basic construction of this cardigan is nothing new, in fact, I'd say it was ancient, harkening back to the earliest woven garments. If you prepared fiber, spun it into thread, dyed the thread, and then wove it on a loom, would you even think of cutting into the resulting fabric? Cutting handwovens to shape them was not only wasteful, it also weakened the integrity of the cloth. Working with rectangles made sense to weavers throughout textile history, and we can borrow from the ingenuity of those who have made garments before us. An online search for the terms "hand woven garments" or "historical hand woven garments" will yield numerous starting points for creative exploration.

# Eitherway

Going against my rule to work complications on one side only, this cowl has a different cable pattern on each side, made oh so much easier by working with a two-chart system, where every row is read as a right-side row, from right to left. The two-sided rectangle becomes a cowl with four different looks. Not only is there a different cable on each side, but the piece can be worn in two different ways, as both cables face outward. Flipping the cowl upside down provides a change of shape. When the slit lays on the bottom, the cowl nestles down on the chest. When the slit is placed at the top, the edges fold down to make a collar-like cowl.

**FINISHED MEASUREMENTS**
10½" (26.5 cm) long x 24" (61 cm) circumference

**YARN**
Jagger Spun Green Line [100% organic merino wool; 166 yards (152 m)/ 1¾ ounces (50 g)]: 3 hanks Pebble

*Note: Cowl uses nearly all of the third skein; you may wish to purchase an additional skein due to variations in individual gauge.*

**NEEDLES**
One pair straight needles, size US 4 (3.5 mm)

One pair straight needles, size US 3 (3.25 mm)

Change needle size if necessary to obtain correct gauge.

**NOTIONS**
Removable stitch marker

**GAUGE**
24 sts and 34 rows = 4" (10 cm) in St st

One 34-st repeat of Cable Chart = 3½" (9 cm)

## SPECIAL ABBREVIATIONS

**2/2 LC (2 over 2 left cross):** Slip 2 sts to cable needle, hold to front, k2, k2 from cable needle.

**2/2 LPC (2 over 2 left purl cross):** Slip 2 sts to cable needle, hold to front, p2, k2 from cable needle.

**2/2 RC (2 over 2 right cross):** Slip 2 sts to cable needle, hold to back, k2, k2 from cable needle.

**2/2 RPC (2 over 2 right purl cross):** Slip 2 sts to cable needle, hold to back, k2, p2 from cable needle.

**LT (left twist):** Slip 1 stitch knitwise, slip a second stitch knitwise, slip both stitches back to the left-hand needle in their new orientation (just like for the beginning of ssk); knit into the back of the second stitch (approaching from the back), then knit into the back of both stitches and slip both from the needle.

**RT (right twist):** K2tog, leaving the original sts on the left-hand needle, then knit the first st only and slip both sts from needle.

## SPECIAL TECHNIQUES

**Alternating Cable Cast-On:** Make a loop (using a slipknot) with the working yarn and place it on the left-hand needle (first stitch cast on), knit into slipknot, draw up a loop but do not drop stitch from left-hand needle; place new loop on left-hand needle; *bring yarn to front, insert tip of right-hand needle from behind into space between last 2 stitches on left-hand needle and draw up a loop; place loop on left-hand needle; bring yarn to back, insert tip of right-hand needle from front into space between last 2 stitches on left-hand needle and draw up a loop.

Repeat from * for remaining stitches to be cast on.

**Tapestry Needle Bind-Off:** This bind-off is to be used with 1×1 Rib, and is a great match with the Alternating Cable Cast-On. Using a blunt tapestry needle, thread a length of yarn approximately 4 times the width of the piece to be bound off.

**Setup:** Working from right to left, insert tapestry needle into first stitch as if to purl, pull yarn through, leaving stitch on needle; insert tapestry needle from the back into second stitch as if to knit, pull yarn through, leaving stitch on needle.

**Step 1:** Insert tapestry needle into first stitch as if to knit, pull yarn through, remove stitch from needle; insert tapestry needle into front of second stitch as if to purl, pull yarn through, leaving stitch on needle.

**Step 2:** Insert tapestry needle into first stitch on needle as if to purl, pull yarn through, remove stitch from needle; insert tapestry needle from the back into second stitch as if to knit, pull yarn through, leaving stitch on needle. Repeat Steps 1 and 2 until 2 stitches remain on the needle. Insert tapestry needle into first stitch on needle as if to knit, removing stitch from needle; insert tapestry needle into first stitch on needle as if to purl, removing stitch from needle.

Thinking of the actions as two steps, instead of four, is more efficient. Plus, you are much less likely to lose your place, and it's easier to find your place when you do lose track of where you are or put down your work.

Cable Pattern – Side B

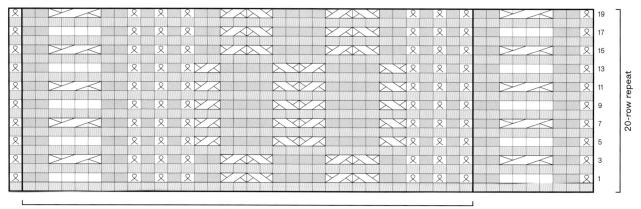

34-st repeat

20-row repeat

19 17 15 13 11 9 7 5 3 1

## PATTERN STITCH

### CABLE PATTERN (SEE CHART)

(panel of 32 sts, increasing to 34 sts; 20-row repeat)

**Setup Row (A):** P1, LT, p1, M1PR, p2, RT, *[p1, k1-tbl] twice, p1, k2, p4, k1, M1L, k2, p4, k2, p1, [k1-tbl, p1], LT, p1, M1PR, p2, RT; repeat from * to last st, p1–1 st increased before repeats and 2 sts increased in each repeat.

**Row 1 (B):** K1-tbl, p2, k4, p2, *k1-tbl, [p1, k1-tbl] twice, p2, LT, RT, p4, LT, RT, p2, k1-tbl, [p1, k1-tbl] twice, p2, k4, p2; repeat from * to last st, k1-tbl.

**Row 2 (A):** P1, LT, p4, RT, *[p1, k1-tbl] twice, p1, k2, p4, 2/2 RC, p4, k2, p1, [k1-tbl, p1] twice, LT, p4, RT; repeat from * to last st, p1.

**Row 3:** K1-tbl, p2, k4, p2, *k1-tbl, [p1, k1-tbl] twice, p2, LT, RT, p4, LT, RT, p2, k1-tbl, [p1, k1-tbl] twice, p2, k4, p2; repeat from * to last st, k1-tbl.

**Row 4:** P1, LT, p4, RT, *[p1, k1-tbl] twice, p1, [2/2 LPC, 2/2 RPC] twice, p1, [k1-tbl, p1] twice, LT, p4, RT; repeat from * to last st, p1.

**Row 5:** K1-tbl, p2, k4, p2, *k1-tbl, [p1, k1-tbl] twice, [LT, p4, RT] twice, k1-tbl, [p1, k1-tbl] twice, p2, k4, p2; repeat from * to last st, k1-tbl.

**Row 6:** P1, LT, p4, RT, *[p1, k1-tbl] twice, p3, 2/2 LC, p4, 2/2 LC, p3, [k1-tbl, p1] twice, LT, p4, RT; repeat from * to last st, p1.

**Row 7:** K1-tbl, p2, 2/2 RC, p2, *k1-tbl, [p1, k1-tbl] twice, [LT, p4, RT] twice, k1-tbl, [p1, k1-tbl] twice, p2, 2/2 RC, p2; repeat from * to last st, k1-tbl.

**Row 8:** P1, LT, p4, RT, *[p1, k1-tbl] twice, p3, k4, p4, k4, p3, [k1-tbl, p1] twice, LT, p4, RT; repeat from * to last st, p1.

**Row 9:** Repeat Row 5.
**Row 10:** Repeat Row 8.
**Row 11:** Repeat Row 7.
**Row 12:** Repeat Row 6.
**Row 13:** Repeat Row 5.
**Row 14:** P1, LT, p4, RT, *[p1, k1-tbl] twice, p1, [2/2 RPC, 2/2 LPC] twice, p1, [k1-tbl, p1] twice, LT, p4, RT; repeat from * to last st, p1.

**Row 15:** Repeat Row 3.
**Row 16:** Repeat Row 2.
**Row 17:** Repeat Row 1.

**Row 18:** P1, LT, p4, RT, *[p1, k1-tbl] twice, p1, k2, p4, k4, p4, k2, p1, [k1-tbl, p1] twice, LT, p4, RT; repeat from * to last st, p1.

**Row 19:** Repeat Row 3.
**Row 20:** Repeat Row 18.
Repeat Rows 1–20 for pattern.

## PATTERN NOTES

This cowl is worked flat, then seamed. Since this piece is two-sided, the sides of the cowl are labeled A and B rather than RS and WS.

The two-sided cable pattern may be worked from text or charts.

If working from the charted pattern, you will be working from two charts, one for side A and one for side B. Both charts are worked from right to left. This makes working a two-sided cable much easier than if all of the symbols were on one chart. When you look at each chart, especially from a distance, you can see the cable formation for that side of the cowl. Work rows in numerical order as for a standard chart, alternating one row from Side A with the next numbered row from Side B.

Cable Pattern – Side A

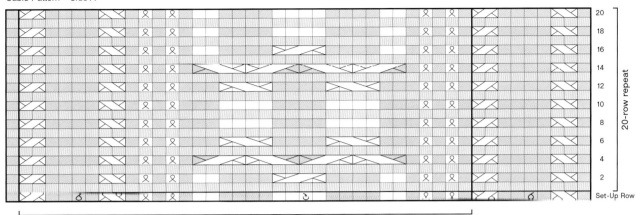

32-st repeat; increases to 34-st repeat on set-up row

| | |
|---|---|
| Work this row on other chart | K1-tbl |
| Knit | M1L |
| Purl | M1RP |

| | |
|---|---|
| LT | 2/2 RC |
| RT | 2/2 LPC |
| 2/2 LC | 2/2 RPC |

## COWL

Using smaller needles and Alternating Cable Cast-On, CO 237 sts.

**Ribbing Row 1 (A):** K2, *p1, k1; repeat from * to last 3 sts, p3.

**Ribbing Row 2 (B):** Slip 2 sts purlwise wyib, *k1, p1; repeat from * to last 3 sts, k1, p2.

Change to larger needles.

**Setup Row (A):** Slip 2 sts purlwise wyib, work Setup Row of Cable Pattern (working from text or chart; if working from chart, work Side A chart), p2–252 sts. Place removable marker on the front of the fabric to mark Side A.

**Row 1 (B):** Slip 2 sts purlwise wyib, work Row 1 of Cable Pattern (if working from chart, work Side B chart) to last 2 sts, p2.

**Row 2 (A):** Slip 2 sts purlwise wyib, work Row 2 of Cable Pattern–Side A to last 2 sts, p2.

Continuing to work first and last 2 edge sts as established (alternating 1 row from Cable Pattern–Side B with 1 row from Cable Pattern–Side A if working

from charts), work Rows 3–20 of Cable Pattern once, Rows 1–20 three more times, then Rows 2–19 once.

Change to smaller needles.

**Decrease Row (A):** Slip 2 sts purlwise wyib, p1, *LT, p1, p2tog, p1, RT, [p1, k1-tbl] twice, p1, k2, p4, k1, k2tog, k1, p3, k2, [p1, k1+tbl] twice, p1; repeat from * to last 11 sts, LT, p1, p2tog, p1, RT, p1, k2–237 sts remain.

**Ribbing Row 2:** Slip 2 sts purlwise wyib, *k1, p1; repeat from * to last 3 sts, k1, p2.

**Ribbing Row 3:** Slip 2 sts purlwise wyib, *p1, k1; repeat from * to last 3 sts, p1, p2tog–236 sts remain.

BO all sts using Tapestry Needle Bind-Off.

## FINISHING

Steam or wet-block.

With side B facing you, sew side seam, working mattress st (see Special Techniques, page 221) in ditch next to 2 slipped sts at edge.

# DESIGN YOUR OWN

## EITHERWAY DESIGN PROCESS

My design process here has everything to do with the reversible fabric and not much to do with the rectangle. I started the process of making this reversible cable pattern by studying a swatch I had on hand featuring the large ropy cable, the one where several two-stitch ribs intertwine with one another. As in the cowl version, the intertwining ribs were filled and separated by two stitches of purl, or reverse stockinette. Turning my swatch over, the two reverse stockinette stitches were knits and, I realized, could easily be worked as little columns of right twists or left twists (basically two-stitch cables).

While the twist could have been worked on the same side as the other cables, it's less intuitive to work purl twists and much easier to work the twists on the side where they will be seen. So the rule of working cables on one side only had to be broken.

Next, I added 1/1 ribs, which are naturally reversible, on each side of the larger cable. I chose to knit into the back of each knit stitch for the look of it (I like to call this half twisted rib). Fully twisted rib would work really well also. To reinforce the idea of the former WS as a second RS, I added some simple four-stitch rope cables to that side. On the original RS they don't show much and seem like slightly bumpy reverse stockinette.

Adding a few twisted columns to the original right side completed the two-sided pattern. I am not sure how many swatches I had to make before I was happy, but it was a few. I love swatching: It's when I can see the possibilities most clearly.

## BOTH SIDES NOW

While designing a two-sided cable can be a challenge, there are many simpler patterns that look great on both sides. The basics—garter stitch, seed stitch, or moss stitch—can always be relied upon. Any knit/purl texture pattern is a good candidate for reversibility, including the Box pattern used for Tilt, page 153, or Woven used for Weave, page 23. I was thinking of only the RS when I made up those last two stitches, but a few tweaks would make them pleasing to the eye on both sides.

To make the wrong side look as if it, too, were a right side, start by swatching the stitch as written. Take a look at the back and determine which elements you'd like to change. For instance, would the single rib of Box look better to you if it were twisted every row, as it is on the other side? Swatch again (maybe a few times!) as you keep making improvements until both sides look like a "right" side to you.

As a rule, I am more concerned with both sides looking good than I am in a truly reversible stitch—that is, one that looks the same on both sides. They are certainly possible and fun to figure out, but I like the idea of a surprise, of things looking different on each side. A reversible or two-sided stitch really comes in handy when you'll catch a glimpse of both sides, as in scarves, wraps, cuffs, and lapels, as well as garments you want to be able to turn inside out for a different look.

# Rib Jacket

Is the Rib Jacket a poncho with sleeves or a very oversized cardigan? The extreme width of the body creates interesting dips and folds, an illusion of complexity that simply doesn't exist. All of the pieces are rectangular. The simple act of binding off a few stitches and casting them back on in the next row forms the lapel, while the collar is merely an extension of the fronts. Seaming is kept to a minimum with some of my favorite techniques. Shoulders are joined with a 3-needle bind-off, as are the two halves of the collar. Sleeves are picked up and worked down, leaving a short side/sleeve seam to sew on each side. Wear your poncho-proportioned jacket open, or close it with a shawl pin.

## SIZES
To fit 30 (34, 38, 42, 46) (50, 54, 58, 62)" [76 (86.5, 96.5, 106.5, 117) (127, 137, 147.5, 157.5) cm] chest

## FINISHED MEASUREMENTS
30¼ (31¾, 34¼, 35¾, 38¼) (39¾, 42¼, 43¾, 46¼)" [77 (80.5, 87, 91, 97) (101, 107.5, 111, 117.5) cm] wide

## YARN
Shibui Knits Twig [46% linen/42% recycled silk/12% wool; 190 yards (174 m)/1.76 ounces (50 g)]: 6 (6, 6, 7, 7) (8, 8, 9, 10) skeins #2041 Pollen (A)

Shibui Knits Silk Cloud [60% kid mohair/40% silk; 330 yards (300 m)/.88 ounces (25 g)]: 4 (4, 4, 5, 5) (5, 6, 6, 6) skeins #2041 Pollen (B)

## NEEDLES
One 24" (60 cm) or longer circular needle, size US 8 (5 mm)

Two spare 24" (60 cm) or longer circular needles, size US 8 (5 mm) or 1 size smaller

One double-pointed needle, size US 6 (4 mm) or 7 (4.5 mm)

Change needle size if necessary to obtain correct gauge.

## NOTIONS
Removable stitch markers

Stitch holders

## GAUGE
20 sts and 23 rows = 4" (10 cm) in Half Twisted Rib, using 1 strand each of A and B held together, after blocking

18 sts and 23 rows = 4" (10 cm) in St st, using 1 strand each of A and B held together, after blocking

*Note: Stockinette stitch is not used is this pattern. However, St st gauge is given here as an alternative way to measure gauge, since rib gauge is often a challenge to measure. If you work the St st gauge, use the same size needle to work the Half Twisted Rib.*

## PATTERN STITCH
### HALF TWISTED RIB
(odd number of sts; 2-row repeat)
**Row 1 (RS):** K1, *k1-tbl, p1; repeat from * to last 2 sts, *k1-tbl, k1.
**Row 2:** K1, *p1, k1-tbl; repeat from * to last 2 sts, p1, k1.

## PATTERN NOTES
The Fronts and Back of this jacket are worked from the bottom up in pieces, then joined at the shoulder with a 3-Needle Bind-Off (see Special Techniques, page 222). The Front collar extensions are joined with a 3-Needle Bind-Off, then sewn to the Back neck. The Sleeves are picked up from the armhole edges and worked flat to the cuffs.

## BACK
CO 151 (159, 171, 179, 191) (199, 211, 219, 231) sts.
Begin Half Twisted Rib; work even until piece measures 18 (18½, 19, 19½, 20) (20½, 21, 21½, 22)" [45.5 (47, 48.5, 49.5, 51) (52, 53.5, 54.5, 56) cm] from the beginning, ending with a WS row.
**Next Row (RS):** Work 61 (65, 71, 75, 81) (85, 91, 95, 101) sts, BO next 29 sts, work to end.
Cut yarn, transfer sts to spare circular needle, and set aside.

### WORK COLLAR EXTENSION

Work even until Collar Extension measures 3" (7.5 cm), ending with a WS row. Cut yarn, place sts on st holder, and set aside.

### LEFT FRONT

CO 89 (93, 99, 103, 109) (113, 119, 123, 129 sts.

Begin Half Twisted Rib; work even until piece measures 12½ (13, 13½, 14, 14½) (15, 15½, 16, 16½)" [32 (33, 34.5, 35.5, 37) (38, 39.5, 40.5, 42) cm] from the beginning, ending with a RS row.

### SHAPE LAPEL

**Next Row (WS):** BO 20 sts, work to end.
**Next Row:** Work to end; using Cable Cast-On, CO 20 sts.
Work even until piece measures 16 (16½, 17, 17½, 18) (18½, 19, 19½, 20)" [40.5 (42, 43, 44.5, 45.5) (47, 48.5, 49.5, 51) cm] from the beginning, ending with a RS row.
**Next Row (WS):** Work 28 sts, M1PR, place remaining 61 (65, 71, 75, 81) (85, 91, 95, 101) sts on spare circular needle—29 sts remain.

### WORK COLLAR EXTENSION

Work even until Collar Extension measures 3" (7.5 cm), ending with a WS row. Cut yarn, place sts on st holder, and set aside.

### JOIN SHOULDERS

With WSs of Left Front and Left Back shoulder together (seam will be on the RS), and beginning at neck edge, join shoulders using 3-Needle Bind-Off. With WSs of Right Front and Right Back shoulder together, and beginning at armhole edge, join shoulders using 3-Needle Bind-Off.

### JOIN COLLAR EXTENSIONS

With RSs of collar extensions together (seam will be on the WS, but will be visible when collar is folded over), join extensions using 3-Needle Bind-Off. Sew edge of extensions to Back neck.

### RIGHT FRONT

CO 89 (93, 99, 103, 109) (113, 119, 123, 129 sts.

Begin Half Twisted Rib; work even until piece measures 12½ (13, 13½, 14, 14½) (15, 15½, 16, 16½)" [32 (33, 34.5, 35.5, 37) (38, 39.5, 40.5, 42) cm] from the beginning, ending with a WS row.

### SHAPE LAPEL

**Next Row (RS):** BO 20 sts, work to end.
**Next Row:** Work to end; using Cable Cast-On (see Special Techniques, page 221), CO 20 sts.
Work even until piece measures 16 (16½, 17, 17½, 18) (18½, 19, 19½, 20)" [40.5 (42, 43, 44.5, 45.5) (47, 48.5, 49.5, 51 cm] from the beginning, ending with a WS row.
**Next Row (RS):** Work 28 sts, M1L, place remaining 61 (65, 71, 75, 81) (85, 91, 95, 101) sts on spare circular needle—29 sts remain.

### SLEEVES

Place removable markers 5¼ (5¾, 6, 6½, 7¼) (7¾, 8, 8¾, 9¼)" [13.5 (14.5, 15, 16.5, 18.5) (19.5, 20.5, 22, 23.5) cm] down from each shoulder seam on Fronts and Back. *Note: The distance between the markers is approximately 1" (2.5 cm) wider than the top of the Sleeve. This makes the Sleeve lie flat and keeps it from bulging at the top.*
With RS facing, using larger needle, pick up and knit 47 (53, 55, 61, 67) (73, 75, 83, 87) sts between markers. Do not join; work back and forth in rows.
Begin Half Twisted Rib; work even until piece measures 7" (18 cm) from pick-up row.
BO all sts in pattern.

### FINISHING

Sew side and sleeve seams.
Block as desired.

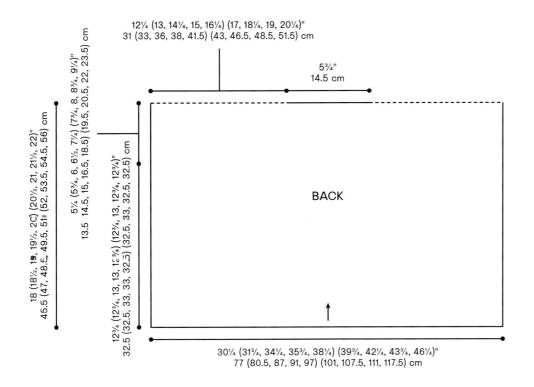

12¼ (13, 14¼, 15, 16¼) (17, 18¼, 19, 20¼)"
31 (33, 36, 38, 41.5) (43, 46.5, 48.5, 51.5) cm

5¾"
14.5 cm

5¼ (5¾, 6, 6½, 7¼) (7¾, 8, 8¾, 9¼)" (19.5, 20.5, 22, 23.5) cm
13.5 14.5, 15, 16.5, 18.5) cm

18 (18½, 19, 19½, 2C) (20½, 21, 21½, 22)"
45.5 (47, 48.5, 49.5, 51) (52, 53.5, 54.5, 56) cm

12¾ (12¾, 13, 13, 12¾) (12¾, 13, 12¾, 12¾)"
32.5 (32.5, 33, 33, 32.5) (32.5, 33, 32.5, 32.5) cm

BACK

30¼ (31¾, 34¼, 35¾, 38¼) (39¾, 42¼, 43¾, 46¼)"
77 (80.5, 87, 91, 97) (101, 107.5, 111, 117.5) cm

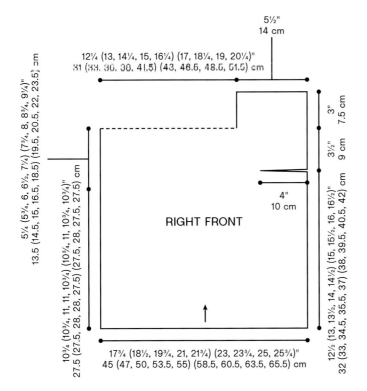

5½"
14 cm

12¼ (13, 14¼, 15, 16¼) (17, 18¼, 19, 20¼)"
31 (33, 36, 38, 41.5) (43, 46.5, 48.5, 51.5) cm

3"
7.5 cm

3½"
9 cm

5¼ (5¾, 6, 6½, 7¼) (7¾, 8, 8¾, 9¼)" (19.5, 20.5, 22, 23.5) cm
13.5 (14.5, 15, 16.5, 18.5) cm

4"
10 cm

RIGHT FRONT

10¾ (10¾, 11, 11, 10¾) (10¾, 11, 10¾, 10¾)"
27.5 (27.5, 28, 28, 27.5) (27.5, 28, 27.5, 27.5) cm

12½ (13, 13½, 14, 14½) (15, 15½, 16, 16½)"
32 (33, 34.5, 35.5, 37) (38, 39.5, 40.5, 42) cm

17¾ (18½, 19¾, 21, 21¾) (23, 23¾, 25, 25¾)"
45 (47, 50, 53.5, 55) (58.5, 60.5, 63.5, 65.5) cm

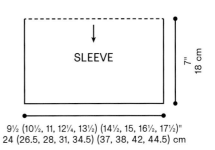

SLEEVE

7"
18 cm

9½ (10½, 11, 12¼, 13½) (14½, 15, 16½, 17½)"
24 (26.5, 28, 31, 34.5) (37, 38, 42, 44.5) cm

# DESIGN YOUR OWN

### DESIGNING RIB JACKET

This piece started with the idea of a wide rectangular body that extends beyond the shoulder—in this case, way beyond, extending practically to the elbow. This proportion means that the side seams will dip down considerably when your arms are relaxed and resting by your side. At the same time, the excess fabric at the bottom edge compresses toward the center, forming lovely ripples along the bottom edge. I know some might consider that a flaw, but I consider the dips and folds interesting, much more interesting than a straight and flat swath of fabric across the belly. At first glance one might assume that there were short rows forming the arch at the bottom edge and shaping forming the folds and drapes. The downward and inward drape of the rectangle makes the garment look more complex than it is: It is very easy to knit.

A few more details complete the design. For the front, I chose a length that covers the waist and hits at high hip. A few extra inches in the back offer extra coverage. I like narrow sleeves to balance the amount of fabric in the body. Not only are these sleeves narrow, they are pretty short, too, which felt like the right proportions to me. I made sure that the fronts overlap by a few inches so there is plenty of fabric for pinning and also a generous fold back when not pinned.

### RELEASING TENSION

As with all of the designs in this chapter, the basic rule is that everything is a rectangle. There is no increasing or decreasing. However, I did allow myself the luxury of binding off and casting back on again, and of making a horizontal slit at the center front edge. This slit releases tension while at the same time forms the lapel. Without the slit, the front edge would be pulled up even higher and would be difficult to fold down. Since the front edge becomes the edge of the collar, it takes up length as it curls around the neck and quite a bit more if the collar is folded. In the Eitherway cowl (page 27), a split made by stopping a seam only halfway releases tension and allows the bottom edge to splay open on the shoulder. Later in the book, a small slit at the center back neck of Hussar (page 71) relieves a little tension at the top edge, allowing the high collar to lie comfortably without the addition of any shaping. It's a trick that comes in handy when you want to keep things simple but need a way to add a little room.

# Trio

Two rectangles and a tube combine to form this versatile neck and shoulder warmer. Worn atop a coat or underneath, the added protection from the elements will be welcome on a chilly day. Wear Trio with the points in the front and back or turn the cowl 90 degrees with a point on each shoulder for a different look. The hem at the top edge adds stability and prevents curling, while a picked-up and bound-off edge along the sides of the rectangles is enough to prevent curling there. The interplay of three colors may add a fun touch you were looking for, or you can knit the piece in one color for elegant simplicity.

### FINISHED MEASUREMENTS

15½" (39.5 cm) circumference

6" (15 cm) length from neck, worn with points on shoulders

9" (23 cm) length from neck, worn with points in center front and back

### YARN

Handspun Hope Worsted [100% organic merino wool; 123 yards (121 m)/3½ ounces (100 g)]: 1 skein each Onionskin (A), Voca Blush (B), and Voca Peach (C)

### NEEDLES

One 16" (40 cm) circular needle, size US 8 (5 mm)

Change needle size if necessary to obtain correct gauge.

### NOTIONS

Stitch marker

Removable stitch marker

### GAUGE

17 sts and 26 rows = 4" (10cm) in St st

## PATTERN NOTES

The base rectangles are worked flat. The second rectangle is picked up from the first rectangle, then sewn to the opposite end of the rectangle. The neckband is picked up from both rectangles and worked in the round.

## RECTANGLE 1

Using A, CO 27 sts.
Begin St st; work even until piece measures 16" (40.5 cm) from the beginning, ending with a WS row.
BO all sts.

## RECTANGLE 2

Place a marker 6" (15 cm) up from bottom edge along right edge of Rectangle 1.
With RS facing, using B and beginning at CO edge, pick up and knit 27 sts along right edge to marker.
Begin St st; work even until piece measures 16" (40.5 cm) from the beginning, ending with a WS row.
BO all sts.
Sew BO edge of Rectangle 1 to top 6" (15 cm) of left edge of Rectangle 2.

## NECKBAND

With RS facing, using C, beginning where A and B meet on the inside neck edge, pick up and knit 90 sts around inside edge. Join for working in the rnd; pm for beginning of rnd.
Begin St st (knit all rnds); work even until piece measures 6½" (16.5 cm) from pick-up rnd.
Purl 1 rnd (turning rnd).
Knit 1" (2.5 cm) from turning rnd.
Fold live sts to WS at turning rnd. Sew live sts to WS 1" (2.5 cm) up from turning rnd, being careful not to let sts show on RS. *Note: If you prefer, you may BO live sts, then sew to WS.*

## FINISHING

With RS facing, using A, pick up and knit 67 sts along outside edge of Rectangle 1. BO all sts knitwise .
With RS facing, using B, pick up and knit 67 sts along outside edge of Rectangle 2. BO all sts knitwise.
Block to flatten edges.

# DESIGN YOUR OWN

### DESIGNING TRIO

When I first thought of this design, it was exactly as it is shown now. The base is two rectangles, each knit on or sewn to the side of the other, front and back identical. Try it with a piece of paper and you'll see that the rectangles, joined, form a three-dimensional, rounded diamond shape. I determined the length needed for each rectangle by draping a dress form with my knitted pieces. Since they were so small and quick to knit I didn't feel the need for a fleece model. A third rectangle—let's consider a tube a rectangle in the round—is picked up and knit upward, forming the neck piece.

After the first two rectangles were knit, but before they were joined, I started to have doubts. Would this formation tug down too much in the back? Did it make sense to have the back and front identical in shape? Was there a way to raise the back neck and still keep things

simple? What if the cast-on edge of the first rectangle and the bound-off end of the second were joined? There would be no point in the back and the back neck would be higher than the front. I ripped it back to a length better for this structure, so the meeting of the rectangles and change of color would be in the center back, and I grafted the (not yet) bound-off edge to the cast-on edge and started to knit the tube.

Trying it on again, I realized that it wasn't working. If I had been willing to add short rows to keep the neck edge shorter than the lower edge, I think it would have been good. But I was determined to keep this one simple and totally square, so the reconfigured idea will have to wait for another day. I returned to my original plan. Turns out, to make the back neck higher, all you need to do is wear the piece pulled forward a bit. I am once again happy that I am designing in stretchy knit fabric and not in something less forgiving, like steel.

### THINK AGAIN

I was so certain that the points of Trio should fall at the center front when worn. That's how I had envisioned it from the idea's inception. My reconfigurations and their abandonment, described above, were based on wearing it that way. Sometimes it's hard, in the midst of deadlines, to think differently, to let go of an idea, or at least let in another possibility. Finally, though, while looking at Trio on my dress form, it occurred to me to rotate it 90 degrees, placing the points on the shoulders. I was astonished. I may like it even better worn this way. The lesson is to stand back, relax, and say "what if" at every phase of a design, no matter how simple the design may be. You are not wasting time. Even if these creative thoughts don't end up affecting the piece you are working on, it may well spur on or inform a future idea.

# Impatiens

The ultimate in relaxing knitting, this brightly lined hat is nothing more than a tube, knit blissfully in the round. One row of purl forms a crisp fold just after the change of color. The floral crown comes together after the knitting is done. A few stitches sewn with yarn and a tapestry needle pull the cast-on and bound-off edges together in six loops, forming the flower shape and exposing the otherwise hidden lining color. It's the nature of stockinette edges to want to curl; I encouraged the curl a bit with my fingers to add to the floral illusion.

## FINISHED MEASUREMENTS
20" (51 cm) circumference

## YARN
Sugar Bush Crisp [100% extrafine superwash merino wool; 95 yards (87 m)/1¾ ounces (50 g)]: 2 skeins each #2005 Clay (MC) and #2008 Rupert's Rose (A)

## NEEDLES
One 16" (40 cm) circular needle, size US 7 (4.5 mm)

One 16" (40 cm) circular needle, size US 6 (4 mm)

Change needle size if necessary to obtain correct gauge.

## NOTIONS
Stitch marker

Removable stitch markers

Waste yarn

## GAUGE
20 sts and 30 rows = 4" (10 cm) in St st using larger needles

## PATTERN NOTES

This hat is worked in two layers, then one is folded inside the other and the top is folded into sixths and sewn into a flower shape.

## HAT
### LINING

Using smaller needle and A, CO 100 sts. Join for working in the rnd, being careful not to twist sts; pm for beginning of rnd. Begin St st (knit all rnds); work even until piece measures 8¼" (21 cm) from the beginning.
Change to MC; knit 1 rnd, purl 1 rnd (turning rnd).

### OUTSIDE

Change to larger needle.
Work even in St st until piece measures 8½" (21.5 cm) from turning rnd.
BO all sts knitwise.

## FINISHING

Steam or wet-block the piece to eliminate some of the rolling.
Fold CC at turning rnd to inside of Hat. Using waste yarn, baste CO edge in A and BO edge in MC together at top edge. Divide basted top of Hat evenly into 6 sections [every 3⅓" (8.5 cm)] and place removable markers between sections, making sure markers catch both layers. Fold top in half at 2 opposite markers and, using tapestry needle and MC, working 1" (2.5 cm) down from top edge, sew through all 4 layers of fabric, tacking them together. Fold each of the halves in thirds and, working 1" (2.5 cm) down from top edge, tack folds together at center, working through all layers and forming a flower shape. Tack folds of flower shape together at center of top edge to hold flower neatly in place. Remove basting. Encourage free edges to roll.

# DESIGN YOUR OWN

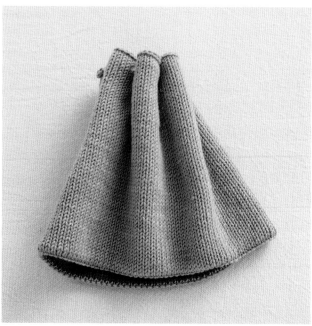

### DESIGNING IMPATIENS

When designing this hat, I started with the idea of a tube, folded inside itself, forming both the outside of the hat and a lining, and I worked from there. While the idea is very simple, there are still a few things to think about.

First, the lining section wants to be a bit smaller than the outside. Measure the top edge of a mug, or any cylinder with some thickness. If you compare the measurement around the inside of the mug and the measurement around the outside, you'll find a difference between the two. The outside is larger and the inside smaller. In lieu of any fancy mathematics to determine the difference between the outside circumference of the hat and the inside circumference, I determined the number of stitches required with the outside circumference using the gauge I wanted for outside of the hat and used a needle one size

smaller for the inside, or lining. I liked the idea of keeping it simple.

Second, deciding how tall to make the hat required a model, which I made out of fleece.

Third, the round of purl I used as a nice crisp turning edge isn't a necessity. Working the tube in all stockinette stitch can be lovely as well.

Fourth, tacking or sewing the top of the hat together to form a pleasing flower was the hardest part of this design. Eight petals would have been much easier to exeute, by folding the opening in half 3 times, instead of having to divide the top into sixths. Divided in eight, though, the petals were too small. I also discovered that tacking only at the very top edge wasn't enough to hold the flower shape. A second set of stitches, about an inch down from the top edge, added the stability needed.

### PULL IT TOGETHER

What else could be pulled together to form the shape needed without actual shaping?
My first thoughts go to other places where the basic form is a tube. Sleeve cuffs could be shaped with loops all around, like the top of Impatiens, but with the opening left large enough for a wrist. A sweater yoke could be worked straight and similarly gathered up dramatically at the neck edge. Both of those examples of shaping occur at the opening or end of a tube. How about forming tiers of tubes by shaping the top edge with loops spaced all around, then picking up stitches to work a smaller tier above? A waistline could be shaped with loops all around instead of small gathers. Thinking about shaping with folds and loops led me to the next design in the book, Blouse (page 47).

# Blouse

The large box pleat at the base of a simple split neck is the centerpiece of Blouse. This pullover is knit in one piece and transformed with the addition of several folds secured by a few lines of hand sewing. Knit-in guidelines mean the folding and sewing can be executed easily with little measuring or guesswork. Double-looped pleats at the cuffs not only add visual interest and style, they have a practical reason for existing as well. The pleats reduce the circumference of the opening so voluminous sleeves aren't dragging through your dinner plate.

**FINISHED MEASUREMENTS**
40 (44½, 48, 52½, 57) (60½, 65, 68½, 73)" [101.5 (113, 122, 133.5, 145) (153.5, 165, 174, 185.5) cm] chest

*Note: This piece is intended to be worn with approximately 10" (25.5 cm) positive ease.*

**YARN**
Purl Soho Understory [50% baby alpaca/25% baby yak/25% silk; 250 yards (228 m)/3½ ounces (100 g)]: 5 (6, 6, 7, 7) (8, 8, 9, 9) skeins #4350 Violet Gray

**NEEDLES**
One 24" (60 cm) or longer circular needle, size US 7 (4.5 mm)

Change needle size if necessary to obtain correct gauge.

**NOTIONS**
Stitch markers

Removable stitch markers

**GAUGE**
18 sts and 26 rows = 4" (10 cm) in St st

## PATTERN STITCH

**1×1 RIB**
(even number of sts)
**All Rows:** *K1, p1; repeat from * to end.

## PATTERN NOTES

This top is worked flat in one piece beginning at the bottom Front. The piece is divided for the neck and stitches are bound off at the same time to prepare for the front pleat. The Front is continued in two pieces, then stitches are cast on to make the Sleeves, and the pieces are worked separately to the end of the Back neck, where the pieces are joined and worked to the end of the Sleeves. After binding off the Sleeve stitches, the Back is worked to the hem. After working the neckband, the Front and Sleeve pleats are created.

## FRONT

Using Long-Tail Cast-On (see Special Techniques, page 221), CO 144 (154, 162, 172, 190) (198, 208, 216, 226) sts.
Begin 1×1 Rib; work 2 rows even.
Purl 5 rows.
Begin St st, beginning with a knit row; work even until piece measures 15½ (15½, 15¼, 15¼, 15¼) (15½, 15¾, 16¼, 16½)" [39.5 (39.5, 38.5, 38.5, 38.5) (39.5, 40, 41.5, 42 cm] from the beginning, ending with a WS row.

## PREPARE FRONT PLEAT

**Row 1 (RS):** K45 (50, 54, 59, 64) (68, 73, 77, 82), pm, p54 (54, 54, 54, 62) (62, 62, 62, 62), pm, knit to end.
**Row 2:** Purl.
**Row 3:** Knit to marker, sm, purl to marker, sm, knit to end.
**Row 4:** Purl to marker, sm, work 1×1 Rib to marker, sm, purl to end.
**Row 5:** Knit to marker, remove marker, join a second ball of yarn, BO the next 54 (54, 54, 54, 62) (62, 62, 62, 62) sts in pattern (removing marker), knit to end—45 (50, 54, 59, 64) (68, 73, 77, 82) sts remain each side.
Working both sides at the same time, work 1" (2.5 cm) even in St st, ending with a WS row.

## MAKE SLEEVES

**Next Row (RS):** Using Cable Cast-On (see Special Techniques, page 221), CO 38 (38, 38, 41, 41) (41, 44, 44, 44) sts, knit to BO sts; on second side, knit to end.
**Next Row:** Using Cable Cast-On, CO 38 (38, 38, 41, 41) (41, 44, 44, 44) sts, p2, k2, knit to end of side; on second side, purl to last 4 sts, k2, p2—83 (88, 92, 100, 105) (109, 117, 121, 126) sts each side.
**Row 1 (RS):** Slip 2 sts purlwise wyib, knit to end of first side; on second side, knit to end.
**Row 2:** Slip 2 sts purlwise wyif, k2, purl to end of first side; on second side, purl to last 4 sts, k2, p2.
Work even as established until Sleeve measures 8¾ (9¼, 9¾, 10, 10¼) (10¼, 10½, 10½, 10¾)" [22 (23.5, 25, 25.5, 26) (26, 26.5, 26.5, 27.5) cm] from Sleeve CO. Place removable marker at each end of row for shoulder.

## BACK

Work even until Sleeve measures 4" (10 cm) from shoulder markers, ending with a WS row.

**Joining Row (RS):** Slip 2 sts purlwise wyib, knit to end of first side; with yarn attached to first side (cut yarn attached to second side), knit across second side to end–166 (176, 184, 200, 210) (218, 234, 242, 252) sts.

**Next Row:** Slip 2 sts purlwise wyif, k2, purl to last 4 sts, k2, p2.

**Next Row:** Slip 2 sts purlwise wyib, knit to end.

Work even until Sleeve measures 8¾ (9¼, 9¾, 10, 10¼) (10¼, 10½, 10½, 10¾)" [22 (23.5, 25, 25.5, 26) (26, 26.5, 26.5, 27.5) cm] from shoulder markers [17½ (18½, 19½, 20, 20½) (20½, 21, 21, 21½)" [44.5 (47, 49.5, 51, 52) (52, 53.5, 53.5, 54.5) cm] from Sleeve CO, ending with a WS row.

BO 38 (38, 38, 41, 41) (41, 44, 44, 44) sts at beginning of next 2 rows–90 (100, 108, 118, 128) (136, 146, 154, 164) sts remain.

Work even until piece measures 16¾ (16¾, 16½, 16½, 16½) (16¾, 17, 17½, 17¾)" [42.5 (42.5, 42, 42, 42) (42.5, 43, 44.5, 45) cm] from underarm, ending with a WS row.

Purl 5 rows.

Work 1 row in 1×1 Rib.

BO all sts in pattern.

## FINISHING

Sew side and sleeve seams.

## NECKBAND

With RS facing, using circular needle and beg at base of Right Front neck, pick up and knit 65 (67, 71, 71, 73) (73, 73, 73, 75) sts from Right Front neck edge to center Back neck, pick up and knit 1 st at center Back (place removable marker on this st), pick up and knit 65 (67, 71, 71, 73) (73, 73, 73, 75) sts to the bottom of Left Front neck–131 (135, 143, 143, 147) (147, 147, 147, 151) sts. Do not join; work back and forth in rows.

**Setup Row:** Knit to marked st, p1, knit to end.

**Row 1 (RS):** Knit to 1 st before marked st, s2kp2, knit to end–129 (133, 141, 141, 145) (145, 145, 145, 149) sts remain.

**Row 2:** Knit to marked st, p1, knit to end.

**Row 3:** *P1, k1; repeat from * to 2 sts before marked st, p1, s2kp2, p1, **k1, p1; repeat from ** to end–127 (131, 139, 139, 143) (143, 143, 143, 147) sts remain.

**Row 4:** P1, *k1, p1; repeat from * to end. BO in pattern to 1 st before marked st, s2kp2, BO in pattern to end.

## FRONT PLEAT

Place removable marker at center of Row 5 of Prepare Front Pleat section (BO row). Pin bottom corners of Front opening together. Pin marked center of Row 5 to neckline just above corners of Front. Fold sides of pleat flat so that you have half of pleat on either side of neck opening for a box pleat. With tapestry needle, sew pleat to Front by sewing between garter st ridges using running st or backstitch.

## SLEEVE PLEATS

Lay piece flat with Sleeve folded at seam and shoulder edge. Place removable marker at top fold. Measure 4" (10 cm) down from marker on front and back of Sleeve and place removable markers at cuff edge. With yarn and tapestry needle and a running stitch, sew both layers together from cuff edge to 2" (5 cm) in from cuff, sewing parallel to fold. Reverse direction and sew back to cuff. Do not cut yarn. Fold marked top edge down to seam you just made, forming two 2" (5 cm) folds, one on either side of center. Continuing with the yarn and tapestry needle, sew each fold in place, sewing close to first seam to secure pleat.

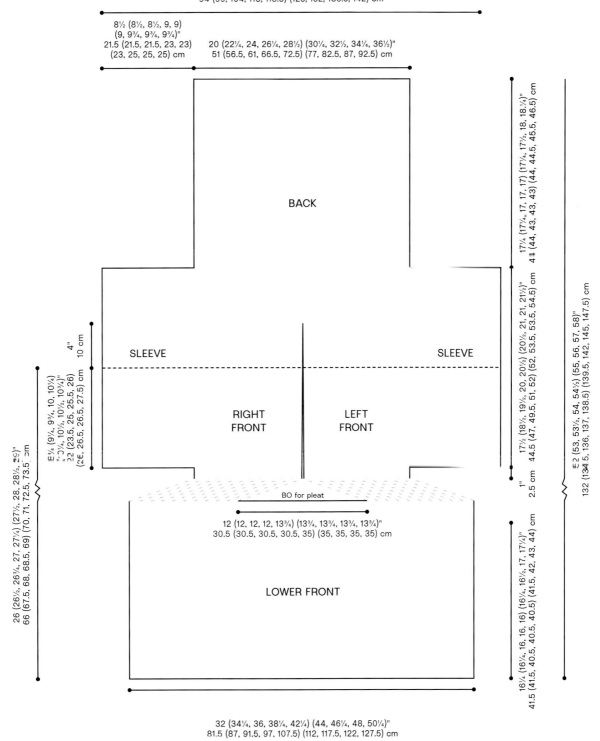

37 (39, 41, 44½, 46¾) (48½, 52, 53¾, 56)"
94 (99, 104, 113, 118.5) (123, 132, 136.5, 142) cm

8½ (8½, 8½, 9, 9)
(9, 9¾, 9¾, 9¾)"
21.5 (21.5, 21.5, 23, 23)
(23, 25, 25, 25) cm

20 (22¼, 24, 26¼, 28½) (30¼, 32½, 34¼, 36½)"
51 (56.5, 61, 66.5, 72.5) (77, 82.5, 87, 92.5) cm

BACK

4"
10 cm

SLEEVE

SLEEVE

RIGHT
FRONT

LEFT
FRONT

9¼ (9¼, 9¾, 10, 10¼)
(10¼, 10½, 10½, 10¾)"
23 (23.5, 25, 25.5, 26)
(26, 26.5, 26.5, 27.5) cm

BO for pleat

12 (12, 12, 12, 13¾) (13¾, 13¾, 13¾, 13¾)"
30.5 (30.5, 30.5, 30.5, 35) (35, 35, 35, 35) cm

LOWER FRONT

17¼ (17¼, 17, 17, 17) (17¼, 17½, 18, 18¼)"
44 (44, 43, 43, 43) (44, 44.5, 45.5, 46.5) cm

17½ (18½, 19½, 20, 20½) (20½, 21, 21, 21½)"
44.5 (47, 49.5, 51, 52) (52, 53.5, 53.5, 54.5) cm

1"
2.5 cm

52 (53, 53½, 54, 54½) (55, 56, 57, 58)"
132 (134.5, 136, 137, 138.5) (139.5, 142, 145, 147.5) cm

16¼ (16¼, 16, 16, 16) (16¼, 16½, 17, 17¼)"
41.5 (41.5, 40.5, 40.5, 40.5) (41.5, 42, 43, 44) cm

26 (26½, 26¾, 27, 27¼) (27½, 28, 28½, 29)"
66 (67.5, 68, 68.5, 69) (70, 71, 72.5, 73.5) cm

32 (34¼, 36, 38¼, 42¼) (44, 46¼, 48, 50¼)"
81.5 (87, 91.5, 97, 107.5) (112, 117.5, 122, 127.5) cm

NOTE: Schematic is shown with Lower Front and Right and Left Fronts separated for the purpose of measurements;, however, once sts are BO for pleat, Right and Left Fronts continue from sts left on needle from Lower Front (shown with series of dashed gray lines). The excess Lower Front fabric will be folded into a pleat in the center during Finishing.

# DESIGN YOUR OWN

## DESIGNING BLOUSE

I wanted to shape this garment without any actual shaping. Pleats made it possible to change the width of the front and rein in the sleeves while adding a great deal of visual interest at the same time. This pullover was insanely simple to knit. Made in just one piece from the front up, sleeves are cast on and bound off, a split forms the neck, and all is worked over the shoulders without requiring a seam. The schematic was trickier for me to wrap my head around. I started with drawing the schematic as it would be without the box pleat in the front. Playing around with my swatches, I made an informed decision about how big I wanted that center front box pleat to be. Calculating how much extra fabric to add for the pleat, I could then devise a way to note that on the schematic (page 49).

Diving into writing the instructions, I used a couple of garter stitches along with a two-stitch I-cord as a self-finishing edge at the sleeve openings and added garter stitch ridges at the bottom of the neck opening to prevent curling and as a sewing guide for the box pleat. I was crossing my fingers a bit, hoping that the knit fabric would be stable enough to hold the weight of the fold. I couldn't think of a way to test it without knitting it, so I plowed ahead. The one large, square-edged piece of knitting was definitely ungainly when the knitting was complete, but pleating and the underarm seams pulled it together quickly. The extra bit of hand sewing was worth the effort. Three pleats (or should I count it as five?) in exchange for increasing, decreasing, and keeping track of shaping. I think it's a great trade-off.

## SELF-FINISHED EDGES

While designing pieces for this book, I tried to adhere to the philosophy of easier is better, which led to avoiding picked-up and knit ribbings and other fussy finishes. While there are a few instances of adding ribbing to a neckline or cuff, you'll find quite a few self-finished edges worked as you go. Here are a few techniques I use frequently for self-finishing vertical edges.

1. I-cord +: Two-stitch I-cord followed by a pair of garter stitches can make a lovely full edge that also resists curling. Blouse and Floret (page 59) both use this self-finishing technique. The I-cord can also be followed by other non-curling stitches, like moss stitch. See the front edge of Forty-Five° (page 101) for an example. I-cord also has the advantage of looking almost identical on both sides, so it works well anywhere the edge might turn over, like a scarf, a wrap, or on a lapel that folds back. The neck and side vent edges of Kite (page 95) are both finished with a two-stitch I-cord, this time followed by an eyelet and decrease, another stable alternative.

2. Ribbing: Ribbing can be tricky to use on a vertical edge because, if knit with the same size needle as the rest of the row, ribbing wants to be taller than stockinette stitch and can also look a bit sloppy if not knit on a smaller needle. One solution is to use a smaller needle for the ribbing, but that's not an easy-to-execute solution, requiring several double-pointed or circular needles to be used in the same row. When designing both Longitude (page 81) and Outward (page 159) I used fully twisted 1×1 Rib, with all rib stitches knit through the back loop, keeping the stitches neat. I then added one garter stitch at the end for neatness and to help keep the edge compressed.

3. Garter edges: Two or more garter stitches can sometimes be enough of a finish, without adding a big visual impact. Afloat (page 145), Weave (page 23), and Pyramid (page 107) are all knit with a two-stitch garter edging worked as you go, as is Georgia (page 201).

4. Let it roll: Occasionally, I leave an edge to its own devices and let it roll as it will. The vertical neck edge of Anne² (page 181) rolls inward beautifully, as does the sideways knit neckline of Facet (page 117). In the case of Centrale (page 133), the armhole edges are left to roll inward.

5. Non-rolling yarn: Sometimes the natural qualities of a yarn do the work for you. Mohair, mohair mixes, and other brushed yarns often lie flat in stockinette stitch, no special edges required. I was able to leave the armhole and neck edges of Skyward (page 175) unfinished with good results, and the long flounce down the center of Jabot (page 209) remains uncurled even though it is knit entirely of stockinette stitch.

# CHAPTER 3
# MANIPULATE

Flat, rectangular surfaces are magically transformed into
three-dimensional wonders with a bit of repetitive, geometrical
stitch work. With the help of knit-in guide stitches, extra
knitted fabric is folded into box pleats and cinched into
sculptural florals, while tucks are knit together as you go.

# Folded Headband

A knitter's equivalent of a crown, this headband has a purchased band of plastic or metal as its base. The band is wrapped in fleece as padding and covered with a simple-to-knit tube made fancy with some basic smocking. Spaced rows of garter stitch define the folds and act as guides for the sewn stitches that hold the smocked folds.

## FINISHED MEASUREMENTS

Approximately 5" (12.5 cm) circumference x 17" (40 cm) end to end

To fit a ½–1" (13–25 mm) headband

## YARN

Julie Asselin Leizu Fingering Simple [90% SW merino/10% silk; 475 yards (438 m)/4 ounces (115 g)]: 1 skein Misty (Limited Edition)

## NEEDLES

One pair straight needles, size US 3 (3.25 mm)

Change needle size if necessary to obtain correct gauge.

## NOTIONS

½–1" (13–25 m) wide plastic headband

Sheep's wool or fiber fill stuffing

## GAUGE

28 sts and 40 rows = 4" (10 cm) in St st

## NOTE

The headband is worked in stockinette stitch with garter stitch lines used to aid in the folding and smocking.

## HEADBAND

Using Long-Tail Cast-On (see Special Techniques, page 221), CO 40 sts. Begin St st, beginning with a purl row Work even until piece measures 1½" (4 cm) from the beginning, ending with a RS row.
**\*Garter Stitch Row (WS):** Knit.
[Knit 1 row, purl 1 row] 7 times, knit 1 row. Repeat from \* 14 more times.
[Knit 1 row, purl 1 row] 7 times.
BO all sts knitwise.

## FINISHING

Sew side edges together. Fold tube flat with seam at center back.

## SMOCKING

*Note: Use working yarn and tapestry needle to make tacks. Each garter st line will be tacked twice, on opposite sides of the Headband. Make each tack small and invisible.*

**Step 1:** Fold the lowest garter st line to CO edge in center back and make a small tack to hold in place.
**Step 2:** Fold the same garter st line to CO edge in center front and tack in place.
**Step 3:** In the center of one side, halfway between center front and center back, fold the lowest untacked garter st line down to the previous garter st line and tack in place. Tack the same garter st line in the same manner on the opposite side.
**Step 4:** In center back, fold lowest unused garter st line to previous garter st line and tack in place.
Tack the same garter st line in the same manner at center front.
Repeat Steps 3 and 4 seven more times.
**Step 5:** In the center of one side, fold BO edge to previous garter st line and tack in place. Repeat for opposite side of BO edge.
Wrap plastic headband with stuffing and wrap yarn loosely around stuffing to hold it in place. Insert padded headband into knit tube and sew ends closed, making pleats at side so sewn end is smaller than width of headband.

# DESIGN YOUR OWN

### DESIGNING HEADBAND

In the eighties, a heyday for headbands, I covered a metal and raffia headband with a tube of a rust colored alpaca/wool yarn and proceeded to live in it every day. I adored my headband so much that it felted from wear, and I loved it even more. Eventually, I tired of wearing headbands and moved on, waiting for the look to come back and seem good to me again. Finally, that day has come. I am seeing headbands in fashion magazines and on celebrities like our amazing youth poet laureate, Amanda Gorman. This headband is the folded version of my headband from the eighties, designed on the fly, as I describe next.

### DESIGN ON THE FLY

Try designing as you go if your project is small. Sometimes an idea seems to have too many variables to work out before you start—or, I should say, it doesn't seem worth figuring them all out beforehand. In the case of the folded headband, I hadn't worked out the exact pattern of smocking I was going to use, but with deadlines quickly approaching I needed someone to get knitting on the piece, and I sent some quick instructions to a helpful local knitter. My idea of spacing out stockinette with garter ridges worked well, but I miscalculated how much length would be needed to cover the headband once the knitting was in its final smocked configuration.

I didn't really know what I was doing until I sewed the seam, forming a tube. I had figured out where I wanted to place the smocking stitches and inserted the headband. I made sure there was enough of the padding around the plastic headband to fill out the smocked knitting tube, just enough to make it rounded and at the same time show the folds. Then, I alternated knitting and smocking until I had enough to cover the padded band. I finished by pleating the ends and closing them up. This *may* be a lesson on why you should make a perfect swatch with the correct smocking or folding before you begin, but sometimes it's fun to hurtle headlong into the unknown and handle the questions as they come. Be sure to keep a good attitude about ripping back and changing your mind.

# Floret

Luxuriously sized and made deeply three dimensional with sewn-in smocking, this wrap is an easy, albeit significant, knit. Mostly stockinette, I-cord, and garter edges make a satisfying rounded border down each side while the cast-on and bound-off edges are left to freely fold and flutter. Purl stitches are knit in as guides to make the smocking very simple to accomplish, with no counting or fussy measuring.

**FINISHED MEASUREMENTS**
13" (33 cm) wide × 72" (183 cm) long after smocking

**YARN**
Quince & Co. Chickadee [100% American wool; 181 yards (166 m)/1¾ ounces (50 g)]: 13 skeins Shell

**NEEDLES**
One pair straight needles, size US 4 (3.5 mm)

Change needle size if necessary to obtain correct gauge.

**GAUGE**
24 sts and 34 rows = 4" (10 cm) in St st

40 sts and 51 rows = 4" (10 cm) after smocking

## PATTERN STITCH

### SMOCKING PLACEMENT PATTERN (SEE CHART)

(multiple of 20 sts + 10; 32 row repeat)
*Note: Slip all slipped sts purlwise with yarn to WS (wyif when working RS rows; wyib when working WS rows).*
**Row 1 (RS):** Slip 2, knit to end.
**Row 2:** Slip 2, k2, purl to last 4 sts, k2, p2.
**Rows 3–16:** Repeat Rows 1 and 2.
**Row 17:** Slip 2, k3, *k5, p1, k8, p1, k5; repeat from * to last 5 sts, knit to end.
**Row 18:** Slip 2, k2, p1, *[p6, k1] twice, p6; repeat from * to last 5 sts, p1, k2, p2.
**Row 19–30:** Repeat Rows 1 and 2.
**Row 31:** Slip 2, k3, *[k6, p1] twice, k6; repeat from * to last 5 sts, knit to end.
**Row 32:** Slip 2, k2, p1, *p5, k1, p8, k1, p5; repeat from * to last 5 sts, p1, k2, p2.
Repeat Rows 1–32 for pattern.

## PATTERN NOTES

This shawl is worked entirely in the Smocking Placement Pattern, which forms a series of rectangles with purls at each corner. These purl stitches are used as guides to smock the wrap.

## SHAWL

CO 110 sts.
Begin Smocking Placement Pattern; work Rows 1–32 a total of 28 times, then work Rows 1–15 once more.
**BO Row (RS):** Slip 2, k1, pass slipped sts over k1, bind off all sts knitwise in the usual manner to last 2 sts, p2tog, BO last st. Fasten off.

## FINISHING

Block as desired.

## SMOCKING

Cut a 12" (30.5 cm) length of yarn. Using tapestry needle, thread yarn through purl sts of each smocking rectangle as shown in Smocking Diagram. Pull end up firmly and tie several times to secure. Sew a few sts to secure center and cut yarn, leaving a 1½" (4 cm) tail, and hide ends in cavity behind center. Complete this step for remainder of Scarf.
Once all centers are gathered and secured, you'll see flowers with four petals around some, but not all centers; some need to be coaxed. Once petals are coaxed (see photo), they need to be secured with a few sts. Make a small tack about halfway down from surface where shown with arrows on photo. Bring ends to WS and cut yarn, leaving a 1½" (4 cm) tail.

# DESIGN YOUR OWN

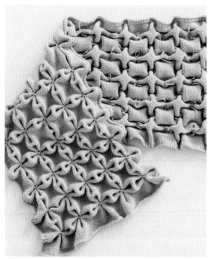
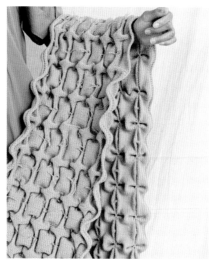

### DESIGNING FLORET

I loved the idea of smocking that pulls the knitted fabric into florets with deeply dimensional petals. I first saw the concept on Pinterest while searching for folded, pleated, and smocked ideas and it appeared to me almost miraculous. The four corners of a square are gathered together, forming a four-petaled flower on one side and a box shape on the other. Most effective in multiples, the shapes appear when the smocking is done in a grid with several rows and columns. More often used on woven fabrics, I set about adapting the idea to hand knitting. First, I was determined to find a way to take the measuring and marking out of the smocking process. I realized that a few purl stitches defining the corners of the square would be the perfect smocking guide—not only are they pre-measured and easy to see, but the loops of the purl stitches are easy to thread the tapestry needle through, with no guesswork. The second modification needed was some additional petal-defining tacking. While firmly woven fabrics have enough body to keep the petal shapes made by cinching the four corners of the squares, handknit fabric does not. When any weight or tension was applied, the petals wanted to fold up, becoming straight lines from one cinched center to the next. A small tack sewn in between the centers, in both directions, helps hold the floret shapes. Still, the piece is long and heavy, and you may find yourself tweaking the florets when you wear it. If you are choosing between two gauges, go with the tighter one, as a looser, floppier fabric will result in looser, floppier florets.

A third consideration, unique to hand knitting, is the treatment of the many yarn ends left after the cinching and making tacks. While sewing threads can be cut short and practically disappear, yarn ends are more evident. I hid the cinching ends in the deep pocket behind the cinch, but there was nowhere to hide the ends left after sewing a tack. Weaving all those ends in didn't appeal to me, not only because of the tedium, but also because I thought it wouldn't look good. I left the ends as a feature of the back of the wrap, trimming them all to about 1½" (4 cm), so they definitely show. Those well-versed in knots that stay knotted may prefer to trim the ends short.

### PLANNING FOR SMOCKING

I decided on the goal width and length of this wrap by studying wide scarves, throws, and wraps I thought worked well, both my own designs and others. Armed with a swatch with the called-for edging and several repeats of the smocking guide pattern, I knit a swatch, measured it, then smocked it and measured it again. These two measurements got me as close as I could get to predicting the finished measurements of the piece. Still, I goofed somehow, and initially called for only half of the rows needed and, coincidentally, half of the yarn too. Can you spot the change of dye lot? (It's smack in the middle of the wrap!) The swatch told the right story, but when will I remember to always double-check my work?

For best results, when calculating for smocking, make two identical swatches containing several repeats in both the width and length. Block both swatches. I recommend treating the swatch as you would your finished garment, so if your finished piece will be washed, wash the swatch. Smock one of the pieces. It will now be easy to measure how much width and height are lost in each repeat of the smocking pattern.

## Smocking Diagram

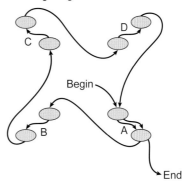

## Smocking Placement Pattern

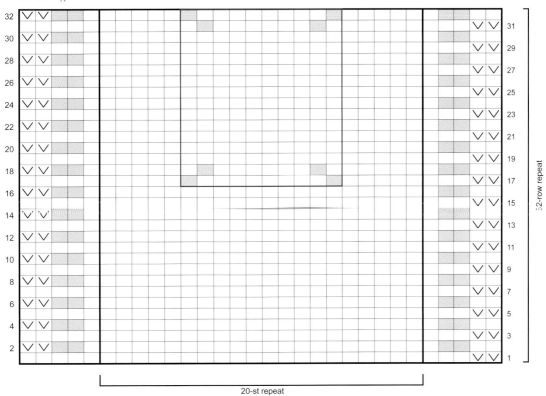

20-st repeat

32-row repeat

☐ Knit on RS, purl on WS.

▨ Purl on RS, knit on WS.

▽ Slip 1 wyib on RS, slip 1 wyif on WS.

☐ Smocking rectangle

# Multiflora

A variation on Floret (page 59), the Multiflora cowl gives you a taste of easy, yet astounding, smocking without a big commitment. Adding a stockinette stitch lining provides stability, keeping the cowl from flopping and at the same time helping the florets keep their shape. The smocked outside layer and the stockinette stitch lining are knit flat separately and joined at the edges with mattress stitch, leaving intriguing loops of the flower shapes extending past the seam.

## FINISHED MEASUREMENTS
7" (18 cm) wide × 25" (63.5 cm) circumference

## YARN
Ancient Arts Nettle Soft DK [68% superwash merino/32% nettle; 263 yards (240 m)/3½ ounces (100 g)]: 3 skeins Lichen in My Crevices

## NEEDLES
One pair straight circular needles, size US 4 (3.5 mm)

Change needle size if necessary to obtain correct gauge.

## GAUGE
24 sts and 32 rows = 4" (10 cm) in St st

35½ sts and 51 rows = 4" (10 cm) after smocking

## PATTERN STITCH

### SMOCKING PLACEMENT PATTERN (SEE CHART)
(multiple of 20 sts + 2; 32-row repeat)
**Row 1 (RS):** Knit.
**Row 2:** Purl.
**Rows 3–8:** Repeat Rows 1 and 2.
**Row 9:** K1, *k5, p1, k8, p1, k5; repeat from * to last st, k1.
**Row 10:** P1, *[p6, k1] twice, p6; repeat from * to last st, p1.
**Rows 11–22:** Repeat Rows 1 and 2.
**Row 23:** K1, *[k6, p1] twice, k6; repeat from * to last st, k1.
**Row 24:** P1, *p5, k1, p8, k1, p5; repeat from * to last, p1.
**Rows 25–32:** Repeat Rows 1 and 2.
Repeat Rows 1–32 for pattern.

## PATTERN NOTES
The inside of this cowl is worked in stockinette stitch. The outside is worked in the Smocking Placement Pattern, which forms a series of rectangles with purls at each corner. These purl stitches are used as guides to smock the outside, which is then sewn to the inside.

## COWL

### OUTSIDE
CO 62 sts.
Begin Smocking Placement Pattern; work Rows 1–32 ten times.
Graft live sts to CO edge (see Special Techniques, page 221), or BO all sts and sew BO edge to CO edge.

## INSIDE
CO 40 sts.
Begin St st; work even until piece measures 25" (63.5 cm) from the beginning.
Graft live sts to CO edge, or BO all sts and sew BO edge to CO edge.

## SMOCKING
Cut a 12" (30.5 cm) length of yarn. Using tapestry needle, thread yarn through purl sts of each smocking rectangle as shown in Smocking Diagram. Pull end up firmly and tie several times to secure. Sew a few sts to secure center, bring yarn to back, tie several times to secure, then cut yarn, leaving a 1½" (4 cm) tail. Complete this step for remainder of Cowl.
Once all centers are gathered and secured, you'll see flowers with four petals around some, but not all centers; some need to be coaxed. Once petals are coaxed (see photo), they need to be secured with a few sts. Make a small tack about halfway down from surface where shown with arrows on photo. Bring ends to WS and cut yarn, leaving a 1½" (4 cm) tail.

## FINISHING
With WSs together, pin Inside to Outside and sew side edges together with mattress st (see Special Techniques, page 221).

# DESIGN YOUR OWN

## DESIGNING MULTIFLORA

Loving the dramatic curved folds of Floret (page 59), I thought that a smaller version might be appreciated. As described in the design lesson following Floret, I calculate the amount of length and width taken up by the smocking by making two swatches, one smocked and one left un-smocked. I measured a few cowls I've been wearing in the past few years and added some extra length, knowing I would be adding a lining. In combination, the lining and the dimensional smocking add a good deal of thickness. The lining was written to approximate the length and width of the outer portion after smocking. Pinning the lining and smocked-out portion of the cowl together, I tested the length on both my dress form and myself before I joined it all, just in case it turned out I'd prefer one more repeat, for a little more length.

## ALTERNATE CONSTRUCTION

Could this lined cowl be knit in one piece, eliminating the sewing altogether? Maybe. You might try knitting the two pieces as one for the rounds that will not take part in the cinching process. Going strictly by the chart, I would knit in the round for 8 rounds, then work back and forth for the next 16 before going back to knitting in the round for the last 8 rows of the pattern. Counting the lining rows of the cowl, or going by the row gauge instructions for the lining, there are 20 rows of lining for 32 rows of the smocked piece. That leads me to believe that you would want to knit rows 1–10 in the round, 11–22 back and forth on the portion to be smocked, and go back to knitting in the round for rows 25–32. I haven't tested this theory. I dismissed the idea as too complicated, but if you are seaming averse, it may be worth a try. Some test swatches would be in order.

Smocking Diagram

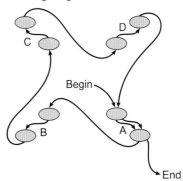

## Smocking Placement Pattern

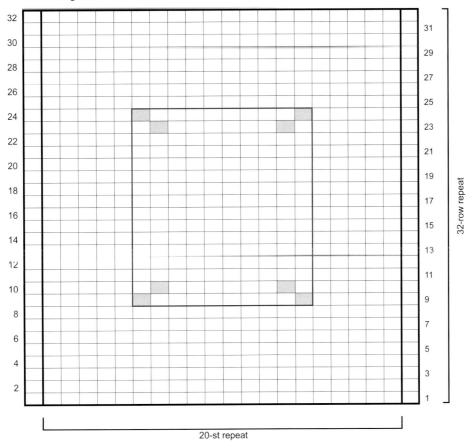

20-st repeat

☐ Knit on RS, purl on WS.

▨ Purl on RS, knit on WS.

☐ Smocking rectangle

# Smocked

Why not knit for your bed or couch? This square pillow cover provides the opportunity to experiment with a multilayered knit fabric that might not suit garment making. Box pleats with the addition of smocking make a highly dimensional surface perfect for catching light and shadows in an interior setting. Ribs and garter ridges become guidelines for the vertical pleats and horizontal stay stitching, so only the most rudimentary hand-sewing skills are required.

## SIZES
16 × 16" (40.5 × 40.5 cm)

## YARN
Rowan Softyak DK [76% cotton/15% yak, 9% nylon; 148 yards (135 m)/1¾ ounces (50 g)]: 6 balls #246 Lantana

## NEEDLES
One pair straight needles, size US 7 (4.5 mm)

Change needle size if necessary to obtain correct gauge.

## NOTIONS
Pins

16 × 16" (40.5 × 40.5 cm) pillow form

## GAUGE
20 sts and 32 rows = 4" (10 cm) in St st

## PATTERN STITCH

### PILLOW PATTERN (SEE CHART)
(multiple of 27 sts + 3; 28-row repeat)
**Row 1 (RS):** *K6, p1, k16, p1, k3; repeat from * to last 3 sts, k3.
**Rows 2–7:** Knit the knit sts and purl the purl sts as they face you.
**Row 8:** Knit.
**Row 9:** Repeat Row 1.
**Rows 10 and 11:** Repeat Rows 8 and 9.
**Rows 12–28:** Repeat Row 2.
Repeat Rows 1–28 for pattern.

## PATTERN NOTE
The Front is worked in stockinette st with purl columns and horizontal garter st lines that will be used to create the pleats and smocking. The Back is worked in two pieces that are overlapped when sewn to the Front, leaving an opening for the pillow form. Before pleating and smocking, the Front will be much wider than the Back pieces.

## BACK (MAKE 2)
Using Long-Tail Cast-On (see Special Techniques, page 221), CO 80 sts.
Knit 10 rows.
Change to St st, beginning with a knit row; work even until piece measures 10" (25.5 cm) from the beginning, ending with a WS row.
BO all sts.

## FRONT
Using Long Tail Cast On, CO 102 sts.
Begin Pillow Pattern (working pattern from text or chart); work Rows 1–28 four times, then work Rows 1–17 once.
BO all sts knitwise.

## SMOCKING
Steam or wet-block to smooth and flatten. Lay Front on a flat surface with WS facing up. There are 7 pairs of vertical knit columns, each pair made by one repeat of Pillow Pattern. Sew each pair of columns together, sewing left leg of st in first column of a pair to right leg of st in second column of the pair. When you have finished all 7 pairs, you will have 7 tubes on the RS. Flatten each tube so seam is in center back of tube, forming a pleat; pin sides of each pleat so that garter st lines on pleat line up with garter st lines beneath pleat. Using tapestry needle and yarn, sew a running st between lines of garter st to secure pleats.
To smock the pleats, fold up sides of pleat halfway between garter st lines, and tack sides together using a few small sts in the center (see photo). Smock every other pleat in first row, then smock alternate pleats on following rows (see photo).

## FINISHING
Sew BO edge of one Back piece to Front along sides, top, and bottom, leaving top of pleats unsewn so tubes are open at ends. Sew BO edge of second Back piece to Front, overlapping first Back piece. Insert pillow form.

# DESIGN YOUR OWN

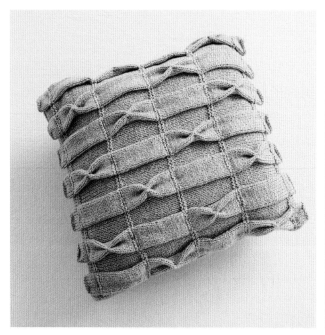

### DESIGNING SMOCKED

How much thinking goes into designing a square pillow? I've long admired Colette Wolff's book *The Art of Manipulating Fabric* and have been inspired by her explanations of flounces, tucks, rushes, pleats, and more for many years now. The tucking and smocking of Smocked was inspired by one of the tucking formations shown in Colette's book, along with similar inspirations found on Pinterest. Hand-knitted fabric, knit in worsted-weight yarn, is quite different from a lightweight woven, so the tucked arrangement in her book was only a starting point. I folded swatches to figure out the size of the pleat I wanted. I tested the idea of a purl rib as a vertical folding line. I played with different ways to sew the pleat together on the wrong side. I tested the idea of two garter ridges as a guide so I would know exactly where to sew and ended up liking the horizontal elements they gave the overall design. I practiced sewing the pleats down between my garter guidelines and determined that the easiest method was the best—running stitch does the trick. I decided that the pleats should not be fastened down where the front meets the back, but should instead be left open to form a sculptural edging. I decided to make the back out of two overlapping pieces so the pillow insert could be easily removed. Sometimes it takes a lot of little details and a lot of small decisions to create something that, at first glance, seems rather simple.

### KNIT-IN GUIDES

I didn't want knitters to have to count stitches or measure to determine where the box pleats would be and where to sew. While knitting Smocked, vertical and horizontal guidelines are knit as you go. Single reverse stockinette stitch ribs help to fold the box pleats and make sewing them together easy. Horizontally, two garter ridges add interest while making it clear where to place your running stitch. They help hide the running stitch as well. Elsewhere in this book, guide stitches make light work of what might be tedious. Ruche (page 187) alternates stockinette and reverse stockinette stitch on the edges of the ruched sleeve to define where to pick up stitches, leaving the space between to pull up in a loop. Floret (page 59) and Multiflora (page 63) use a few purl stitches to define the path of hand-sewn smocking threads, which totally transform the surface. Use these examples and others from this book to get your mind thinking about how a few guidelines or guide stitches can make folding, gathering, or cinching an easily accomplished task.

## Pillow Pattern

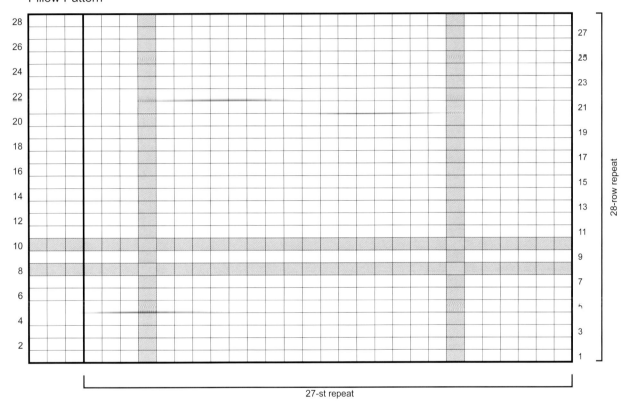

27-st repeat

28-row repeat

☐ Knit on RS, purl on WS.

▨ Purl on RS, knit on WS.

# Hussar

Named as a nod to the military jackets worn by the Hussar horsemen of Hungary, in this version, golden braided cord is replaced with repetitive tucks set on a diagonal. All focus is placed on the front band, which is worked first, getting the harder part out of the way. The rest of the sweater is a very simple shape with the bottom and sleeve edging worked as you go.

## FINISHED MEASUREMENTS

40 (44, 48, 52, 56) (60, 64, 68, 72)" [101.5 (112, 122, 132, 142) (152.5, 162.5, 172.5, 183 cm] chest, with fronts overlapped

*Note: This piece is intended to be worn with approximately 10" (25.5 cm) positive ease.*

## YARN

Harrisville Designs Shear [100% CVM and Romeldale wool; 320 yards (292 m)/3½ ounces (100 g)]: 6 (6, 7, 7, 8) (8, 9, 9, 9) skeins #YCL005 Fawn Brown

## NEEDLES

One 29" (60 cm) or longer circular needle, size US 6 (4 mm)

One double-pointed needle, size US 4 (3.5 mm) or 5 (3.75 mm)

Change needle size if necessary to obtain correct gauge.

## NOTIONS

Removable stitch markers

Waste yarn

Crochet hook size US G-6 (4 mm)

## GAUGE

21 sts and 30 rows = 4" (10 cm) in St st after blocking

21 sts and 40 rows = 4" (10 cm) in garter st (knit every row) after blocking

## PATTERN NOTE

This garment is worked flat in one piece, beginning with the Front Bands, which are worked on the bias from the bottom up, with pleats. The Body begins at the center Back with a Provisional Cast-On (see Special Techniques, page 221). The Left Back is worked first, then stitches are cast on for the Left Front, and the Back and Front are worked at the same time. Stitches are then bound off for the sides and the Sleeves are worked flat to the cuff. The Right Back is picked up and worked from the Provisional Cast-On, and the right Front and Sleeve are worked as a mirror image to the left.

## RIGHT FRONT BAND

CO 3 sts.
Purl 1 row.

## INCREASE SECTION

**Row 1 (RS):** K1, M1R, k1, M1L, k1—5 sts.
**Row 2:** P2, k1, p2.
**Row 3:** K2, M1R, k1, M1L, k2—7 sts.
**Row 4:** P2, k3, p2.
**Row 5:** K2, M1R, knit to last 2 sts, M1L, k2—2 sts increased.
**Row 6:** P2, knit to last 2 sts, p2.
Repeat Rows 5 and 6 twelve more times—33 sts.

## STRAIGHT TUCK SECTION

**Row 1 (RS):** K2, M1R, knit to last 3 sts, k2tog, k1.
**Row 2:** Purl.
**Row 3:** Knit.
**Row 4:** Purl.
**Rows 5–12:** Repeat Rows 3 and 4 four times.
With WS facing, using dpn, pick up (but do not knit) 33 sts, picking up the bottommost purl bumps above last garter tunnel, including a loop from one of the ends; turn to RS. *Note: The garter tunnel is the knit row between garter ridges; the bottommost purl bumps are the U-shaped bumps just above the tunnel.*
**Row 13 (RS):** Holding dpn behind front needle, *k2tog (1 st from front needle together with 1 st from dpn); repeat from * to end.
**Row 14:** P2, knit to last 2 sts, p2.
**Row 15:** K2, M1R, knit to last 3 sts, k2tog, k1.
**Row 16:** P2, knit to last 2 sts, p2.
**Rows 17–20:** Repeat Rows 15 and 16 twice.
Repeat Rows 1–16 sixteen (16, 16, 17, 17) (17, 18, 18, 18) more times.
You should now have 17 (17, 17, 18, 18) (18, 19, 19, 19) tucks and 4 garter ridges.
Repeat Rows 15 and 16 seventeen (17, 17, 19, 19) (19, 21, 21, 21) more times; you should have a total of 21 (21, 21, 23, 23) (23, 25, 25, 25) garter ridges since last tuck.

## DECREASE SECTION

**Row 1 (RS):** K1, ssk, knit to last 3 sts, k2tog, k1—2 sts decreased.
**Row 2:** P2, knit to last 2 sts, p2.
Repeat Rows 1 and 2 thirteen more times—5 sts remain.
**Row 3:** K1, s2kp2—3 sts remain.
BO all sts purlwise.

## LEFT FRONT BAND

CO 3 sts.
Purl 1 row.

### INCREASE SECTION

**Row 1 (RS):** K1, M1R, k1, M1L, k1—5 sts.
**Row 2:** P2, k1, p2.
**Row 3:** K2, M1R, k1, M1L, k2—7 sts.
**Row 4:** P2, k3, p2.
**Row 5:** K2, M1R, knit to last 2 sts, M1L, k2—2 sts increased.
**Row 6:** P2, knit to last 2 sts, p2.
Repeat Rows 5 and 6 twelve more times—33 sts.

### STRAIGHT TUCK SECTION

**Row 1 (RS):** K1, ssk, knit to last 2 sts, M1L, k2.
**Row 2:** Purl.
**Row 3:** Knit.
**Row 4:** Purl.
**Rows 5–12:** Repeat Rows 3 and 4 four times.
With WS facing, using dpn, pick up (but do not knit) 33 sts, picking up the bottommost purl bumps above last garter tunnel, including a loop from one of the ends; turn to RS. *Note: The garter tunnel is the knit row between garter ridges; the bottommost purl bumps are the U-shaped bumps just above the tunnel.*
**Row 13 (RS):** Holding dpn behind front needle, *k2tog (1 st from front needle together with 1 st from dpn); repeat from * to end.
**Row 14:** P2, knit to last 2 sts, p2.
**Row 15:** K1, ssk, knit to last 2 sts, M1L, k2.
**Row 16:** P2, knit to last 2 sts, p2.
**Rows 17–20:** Repeat Rows 15 and 16 twice.
Repeat Rows 1–20 sixteen (16, 16, 17, 17) (17, 18, 18, 18) more times.
You should now have 17 (17, 17, 18, 18) (18, 19, 19, 19) tucks and 4 garter ridges.
Repeat Rows 15 and 16 seventeen (17, 17, 19, 19) (19, 21, 21, 21) more times; you should have a total of 21 (21, 21, 23, 23) (23, 25, 25, 25) garter ridges since last tuck.

## DECREASE SECTION

**Row 1 (RS):** K1, ssk, knit to last 3 sts, k2tog, k1–2 sts decreased.
**Row 2:** P2, knit to last 2 sts, p2.
Repeat Rows 1 and 2 thirteen more times–5 sts remain.
**Row 3:** K1, s2kp2–3 sts remain.
BO all sts purlwise.

## LEFT BACK/FRONT/SLEEVE

### LEFT BACK

Using waste yarn, crochet hook, and Provisional Cast-On, CO 136 (136, 136, 143, 143) (143, 150, 150, 150) sts.
**Setup Row (WS):** P2, k2, purl to end.
**Row 1:** Knit.
**Row 2:** P2, k2, purl to end.
Repeat Rows 1 and 2 until piece measures 3½ (3½, 3½, 4, 4) (4, 4½, 4½, 4½)" [9 (9, 9, 10, 10) (10, 11.5, 11.5, 11.5) cm] from the beginning, ending with a WS row. Cut yarn and leave sts on right-hand end of needle.

### ESTABLISH LEFT FRONT

Lay Left Front Band on a flat surface with RS facing up, with CO edge at the bottom and BO corner at the top; place marker along right edge of Band 4 (4, 4, 4½, 4½) (4½, 5, 5, 5)" [10 (10, 10, 11.5, 11.5) (11.5, 12.5, 12.5, 12.5) cm] down from BO corner. With RS facing, using unoccupied end of needle (Back sts are on the other end), pick up and knit 136 (136, 136, 143, 143) (143, 150, 150, 150) sts along right edge of Left Front Band, between CO edge and marker, knit across Back sts–272 (272, 272, 286, 286) (286, 300, 300, 300) sts.
**Setup Row (WS):** P2, k2, purl to last 4 sts, k2, p2.
**Row 1:** Knit.
**Row 2:** P2, k2, purl to last 4 sts, k2, p2.
Repeat Rows 1 and 2 until piece measures 6½ (7½, 8½, 9, 10) (11, 11½, 12½, 13½)" [16.5 (19, 21.5, 24, 26.5) (29, 32, 34.5, 37) cm] from pick-up row, ending with a WS row.

### ESTABLISH LEFT SLEEVE

BO 101 (99, 97, 102, 100) (97, 101, 100, 98) sts at beginning of next 2 rows–70 (74, 78, 82, 86) (92, 98, 100, 104) sts remain. Work even in St st across all sts, discontinuing edge sts on WS rows, until piece measures 14½ (14½, 14½, 14½, 14½) (14, 14, 13, 12½)" [37 (37, 37, 37, 37) (35.5, 35.5, 33, 32) cm] from BO row, ending with a RS row.
Knit 4 rows.
BO all sts knitwise.

## RIGHT BACK/FRONT/SLEEVE

### RIGHT BACK

Carefully unzip provisional cast-on and place 136 (136, 136, 143, 143) (143, 150, 150, 150) Back sts on needle. Join yarn ready to work a RS row. Place removable marker at both ends of last row.
**Row 1 (RS):** Knit.
**Row 2:** Purl to last 4 sts, k2, p2.
Repeat Rows 1 and 2 until piece measures 3½ (3½, 3½, 4, 4) (4, 4½, 4½, 4½)" [9 (9, 9, 10, 10) (10, 11.5, 11.5, 11.5) cm] from markers, ending with a RS row. Do not cut yarn; leave sts on right-hand end of needle.

### ESTABLISH RIGHT FRONT

Lay Right Front Band on a flat surface with RS facing up, with CO edge at the bottom and BO edge at the top; place marker along left edge of Band 4 (4, 4, 4½, 4½) (4½, 5, 5, 5)" [10 (10, 10, 11.5, 11.5) (11.5, 12.5, 12.5, 12.5) cm] down from BO edge. With RS facing, using left-hand end of needle (Back sts are on right-hand end, with RS facing) and yarn attached to Back, pick up and knit 136 (136, 136, 143, 143) (143, 150, 150, 150) sts along left edge of Right Front Band, between marker and CO edge–272 (272, 272, 286, 286) (286, 300, 300, 300) sts.
**Setup Row (WS):** P2, k2, purl to last 4 sts, k2, p2.
**Row 1:** Knit.
**Row 2:** P2, k2, purl to last 4 sts, k2, p2.
Repeat Rows 1 and 2 until piece measures 6½ (7½, 8½, 9, 10) (11, 11½, 12½, 13½)" [16.5 (19, 21.5, 24, 26.5) (29, 32, 34.5, 37) cm] from pick-up row, ending with a WS row.

### ESTABLISH RIGHT SLEEVE

BO 101 (99, 97, 102, 100) (97, 101, 100, 98) sts at beginning of next 2 rows–70 (74, 78, 82, 86) (92, 98, 100, 104) sts remain. Work even in St st across all sts, discontinuing edge sts on WS rows, until piece measures 14½ (14½, 14½, 14½, 14½) (14, 14, 13, 12½)" [37 (37, 37, 37, 37) (35.5, 35.5, 33, 32) cm] from BO row, ending with a RS row.
Knit 4 rows.
BO all sts knitwise.

### FINISHING

Sew Front Bands together at back neck, leaving top 1½" (4 cm) unsewn. Sew Bands to Back neck. Steam or wet-block to measurements. Sew side and Sleeve seams.

# DESIGN YOUR OWN

## DESIGNING HUSSAR

I set out to design another cardigan made entirely of rectangles, like Weave (page 23), but this time worked side to side and with the addition of a pleated, or tucked, element. I put the fanciness front and center in the wide front bands to maximize the effect (and effort). The garter stitch base of the bands is knit on the bias, starting with increases on both edges. When the band reaches its full width, you increase on one edge while decreasing on the other and the pleating begins. To ensure that the bottom corner of the band matched on both fronts, the band is knit in two pieces, each increasing to full width from the three stitches cast on. If the band were knit in one piece, the decreases on the left front would look quite different from the increases on the right front. Perhaps more important, though, knitting the band in two pieces means that the pleats on one front mirror image the pleats on the other and are at the opposite angle.

## COLLAR SUBSTITUTIONS

The basic rectangular design of Hussar can be changed in so many ways. You might shorten the body, lengthen the sleeves, or even knit it in a different gauge with very little calculation. The easiest variation by far, though, is to switch out the collar/bands. Any scarf pattern made approximately the same width would substitute well and would change the design dramatically. Try colorwork or cables, textures or brioche. While you could keep the diagonal idea if you wanted, it certainly isn't necessary. Drop the split at the back of the neck, and the collar can be knit in one piece. A switch like this makes for a perfect first design project.

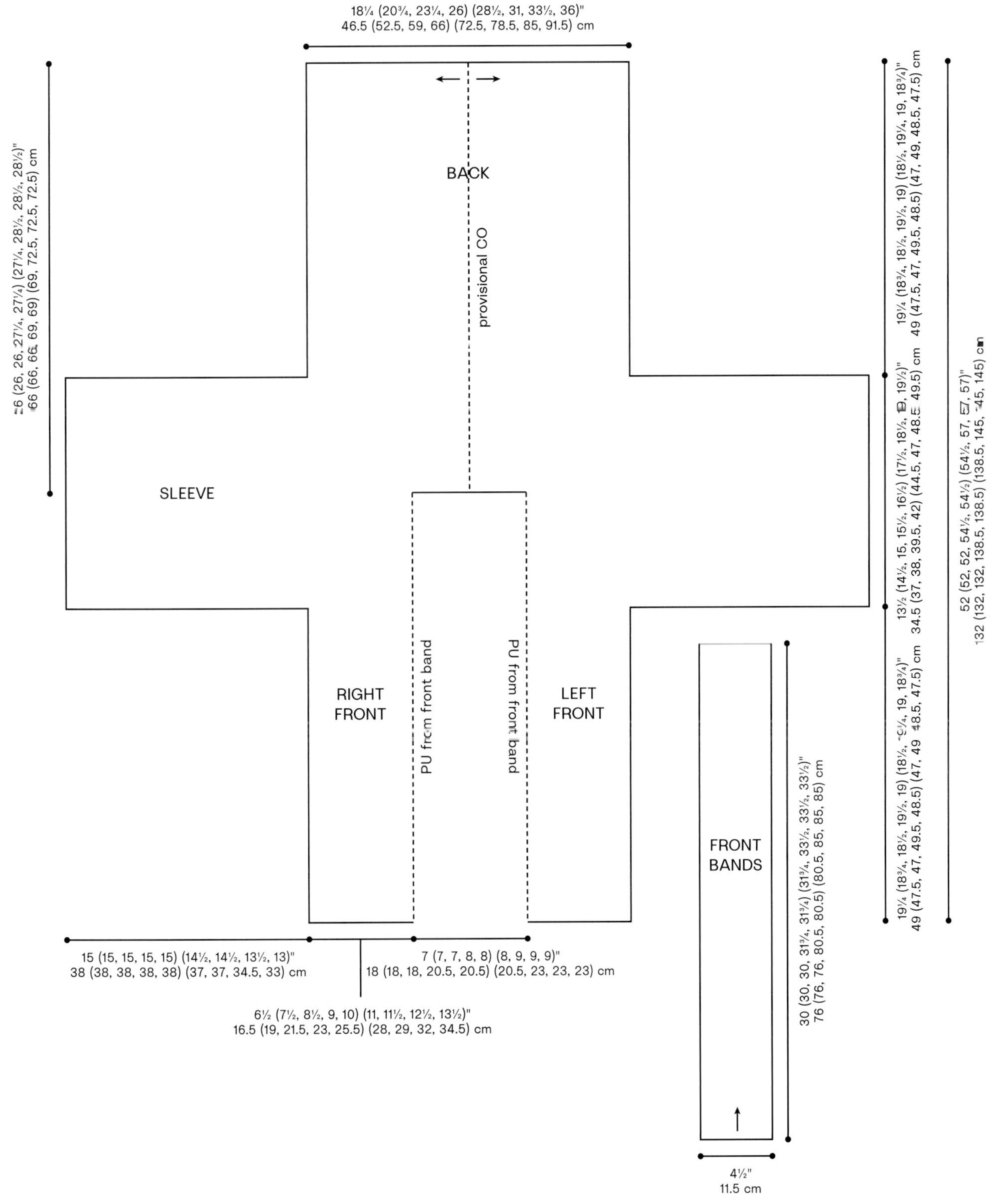

18¼ (20¾, 23¼, 26) (28½, 31, 33½, 36)"
46.5 (52.5, 59, 66) (72.5, 78.5, 85, 91.5) cm

BACK

provisional CO

26 (26, 26, 27¼, 27¼) (27¼, 28¼, 28½, 28½)"
66 (66, 66, 69, 69) (69, 72.5, 72.5, 72.5) cm

SLEEVE

19¼ (18¾, 18½, 19¼, 19) (18½, 19¼, 19, 18¾)"
49 (47.5, 47, 49.5, 48.5) (47, 49, 48.5, 47.5) cm

13½ (14½, 15, 15½, 16½) (17½, 18½, 19, 19½)"
34.5 (37, 38, 39.5, 42) (44.5, 47, 48.5, 49.5) cm

52 (52, 52, 54½, 54½) (54½, 57, 57, 57)"
132 (132, 132, 138.5, 138.5) (138.5, 145, 145, 145) cm

RIGHT
FRONT

PU from front band

PU from front band

LEFT
FRONT

19¼ (18¾, 18½, 19½, 19) (18½, 19¼, 19, 18¾)"
49 (47.5, 47, 49.5, 48.5) (47, 49, 48.5, 47.5) cm

FRONT
BANDS

15 (15, 15, 15, 15) (14½, 14½, 13½, 13)"
38 (38, 38, 38, 38) (37, 37, 34.5, 33) cm

7 (7, 7, 8, 8) (8, 9, 9, 9)"
18 (18, 18, 20.5, 20.5) (20.5, 23, 23, 23) cm

6½ (7½, 8½, 9, 10) (11, 11½, 12½, 13½)"
16.5 (19, 21.5, 23, 25.5) (28, 29, 32, 34.5) cm

30 (30, 30, 31¾, 31¾) (31¾, 33¼, 33½, 33½)"
76 (76, 76, 80.5, 80.5) (80.5, 85, 85, 85) cm

4½"
11.5 cm

# Pinion

This cowl is a variation on the cardigan Hussar (page 71). The gauge is smaller and the length longer, but the bias and pleating techniques are the same. Pinion's pleats are the perfect vehicle for a slowly changing colorway. Each pleat seems to be made of a different color until you are back to the beginning of the color sequence. Wear the cowl as a single loop or wrap it around twice, doubling it up for layers of layers.

**FINISHED MEASUREMENTS**
Approximately 3½" (9 cm) wide × 28" (71 cm) circumference

**YARN**
Spincycle Dyed in the Wool [100% superwashed American wool; 200 yards (183 m)/1¾ ounces (50 g)]: 3 skeins Cold Comfort

*Note: Cowl uses nearly all of 3 skeins; you may wish to purchase an additional skein if you intend to work a longer cowl.*

**NEEDLES**
One 24" (60 cm) or longer circular needle, size US 2 (2.75 mm)

One double-pointed needle size US 1 (2.25) or 0 (2 mm)

**NOTIONS**
Waste yarn and crochet hook size US 2 (2.5 mm) (optional; for provisional cast-on)

**GAUGE**
30 sts and 40 rows = 4" (10 cm) in St st after blocking

## SPECIAL TECHNIQUE (OPTIONAL)

**Kitchener Stitch:** Using a blunt tapestry needle, thread a length of yarn approximately 4 times the length of the section to be joined. Hold the pieces to be joined wrong sides together, with the needles holding the sts parallel, both ends pointing to the right. Working from right to left, insert tapestry needle into first st on front needle as if to purl, pull yarn through, leaving st on needle; insert tapestry needle into first st on back needle as if to knit, pull yarn through, leaving st on needle; *insert tapestry needle into first st on front needle as if to knit, pull yarn through, remove st from needle; insert tapestry needle into next st on front needle as if to purl, pull yarn through, leave st on needle; insert tapestry needle into first st on back needle as if to purl, pull yarn through, remove st from needle; insert tapestry needle into next st on back needle as

if to knit, pull yarn through, leave st on needle. Repeat from *, working 3 or 4 sts at a time, then go back and adjust tension to match the pieces being joined. When 1 st remains on each needle, cut yarn and pass through last 2 sts to fasten off.

## NOTE

Perfectionists may want to use a provisional cast-on so that they can graft live stitches at the end to live stitches from the provisional cast-on. I find it much easier to cast on with the long-tail method and graft the live stitches to the cast-on edge.

## COWL

Using Provisional (Crochet Chain) Cast-On or Long-Tail Cast-On (see Special Techniques, page 221), CO 36 sts.
**Row 1 (RS):** K2, M1R, knit to last 3 sts, k2tog, k1.

**Row 2:** P2, knit to last 2 sts, p2.
**Rows 3–8:** Repeat Rows 1 and 2 three more times. You now have 4 garter ridges.

## STRAIGHT SECTION, WITH TUCKS

**Row 9 (RS):** K2, M1R, knit to last 3 sts, k2tog, k1.
**Row 10:** Purl.
**Row 11:** Knit.
**Row 12:** Purl.
**Rows 13–24:** Repeat Rows 11 and 12 six more times.
With WS facing, using dpn, pick up (but do not knit) 36 sts, picking up the bottommost bumps above last garter tunnel, including a loop from one of the ends. *Note: The garter tunnel is the knit row between garter ridges; the bottommost purl bumps are the U-shaped bumps just above the tunnel.*
**Row 25:** Holding dpn behind front needle, *k2tog (1 st from front needle together with 1 st from dpn); repeat from * to end.
**Row 26:** P2, knit to last 2 sts, p2.
**Row 27:** K2, M1R, knit to last 3 sts, k2tog, k1.
**Row 28:** P2, knit to last 2, p2.
**Rows 29–36:** Repeat Rows 27 and 28 four times.
You should now have 6 garter ridges after the tuck.
Repeat Rows 9–36 thirty-one more times, then repeat Rows 9–28 once more.
You should now have 33 tucks and 2 garter ridges.

## FINISHING

Graft live sts to provisional cast-on using Kitchener st (see left) or graft live sts to cast-on edge (see Special Techniques, page 221).
Steam or wet-block.

# DESIGN YOUR OWN

### DESIGNING PINION

As you have probably figured out by now, even if you haven't designed a knit garment in your life, designing is all about swatching. Swatching is my life. When I set out to make the Pinion cowl, I decided on the yarn I wanted to knit with and knew I would be reusing the tuck idea from Hussar (page 71), but those decisions were only half the battle. After swatching in both stockinette and garter stitch to determine the needle size I liked best for the project, I then worked the tuck pattern from Hussar, starting at the full number of stitches. I didn't need the triangle formed with increasing since I would be joining diagonal start to diagonal end. In the smaller gauge, the original Hussar tucking pattern didn't look full enough to me. The tucks needed to have more rows. I increased

the number of stockinette rows worked before folding the tucks and joining them back to their base. After a few tries I determined the number of rows I liked best. Then my eyes told me that tucks with more rows need more space between them. I increased the number of garter ridges between the tucks until I was happy with the combination.

### CHANGE OF GAUGE

When changing gauges while reworking an idea, don't assume you can simply knit the original stitch pattern as written and all will be well. There will inevitably be a whole host of little decisions to be made specific to the new gauge. Does the same number of stitches in each element—for instance the pleat or tuck—look good to you at the new gauge?

How about the number of rows between elements like garter ridges? Does the number of stitches in the edging still look in proportion to the rest? As I write, I am thinking about the differences I found between the tucks for the front bands of the Hussar cardigan (page 71) and those of Pinion, but the advice is really much more general. For instance, if you were adapting the pleated pattern shown in the pillow Smocked (page 67), you might want to keep the pleat a similar width, which would call for a greater number of stitches, which in turn would call for more rows between the garter stitch lines. I try to not feel rushed while making these determinations, to indulge in the process, while at the same time not taking forever to swatch every possibility.

# Longitude

Seven significant vertical tucks provide the major design element for this generous scarf/stole. The tucks pull in considerably, leaving the stockinette stitch to expand and flutter. A few garter ridges add definition to the area where the plain knitting ends and the tucking begins and vice versa. On the other side, special care has been given to the appearance with the addition of twisted stitches to secure the reverse side of each tuck. After all, there really is no wrong side of a scarf or stole. When worn, both sides are likely to make an appearance.

## FINISHED MEASUREMENTS

14" × 60" (35.5 × 152.5 cm)

## YARN

mYak Tibetan Cloud [100% wool; 328 yards (300 m)/3½ ounces (100 g)]: 4 skeins Ginepro

*Note: Four skeins is enough yarn to make a 72" (183 cm) long shawl.*

## NEEDLES

One pair straight needles, size US 5 (3.75 mm)

Seven double-pointed needles, size US 5 (3.75 mm), for vertical pleats

*Note: Plastic or non-slippery wood is recommended for the double pointed needles, to keep sts from sliding off needles while pleat sts are on hold.*

Change needle size if necessary to obtain correct gauge.

## GAUGE

25 sts and 31 rows = 4" (10 cm) in St st

## PATTERN NOTES

The vertical pleats in this shawl are worked by placing sts on double-pointed needles and working the held sts every other row. On the rows where the held sts aren't worked, a right twist joins the sts on either side of the held sts to create the pleat.

## SHAWL

Using Long-Tail Cast-On (see Special Techniques, page 221), CO 141 sts.

**Row 1 (RS):** K1, k1-tbl, [p1-tbl, k1-tbl] 3 times, knit to last 8 sts, k1-tbl, [p1-tbl, k1-tbl] 3 times, k1.

**Row 2:** K1, p1-tbl, [k1-tbl, p1-tbl] 3 times, purl to last 8 sts, p1-tbl, [k1-tbl, p1-tbl] 3 times, k1.

Repeat Rows 1 and 2 until piece measures 9½" (24 cm) from the beginning, ending with a WS row.

**Row 3:** K1, k1-tbl, [p1-tbl, k1-tbl] 3 times, k4, p1, k7, slip last 7 sts to dpn and hold to front, p1, [k9, p1, k7, slip last 7 sts to dpn and hold to front, p1] 6 times, k4, k1-tbl, [p1-tbl, k1-tbl] 3 times, k1.

**Row 4:** K1, p1-tbl, [k1-tbl, p1-tbl] 3 times, p4, RT, [p9, RT] 6 times, p4, p1-tbl, [k1-tbl, p1-tbl] 3 times, k1.

**Row 5:** K1, k1-tbl, [p1-tbl, k1-tbl] 3 times, k4, p1, k7 from dpn, then slip these same 7 sts back to dpn and knit them again, slip them back to dpn, p1, [k9, p1, k7 from dpn, then slip these same 7 sts back to dpn and knit them again, slip them back to dpn, p1] 6 times, k4, k1-tbl, [p1-tbl, k1-tbl] 3 times, k1.

**Row 6:** Repeat Row 4.

**Rows 7 and 8:** Repeat Rows 5 and 6.

**Row 9:** Repeat Row 5.

**Row 10:** K1, p1-tbl, [k1-tbl, p1-tbl] 3 times, k4, RT, [k9, RT] 6 times, k4, p1-tbl, [k1-tbl, p1-tbl] 3 times, k1.

**Rows 11–14:** Repeat Rows 9 and 10 twice. Repeat Rows 5 and 6 until piece measures 50½" (128.5 cm).

Repeat Rows 9 and 10 three times, then repeat Rows 5 and 6 twice.

Repeat Rows 1 and 2 until piece measures 60" (152.5 cm), ending with a WS row.

BO all sts purlwise.

## FINISHING

Block as desired.

# DESIGN YOUR OWN

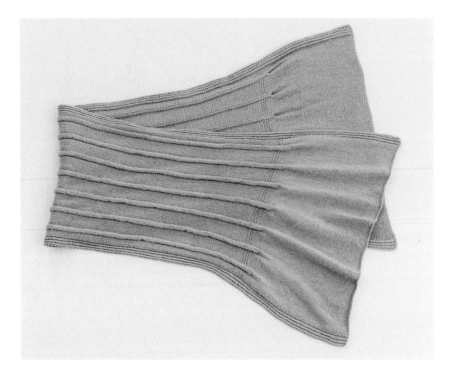

### DESIGNING LONGITUDE

Determined to find a way to make vertical tucks during the knitting process, it occurred to me that slipping stitches, making something like an I-cord for each vertical line, might make a nice, rounded tuck. That idea started a process of experimentation. When testing the idea, I found there were two problems that needed to be solved. First, the slipped stitches weren't stretchy enough to reach the same length as the stockinette. The shortness was predictable, since there were half the number of rows in the tucks. How could I restore the number of rows and still get the rounded vertical tuck? The stitches weren't worked on the wrong side. What if I worked them twice on the right side row so the tuck and the surrounding stitches had the same number of rows, slipping them back to the left needle and working them again? The idea

worked, but there was a second problem to be solved: The wrong side of the tucks didn't look very pretty. When I am designing a shawl or scarf, or anything where the wrong side is bound to face forward, I like that side to look nice, too. I already had a reverse stockinette stitch on either side of the tuck, both for definition and for visual cues for the start and end of the tuck. If I put the tuck stitches on a double-pointed needle, or if they were already on a double-pointed needle from the previous row, they would be out of the way. Then, the two reverse stockinette stitches would be next to each other, which meant that they could be joined with a right twist. The right twists look neat and attractive and pull the fabric together, making the tuck better, too. Admittedly, having seven tucks on seven double-pointed needles is somewhat awkward. If you know you don't have the patience for it, next are some thoughts about how to make vertical tucks in an easier way.

### SIMPLIFIED VERTICAL TUCKS

While it is satisfying to knit vertical tucks in as you go, it's also a bit of knitting gymnastics and takes patience and nerve to accomplish. If you are designing something with vertical tucks, take a look at how the vertical box pleats are made in the pillow Smocked (page 67). Place at least one reverse stockinette stitch on either side of the stockinette stitches that will form the tuck, knit your piece to its desired length, and sew the edges of the reverse stockinette stitches together at the end. Experiment with different types of seaming before you start. Some will look better to you than others, and some will pull in more than others. Both mattress stitch and whip stitch were strong contenders for me.

# CHAPTER 4
# MULTIPLY

Multiple squares, rectangles, and polygons are joined to create unique surfaces. Though these projects are not all made out of squares, the hexagons, pentagons, and octagons are scribed with ribs and twisted stitches to resemble the fold lines of traditional origami. Some squares combine and fold to make not-so-square garments while following a different approach; others expand into three-dimensional space, becoming pyramids.

# Patch

This cardigan is constructed entirely of squares, some knit in garter stitch and some in a textural seeded stitch, while the remainder are mitered squares. In a bid to eliminate excess seaming, each is picked up and knit onto a previously knit unit. The dramatic dolman shape allows plenty of freedom to move as you go about your busy day.

## FINISHED MEASUREMENTS

41 (49, 57)" [104 (124.5, 145) cm] hip circumference, buttoned

*Note: This piece is intended to be worn with approximately 1–3" (2.5–7.5 cm) positive ease.*

## YARN

Brooklyn Tweed Loft [100% American Targhee-Columbia wool; 275 yards (251 m)/1¾ ounces (50 g)]: 3 (3, 4) skeins each Foothills (light green) (A) and Sap (green) (B); 2 (3, 3) skeins Bale (yellow) (C); and 3 (4, 4) skeins Hayloft (rust) (D)

## NEEDLES

One pair straight needles, size US 5 (3.75 mm)

Change needle size if necessary to obtain correct gauge.

## NOTIONS

Removable stitch marker

Nine ½" (13 mm) buttons

## GAUGE

24 sts and 48 rows = 4" (10 cm) in garter st (knit every row)

24 sts and 44 rows = 4" (10 cm) in Dotted Texture

## PATTERN STITCHES

### MITERED SQUARE (61 STS)

(odd number of sts; 2-row repeat)
Place removable marker on center st.
**Row 1 (WS):** Knit to center st, p1, knit to end.
**Row 2:** Knit to 1 st before center st, s2kp2, knit to end—2 sts decreased.
Repeat Rows 1 and 2 until 5 sts remain, ending with Row 2.
Repeat Row 1.
**Last Row:** S3k2p3. Fasten off.

### DOTTED TEXTURE

(even number of sts; 4-row repeat)
**Row 1 (WS):** Purl.
**Row 2:** K1, *k1, p1; repeat from * to last st, k1.
**Row 3:** Purl.
**Row 4:** K1, *p1, k1; repeat from * to last st, k1.
Repeat Rows 1–4 for pattern.

## PATTERN NOTES

This cardigan is constructed of individual squares worked in three stitch patterns and four colors. Most of the squares are worked off of a previous square, either by continuing with a new color or by picking up stitches, but in a few cases, two internal (non-edge) squares must be sewn together. The cardigan could be made with fewer seams, but the instructions would be much more complicated.

The square numbers indicate the order in which the squares are worked, and not the pattern worked for that square.

Squares of the same number may be worked in a different color and stitch pattern for each garment piece. You may find it helpful to refer to the diagram as you work.

Cast on all sts using Long-Tail Cast-On (see Special Techniques, page 221). All stitch patterns begin with a WS row.

## LEFT FRONT

### SQUARE 1

Using A, CO 30 (36, 42) sts; knit every row for 5 (6, 7)" [12.5 (15, 18) cm], ending with a RS row. Do not BO.

### SQUARE 2

Change to C; work Dotted Texture for 5 (6, 7)" [12.5 (15, 18) cm]. BO all sts in pattern.

### SQUARE 3

Using B, pick up and knit 30 (36, 42) sts along edge of Square 2; knit every row for 5 (6, 7)" [12.5 (15, 18) cm], ending with a RS row. Do not BO.

### SQUARE 4

Change to C; work Dotted Texture for 5 (6, 7)" [12.5 (15, 18) cm], ending with a WS row. BO all sts in pattern.

### SQUARE 5

Using D, pick up and knit 30 (36, 42) sts along side edge of Square 1, pick up and knit 1 st in corner (place removable marker on this st), then pick up and knit 30 (36, 42) sts along side edge of Square 3; work Mitered Square.

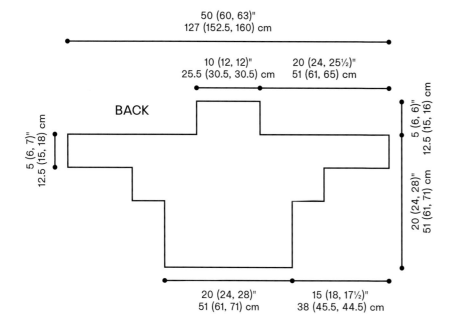

50 (60, 63)"
127 (152.5, 160) cm

10 (12, 12)"
25.5 (30.5, 30.5) cm

20 (24, 25½)"
51 (61, 65) cm

BACK

5 (6, 6)"
12.5 (15, 16) cm

5 (6, 7)"
12.5 (15, 18) cm

20 (24, 28)"
51 (61, 71) cm

20 (24, 28)"
51 (61, 71) cm

15 (18, 17½)"
38 (45.5, 44.5) cm

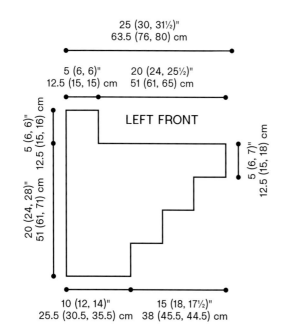

25 (30, 31½)"
63.5 (76, 80) cm

5 (6, 6)"
12.5 (15, 15) cm

20 (24, 25½)"
51 (61, 65) cm

LEFT FRONT

5 (6, 6)"
12.5 (15, 16) cm

5 (6, 7)"
12.5 (15, 18) cm

20 (24, 28)"
51 (61, 71) cm

10 (12, 14)"
25.5 (30.5, 35.5) cm

15 (18, 17½)"
38 (45.5, 44.5) cm

### SQUARE 6

Using A, pick up and knit 30 (36, 42) sts along side edge of Square 3; knit every row for 5 (6, 7)" [12.5 (15, 18) cm], ending with a RS row. Do not BO.

### SQUARE 7

Change to C; work Dotted Texture for 5 (6, 7)" [12.5 (15, 18) cm], ending with a WS row. BO all sts in pattern.

### SQUARE 8

Using B, pick up and knit 30 (36, 42) sts along side edge of Square 6; knit every row for 5 (6, 7)" [12.5 (15, 18) cm], ending with a WS row. BO all sts knitwise.

### SQUARE 9

Using D, pick up and knit 30 (36, 42) sts along side edge of Square 7, pick up and knit 1 st in corner (place removable marker on this st), then pick up and knit 30 (36, 42) sts along side edge of Square 8; work Mitered Square.

### SQUARE 10

Using B, pick up and knit 30 (36, 42) sts along side edge of Square 7; knit every row for 5 (6, 7)" [12.5 (15, 18) cm], ending with a WS row. BO all sts knitwise.

### SQUARE 11

Using D, pick up and knit 30 (36, 42) sts along side edge of Square 6, pick up and knit 1 st in corner (place removable marker on this st), then pick up and knit 30 (36, 42) sts along side edge of Square 10; work Mitered Square.

### SQUARE 12

Using B, pick up and knit 30 (36, 42) sts along side edge of Square 11; knit every row for 5 (6, 7)" [12.5 (15, 18) cm], ending with a WS row. BO all sts knitwise.

### SQUARE 13

Using A, pick up and knit 30 (36, 42) sts along side edge of Square 12; knit every row for 5 (6, 7)" [12.5 (15, 18) cm], ending with a WS row. BO all sts knitwise.

## SIZES 41 AND 49 ONLY:

### SQUARE 14

Using D, CO 30 (36, -) sts, pick up and knit 1 st in corner of Square 12 (place removable marker on this st), then pick up and knit 30 (36, -) sts along edge of Square 13; work Mitered Square.

### SQUARE 15

Using C, pick up and knit 30 (36, -) sts along edge of Square 9; work Dotted Texture for 5 (6, -)" [12.5 (15, -) cm], ending with a WS row. BO all sts in pattern.

## SIZE 57 ONLY:

### SQUARE 14

Using D, pick up and knit 42 sts along side edge of Square 13; knit every row for 2" (5 cm), ending with a WS row. BO all sts knitwise.

### SQUARE 15

Using C, and beginning 1" (2.5 cm) in from right edge of Square 9, pick up and knit 36 sts along edge of Square 9; work Dotted Texture for 6" (15 cm), ending with a WS row. BO all sts in pattern.

## ALL SIZES:

Using C, sew short seams shown on diagram (page 90).

## RIGHT FRONT

### SQUARE 1

Using B, CO 30 (36, 36) sts; knit every row for 5 (6, 6)" [12.5 (15, 15) cm], ending with a WS row. BO all sts knitwise.

## SIZES 41 AND 49 ONLY:

### SQUARE 2

Using A, pick up and knit 30 (36, -) sts along side edge of Square 1; knit every row for 5 (6, -)" [12.5 (15, -) cm], ending with a RS row. Do not BO.

## SIZES 57 ONLY:

### SQUARE 2

Using A, CO 6 sts, pick up and knit 36 sts along side edge of Square 1—42 sts.

Knit every row for 6" (15 cm), ending with a RS row. Do not BO.

## ALL SIZES:

### SQUARE 3

Change to C; work Dotted Texture for 5 (6, 7)" [12.5 (15, 18) cm], ending with a WS row. BO all sts in pattern.

### SQUARE 4

Using B, pick up and knit 30 (36, 42) sts along side edge of Square 2; knit every row for 5 (6, 7)" [12.5 (15, 18) cm], ending with a RS row. Do not BO.

### SQUARE 5

Change to C; work Dotted Texture for 5 (6, 7)" [12.5 (15, 18) cm], ending with a WS row. BO all sts in pattern.

### SQUARE 6

Using A, pick up and knit 30 (36, 42) sts along side edge of Square 5; knit every row for 5 (6, 7)" [12.5 (15, 18) cm], ending with a WS row. BO all sts knitwise.

### SQUARE 7

Using D, pick up and knit 30 (36, 42) sts along side edge of Square 6, pick up and knit 1 st in corner (place removable marker on this st), then pick up and knit 30 (36, 42) sts along side edge of Square 4; work Mitered Square.

### SQUARE 8

Using A, pick up and knit 30 (36, 42) sts along side edge of Square 7; knit every row for 5 (6, 7)" [12.5 (15, 18) cm], ending with a RS row. Do not BO.

### SQUARE 9

Change to C; work Dotted Texture for 5 (6, 7)" [12.5 (15, 18) cm], ending with a WS row. BO all sts in pattern.

### SQUARE 10

Using B, pick up and knit 30 (36, 42) sts along side edge of Square 9; knit every row for 5 (6, 7)" [12.5 (15, 18) cm], ending with a WS row. BO all sts knitwise.

### SQUARE 11

Using D, pick up and knit 30 (36, 42) sts along side edge of Square 10, pick up and knit 1 st in corner (place removable marker on this st), then pick up and knit 30 (36, 42) sts along side edge of Square 8; work Mitered Square.

### SQUARE 12

Using B, pick up and knit 30 (36, 42) sts along side edge of Square 8; knit every row for 5 (6, 7)" [12.5 (15, 18) cm], ending with a WS row. BO all sts knitwise.

### SQUARE 13

Using D, CO 30 (36, 42) sts, pick up and knit 1 st in corner of Square 5 (place removable marker on this st), then pick up and knit 30 (36, 42) sts along side edge of Square 5; work Mitered Square.

### SQUARE 14

Using C, pick up and knit 30 (36, 42) sts along side edge of Square 13; work Dotted Texture for 5 (6, 7)" [12.5 (15, 18) cm], ending with a WS row. BO all sts knitwise.

### SQUARE 15

Using A, pick up and knit 30 (36, 42) sts along side edge of Square 13; knit every row for 5 (6, 7)" [12.5 (15, 5) cm], ending with a WS row. BO
Using C, sew short seams shown on diagram.

## BACK

### SQUARE 1

Using C, CO 30 sts; work Dotted Texture for 5 (6, 7)" [12.5 (15, 18) cm], ending with a WS row. Do not BO.

### SQUARE 2

Change to A; knit every row for 5 (6, 7)" [12.5 (15, 18) cm], ending with a WS row. BO all sts knitwise.

### SQUARE 3

Using B, pick up and knit 30 (36, 42) sts along side edge of Square 1; knit every row for 5 (6, 7)" [12.5 (15, 18) cm], ending with a WS row. BO all sts knitwise.

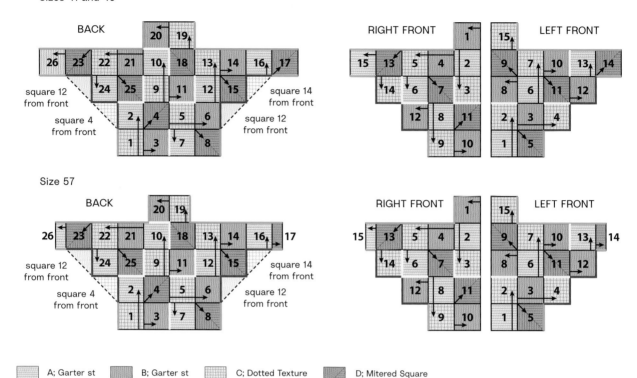

Sizes 41 and 49

BACK

RIGHT FRONT

LEFT FRONT

square 12 from front

square 4 from front

square 14 from front

square 12 from front

Size 57

BACK

RIGHT FRONT

LEFT FRONT

square 12 from front

square 4 from front

square 14 from front

square 12 from front

A; Garter st        B; Garter st        C; Dotted Texture        D; Mitered Square

**SQUARE 4**

Using D, pick up and knit 30 (36, 42) sts along side edge of Square 3, pick up and knit 1 st in corner (place removable marker on this st), then pick up and knit 30 (36, 42) sts along side edge of Square 2; work Mitered Square.

**SQUARE 5**

Using C, pick up and knit 30 (36, 42) sts along side edge of Square 4; work Dotted Texture for 5 (6, 7)" [12.5 (15, 18) cm], ending with a WS row. Do not BO.

**SQUARE 6**

Change to B; knit every row for 5 (6, 7)" [12.5 (15, 18) cm], ending with a WS row. BO all sts knitwise.

**SQUARE 7**

Using A, pick up and knit 30 (36, 42) sts along side edge of Square 5; knit every

row for 5 (6, 7)" [12.5 (15, 18) cm], ending with a WS row. BO all sts knitwise.

**SQUARE 8**

Using D, pick up and knit 30 (36, 42) sts along side edge of Square 7, pick up and knit 1 st in corner (place removable marker on this st), then pick up and knit 30 (36, 42) sts along side edge of Square 6; work Mitered Square.

**SQUARE 9**

Using C, pick up and knit 30 (36, 42) sts along side edge of Square 4; work Dotted Texture for 5 (6, 7)" [12.5 (15, 18) cm], ending with a WS row. Do not BO.

**SQUARE 10**

Change to A; knit every row for 5 (6, 7)" [12.5 (15, 18) cm], ending with a WS row. BO all sts knitwise.

**SQUARE 11**

Using B, pick up and knit 30 (36, 42) sts along side edge of Square 9; knit every row for 5 (6, 7)" [12.5 (15, 18) cm], ending with a WS row. BO all sts knitwise.

**SQUARE 12**

Using A, pick up and knit 30 (36, 42) sts along side edge of Square 6; knit every row for 5 (6, 7)" [12.5 (15, 18) cm], ending with a RS row. Do not BO.

**SQUARE 13**

Change to C; work Dotted Texture for 5 (6, 7)" [12.5 (15, 18) cm], ending with a WS row. BO all sts in pattern.

**SQUARE 14**

Using B, pick up and knit 30 (36, 42) sts along side edge of Square 13; knit every row for 5 (6, 7)" [12.5 (15, 18) cm], ending with a WS row. BO all sts knitwise.

## SQUARE 15

Using D, pick up and knit 30 (36, 42) sts along side edge of Square 12, pick up and knit 1 st in corner (place removable marker on this st), then pick up and knit 30 (36, 42) sts along side edge of Square 14; work Mitered Square.

## SQUARE 16

Using A, CO 30 sts; knit every row for 5 (6, 7)" [12.5 (15, 18) cm], ending with a RS row. BO all sts knitwise.

## SIZES 41 AND 49 ONLY:

## SQUARE 17

Using D, CO 30 (36, -) sts, pick up and knit 1 st in corner of Square 16 (place removable marker on this st), then pick up and knit 30 (36, -) sts along side edge of Square 16; work Mitered Square.

## SIZE 57 ONLY:

## SQUARE 17

Using D, pick up and knit 42 sts along side edge of Square 16; knit every row for 2" (5 cm), ending with a RS row. BO all sts knitwise.

## ALL SIZES:

## SQUARE 18

Using D, pick up and knit 30 (36, 42) sts along side edge of Square 13, pick up and knit 1 st in corner (place removable marker on this st), then pick up and knit 30 (36, 42) sts along side edge of Square 11; work Mitered Square.

## SIZES 41 AND 49 ONLY:

## SQUARE 19

Using C, pick up and knit 30 (36, -) sts along side edge of Square 18; work Dotted Texture for 5 (6, -)" [12.5 (15, -) cm], ending with a WS row. BO all sts in pattern.

## SQUARE 20

Using B, pick up and knit 30 (36, -) sts along side edge of Square 19; knit every row for 5 (6, -)" [12.5 (15, -) cm], ending with a WS row. BO all sts knitwise.

## SIZE 57 ONLY:

## SQUARE 19

Using C, and beginning 1" (2.5 cm) in from corner of Squares 13 and 18, pick up and knit 36 sts along side edge of Square 18; work Dotted Texture for 6" (15 cm), ending with a WS row. BO all sts in pattern.

## SQUARE 20

Using B, pick up and knit 36 sts along edge of Square 19; knit every row for 6" (15 cm), ending with a WS row. BO all sts knitwise.

## ALL SIZES:

## SQUARE 21

Using B, pick up and knit 30 (36, 42) sts along side edge of Square 10; knit every row for 5 (6, 7)" [12.5 (15, 18) cm], ending with a RS row. Do not BO.

## SQUARE 22

Change to C; work Dotted Texture for 5 (6, 7)" [12.5 (15, 18) cm], ending with a WS row. BO all sts in pattern.

## SQUARE 23

Using D, CO 30 (36, 42) sts, pick up and knit 1 st in corner of Square 22 (place removable marker on this st), then pick up and knit 30 (36, 42) sts along side edge of Square 22; work Mitered Square.

## SQUARE 24

Using A, pick up and knit 30 (36, 42) sts along side edge of Square 22; knit every row for 5 (6, 7)" [12.5 (15, 18) cm], ending with a WS row. BO all sts knitwise.

## SQUARE 25

Using D, pick up and knit 30 (36, 42) sts along side edge of Square 24, pick up and knit 1 st in corner (place removable marker on this st), then pick up and knit 30 (36, 42) sts along side edge of Square 21; work Mitered Square.

## SQUARE 26

Using A, pick up and knit 30 (36, 42) sts along side edge of Square 23; knit every row for 5 (6, 2)" [12.5 (15, 5) cm], ending with a WS row. BO all sts knitwise. Using C, sew short seams shown on diagram.

## FINISHING

Block as desired. Sew Fronts and Back together along seams shown in pink and blue on diagram. Some of the Front Squares fold in half diagonally to be sewn to the Back (see pink lines on diagram). *Note: For size 59, when sewing Square 20 to Square 10, end seam 1" (2.5 cm) before corner of Squares 10 and 21.*

## BUTTON BAND

With RS of Left Front facing, pick up and knit 30 (36, 36) sts along edge of Square 15, then 30 36, 42) sts along center Front edge of remaining Squares—150 (180, 204) sts. Knit 10 rows. BO all sts knitwise. Place markers for buttons, the first ½" (1.5 cm) down from top edge, the second where neck Square ends and top body Square begins, the third halfway between the first and second, the fourth 1" (2.5 cm) up from bottom edge, and the remaining 5 spaced evenly between bottom marker and bottom of neck marker.

## BUTTONHOLE BAND

With RS of Right Front facing, pick up and knit 30 (36, 42) sts along edges of Squares 10, 11, 3, and 2, then 30 (36, 36) sts along edge of Square 1—150 (180, 204) sts. Knit 4 rows.
**Buttonhole Row 1 (WS):** *Knit to 1 st before marker, k1-f/b, [k1, pass st over] 3 times; repeat from * until all buttonholes have been worked, knit to end.
**Buttonhole Row 2:** *Knit to BO sts, turn; using Cable Cast-On, CO 3 sts, turn; yb, slip 1 st from right needle back to left needle, k2tog; repeat from * until all buttonholes have been completed, knit to end. Knit 4 rows. BO all sts knitwise. Sew buttons at markers.

# DESIGN YOUR OWN

## DESIGNING PATCH

I had a couple of parameters in mind when I started designing Patch. I knew I was aiming for a high-necked cardigan, and I knew I wanted it built out of multiple squares, some of which would be mitered. I start by mapping out the target width and length on a scale grid on my drawing program or hand drawing on square graph paper: One square equals one inch. As I started to think about filling up the grid in front of me, a few design decisions presented themselves.

1. Since a cardigan is (usually) divided straight up the center, I needed an even number of squares across the front, and therefore, across the back. If I weren't using mitered squares, it would have been easy to make half squares, but I really liked the idea of using mitered squares and sticking to using only

one shape. I also like the occasional interjection of the sharp diagonal line in the mitered square. Drawing squares onto my grid, I took a look at both four squares across and six squares across to see which was closest to my original vision, and four across won. Filling up the length with squares, I had a choice between three, four, or five squares in length. Four was closest to what I was thinking, although three squares in length, maybe with a ribbed bottom edge, would be a good choice too, and you could make a coat by adding many more rows of squares.

2. What did the dimensions of my chosen square mean for the sleeve? Two squares across was a good width for the bottom edge of the sleeve. However, if the sleeve remained 2 squares across at the top it would be too tight, so the sleeve could not be rectangular unless the sleeve squares were larger than the body squares, which I wasn't in favor of—

plus I like the idea of a fairly narrow cuff, and without a way to shape the sleeve, the cuff and top would be the same width.

Diagonal folds to the rescue! The answer to my dilemma was using squares folded on the diagonal, half belonging to the back and half to the front. Represented by triangles on my grid, I played around to decide how much fabric to leave in the underarm, and I went for a fairly dramatic dolman.

Keeping to my decisions above worked for the same sample size, which uses a 5" (12.5 cm) square throughout. The dimensions worked well for 6" (15 cm) squares also. When expanded to 7" (17.5 cm) squares, the lengths and widths were still okay, but I decided that the neck was better in the 6" (15cm) squares. With squares larger than 7" (17.5 cm), sleeve lengths became inhuman in scale, as did the length of the garment.

The resulting three sizes will fit hips 38–58" [96.5–147.5) cm]. Because of its shape, with the extra width provided by the dolman sleeves, Patch is forgiving in fit at the chest but more fitted at the hip.

## BUILDING WITH SQUARES

Figuring out how to build shapes with squares can be a fun puzzle. Think about how your desired shape might be broken down into squares and folded squares. That gives you three basic units to work with—squares, triangles, and rectangles. I based the design for Patch on the premise that all of the squares had to be identical in size, and I didn't stray from that idea until it came time to plan the neckline for the largest size. What if a design were built of squares of different sizes? If each piece of the garment, say the sleeve and the front, could be made from different size squares and didn't have to match up where they met, there would be more flexibility for sizing. Other puzzles might need to be solved, though. Do you like how it looks where the two different grids meet? Is there something you could do to make the point of collision work better? Maybe introducing a new element, like a solid line, would make an attractive transition. Maybe my preconceived notion that everything should match up is too constricting. Get out your computer or pencil and paper and start building your idea. Try to throw those accepted ideas out the window and approach the puzzle with a creative and open mind.

# Kite

Kite's major squares are knit on the bias, from bottom corner to top corner, adorned with eyelet increases and an occasional column of refined lace stitches. Triangular "half squares" fill out the body, and easy rectangles become both the sleeves and the tailored peplum, where the total length can be adjusted. While the neckline appears to be a V in the front, it is merely a split with a few self-finishing stitches worked as you go. What is most unusual is the fold-down in the back, where the top corners of the front and back squares join, forming a point that folds down (see page 96).

## FINISHED MEASUREMENTS

40 (44, 48, 52, 56) (60, 64, 68, 72)" [101.5 (112, 122, 132, 142) (152.5, 162.5, 172.5, 183) cm] chest

Note: This piece is intended to be worn with approximately 10" (25.5 cm) positive ease.

## YARN

Berroco Arno [57% cotton/43% merino wool; 159 yards (145 m)/1¾ ounces (50 g)]: 7 (8, 9, 10, 11) (12, 13, 14, 16) skeins #5033 Twilight Blue

## NEEDLES

One pair straight needles, size US 5 (3.75 mm)

Change needle size if necessary to obtain correct gauge.

## NOTIONS

Stitch markers

Removable stitch markers

Cable needle

## GAUGE

22 sts and 32 rows = 4" (10 cm) in St st

## PATTERN NOTES

The Front and Back are worked separately, beginning with the main upper square. The middle triangles are worked off the upper square, and the lower pieces are worked off the middle triangles. Finally, after sewing the top section of the upper squares together, the Sleeves are picked up and worked flat to the bottom edge.

## UPPER BACK

Using Long-Tail Cast-On (see Special Techniques, page 221), CO 3 sts.
**Setup Row (WS):** Purl.
**Row 1 (RS):** K1, M1R, k1, M1L, k1–5 sts.
**Rows 2 and 4:** Purl.
**Row 3:** K2, M1R, k1, M1L, k2–7 sts.
**Row 5:** K3, yo, k1, yo, k3–9 sts.
**Row 6:** Purl.

## INCREASE SECTION

**Row 7 (RS):** K3, yo, knit to last 3 sts, yo, k3–2 sts increased.
**Rows 8 and 10:** Purl.
**Row 9:** K3, yo, k1, yo, knit to last 4 sts, yo, k1, yo, k3–4 sts increased.
**Row 11:** Repeat Row 7–2 sts increased.
**Row 12:** Purl.
Repeat Rows 7–12 eleven (13, 14, 15, 17) (18, 20, 21, 22) more times, then repeat Rows 7 and 8 1 (0, 1, 1, 1) (1, 0, 1, 1) more time(s)–107 (121, 131, 139, 155) (163, 177, 187, 195) sts.

## SIZES 40, 52, 60, AND 72 ONLY:

**Row 13 (RS):** K3, yo, ssk, yo, knit to last 5 sts, yo, ssk, yo, k3–2 sts increased.
**Row 14:** Purl.
Repeat Rows 7 and 8 zero (-, -, 1, -) (0, -, -, 1) time(s)–109 (-, -, 143, -) (165, -, -, 199) sts.

## ALL SIZES

Place removable markers at beginning and end of last row worked.

## DECREASE SECTION

**Row 1 (RS):** K3, k2tog, knit to last 5 sts, ssk, k3–2 sts decreased.
**Rows 2 and 4:** Purl.
**Row 3:** Repeat Row 1–2 sts decreased.
**Row 5:** K3, [k2tog] twice, knit to last 7 sts, [ssk] twice, yo, k3–4 sts decreased.
**Row 6:** Purl.
Repeat Rows 1–6 eleven (12, 14, 15, 17) (18, 19, 21, 22) more times, repeat Rows 1 and 2 one (1, 0, 2, 0) (1, 1, 0, 2) more time(s), then repeat Rows 5 and 6 zero (1, 0, 0, 0) (0, 1, 0, 0) more time(s)–11 sts remain.
**Row 7 (RS):** K3, k2tog, k1, ssk, k3–9 sts remain.
**Rows 8, 10, and 12:** Purl.
**Row 9:** K3, s2kp2, k3–7 sts remain.
**Row 11:** K2, s2kp2, k2–5 sts remain.
**Row 13:** K1, s2kp2, k1–3 sts remain.
BO all sts.

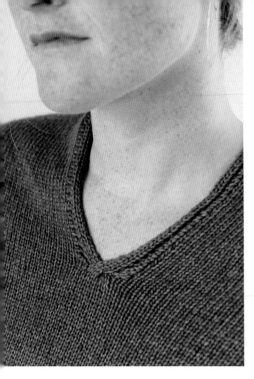

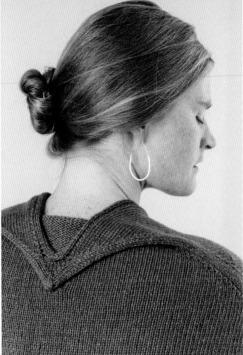

## UPPER FRONT

Work as for Upper Back to beginning of Decrease Section–109 (121, 131, 143, 155) (165, 177, 187, 199) sts. Place markers on either side of center 7 sts.

### DECREASE SECTION

**Row 1 (RS):** K3, k2tog, knit to marker, remove marker, slip 4 sts to cable needle, hold to back, k3, remove marker, join a second ball of yarn, (k2tog, k2) from cable needle, knit to last 5 sts, ssk, k3–53 (59, 64, 70, 76) (81, 87, 92, 98) sts remain each side.
Work both sides at the same time.
**Rows 2, 4, and 6:** Purl.
**Row 3:** K3, k2tog, knit to 5 sts before neck opening, k2tog, yo, k3; on second side, k3, yo, ssk, knit to last 5 sts, ssk, k3–2 sts decreased.
**Row 5:** K3, [k2tog] twice, knit to 5 sts before neck opening, k2tog, yo, k3; on second side, k3, yo, ssk, knit to last 7 sts, [ssk] twice, yo, k3–4 sts decreased.
**Row 7:** K3, k2tog, knit to 5 sts before neck opening, k2tog, yo, k3; on second side, k3, yo, ssk, knit to last 5 sts, ssk, yo, k3–2 sts decreased.
**Row 8:** Purl.
Repeat Rows 3–8 ten (11, 12, 14, 15) (17, 18, 19, 21) more times, then repeat Rows 3 and 4 zero (2, 3, 1, 3) (0, 2, 3, 1) more time(s)–9 sts remain each side.
**Row 9 (RS):** K3, k2tog, k1, slip 3 sts to cable needle, hold to back, continuing with same ball of yarn (cut second ball), k2tog, k1, k3 from cable, k1, ssk, k3–15 sts.
**Rows 10, 12, 14, 16, 18, and 20:** Purl.
**Row 11:** K3, k2tog, k5, ssk, k3–13 sts remain.
**Row 13:** K3, k2tog, k3, ssk, k3–11 sts remain.
**Row 15:** K3, k2tog, k1, ssk, k3–9 sts remain.
**Row 17:** K3, s2kp2, k3–7 sts remain.
**Row 19:** K2, s2kp2, k2–5 sts remain.
**Row 21:** K1, s2kp2, k1–3 sts remain.
BO all sts.

## MIDDLE BACK TRIANGLES

With RS of Upper Back facing, beginning at marker on left side, pick up and knit 79 (85, 93, 101, 109) (117, 125, 133, 141) sts to CO edge.
**Setup Row (WS):** P37 (40, 44, 48, 52) (56, 60, 64, 68), pm, p5, pm, purl to end.

### DECREASE SECTION

**Row 1 (RS):** K3, k2tog, knit to marker, sm, k2tog, yo, k1, yo, ssk, sm, knit to last 5 sts, ssk, k3–2 sts decreased.
**Rows 2 and 4:** Purl.
**Row 3:** Repeat Row 1–2 sts decreased.
**Row 5:** K3, [k2tog] twice, knit to marker, sm, k2tog, yo, k1, yo, ssk, sm, knit to last 7 sts, [ssk] twice, yo, k3–4 sts decreased.
**Row 6:** Purl.
Repeat Rows 1–6 six (7, 8, 9, 10) (11, 12, 13, 14) more times, then repeat Rows 1 and 2 three (2, 2, 2, 2) (2, 2, 2, 2) more times, removing markers on final row–17 sts remain.
**Row 7 (RS):** K3, k2tog, k1, k2tog, yo, k1, yo, ssk, k1, ssk, k3–15 sts remain.
**Rows 8, 10, 12, 14, and 16:** Purl.
**Row 9:** K3, [k2tog] twice, yo, k1, yo, [ssk] twice, k3–13 sts remain.
**Row 11:** K3, k3tog, yo, k1, yo, sssk, k3–11 sts remain.
**Row 13:** K3, k2tog, k1, ssk, k3–9 sts remain.

**Row 15:** K3, s2kp2, k3–7 sts remain.
**Row 17:** K2, s2kp2, k2–5 sts remain.
**Row 19:** K1, s2kp2, k1–3 sts.
BO all sts.
Repeat for opposite side.

## LOWER BACK

With RS of Middle Back Triangles facing, pick up and knit 109 (121, 131, 143, 155) (165, 177, 187, 199) sts along bottom edge of Triangles.
**Setup Row (WS):** P52 (58, 63, 69, 75) (80, 86, 91, 97), pm, p5, pm, purl to end.
**Row 1 (RS):** K3, yo, ssk, knit to marker, sm, k2tog, yo, k1, yo, ssk, sm, knit to last 5, k2tog, yo, k3–2 sts decreased.
**Row 2:** Purl.
Repeat Rows 1 and 2 until piece measures 6 (5½, 5½, 5, 5) (4½, 4½, 4, 4)" [15 (14, 14, 12.5, 12.5) (11.5, 11.5, 10, 10) cm] from pick-up row, ending with a WS row.
**Row 3 (RS):** K3, yo, ssk, purl to last 5 sts, k2tog, yo, k3.
**Row 4:** P5, knit to last 5 sts, purl to end.
Repeat Rows 3 and 4 once more.
BO all sts, working Row 3 as you BO.

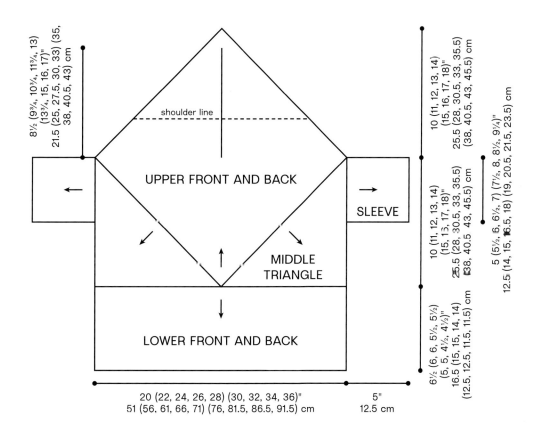

8½ (9¾, 10¾, 11¾, 13) (13¾, 15, 16, 17)" 21.5 (25, 27.5, 30, 33) (35, 38, 40.5, 43) cm

shoulder line

UPPER FRONT AND BACK

← 

SLEEVE

→

MIDDLE TRIANGLE

↑

LOWER FRONT AND BACK

↓

10 (11, 12, 13, 14) (15, 16, 17, 18)" 25.5 (28, 30.5, 33, 35.5) (38, 40.5, 43, 45.5) cm

10 (11, 12, 13, 14) (15, 16, 17, 18)" 25.5 (28, 30.5, 33, 35.5) (38, 40.5, 43, 45.5) cm

5 (5½, 6, 6½, 7) (7½, 8, 8½, 9¼)" 12.5 (14, 15, 16.5, 18) (19, 20.5, 21.5, 23.5) cm

6½ (6, 6, 5½, 5½) (5, 5, 4½, 4½)" 16.5 (15, 15, 14, 14) (12.5, 12.5, 11.5, 11.5) cm

20 (22, 24, 26, 28) (30, 32, 34, 36)" 51 (56, 61, 66, 71) (76, 81.5, 86.5, 91.5) cm

5" 12.5 cm

## MIDDLE FRONT TRIANGLES

Work as for Middle Back Triangles.

## LOWER FRONT

Work as for Lower Back.

## SLEEVES

Sew Upper Back and Front together along Decrease Sections. Place removable markers on Back and Front, 5½ (6, 6½, 7, 7½) (8, 8½, 9, 9¾)" [14 (15, 16.5, 18, 19) (20.5, 21.5, 23, 25) cm] down from point where Back and Front corners meet. *Note: The distance between the markers is approximately 1" (2.5 cm) wider than the top of the sleeve. This makes the sleeve lie flat and keeps it from bulging at the top.* With RS facing, pick up and knit 55 (61, 67, 71, 77) (83, 89, 93, 101) sts between markers.

**Setup Row (WS):** P25 (28, 31, 33, 36) (39, 42, 44, 48), p5, pm, purl to end.

**Row 1 (RS):** K3, yo, ssk, knit to marker, sm, k2tog, yo, k1, yo, ssk, sm, knit to last 5 sts, k2tog, yo, k3—2 sts decreased.

**Row 2:** Purl.

Repeat Rows 1 and 2 until piece measures 4½" (11.5 cm) from pick-up row, ending with a WS row.

**Row 3 (RS):** K3, yo, ssk, purl to last 5, k2tog, yo, k3.

**Row 4:** P5, knit to last 5 sts, p5.

Repeat Rows 3 and 4 once.

BO all sts, working Row 3 as you BO.

## FINISHING

Block as desired. Sew underarm and side seams, leaving the Lower Front and Back unsewn for side slit.

# DESIGN YOUR OWN

## DESIGNING KITE

The concept for Kite began with the idea of having large squares, knit on the diagonal, taking up the top half of the garment. Often, I have the kernel of an idea like this and can't fully visualize the construction or the final outcome until I start playing with shapes on a grid, building a schematic. Determining the width of a normal oversized pullover for the sample size gave me a starting point, and fitting the bias square into that width furthered my thought process. Adding smaller half squares (aka triangles) filled out the lower sides. I liked the look of my schematic so far. Though, left there, it looked as if the garment would be quite short—how could I estimate the length of the garment when worn, with such an odd shape at the top? There were no shoulder seams except the diagonal seams joining the front and back squares. I had to do

some guesswork. I postulated that, when worn, a person's shoulders would stop the garment at the place where the square measured about the same as the shoulders from shoulder to shoulder, which I estimated by adding a few inches to the shoulder width I knew was right for a sweater with set-in sleeves. From there, I could see how much more length I might add to the bottom edge to get to the length I was aiming for. This additional length could be easily added as a rectangle. Another pair of rectangles became the short sleeves. I spent time figuring out the order the pieces would be knit in, so all could be knit onto a previously knit piece, leaving only two sleeve/underarm seams to be joined. The large square in the front still needed a neck opening. I'll tell you about that in the next section.

## GRACEFUL OPENINGS

A few years back, I learned that a neck opening can be nothing more than a slit. In a normally constructed sweater, one with shoulder seams or, at least, defined shoulders, like Weave (page 23), the slit should extend into the back by a few inches, so the opening can spread open to make room for a human neck without pulling the front upward. In the novel construction of Kite, the slit goes from the center of its large front square to near the top corner, a few inches of which is folded to the back when worn, which allows the neck room needed. It might go without saying, but remember, in total, the slit has to be deep enough to leave enough room for a head to fit through. The opening in the front, while only a split, will appear like a V-neck when worn. I used one of my favorite tricks at the opening and closing of the divide. I worked a four-stitch cable at the base at the same time the second ball of yarn is joined. Work to 2 sts before the split will happen, place two stitches on a cable needle (in front or back, it doesn't matter) and knit two. With new yarn, work the stitches from your cable needle and complete the row. You'll be working each side of the split with two separate balls of yarn until it's time to rejoin the sides. At that point, working the entire row with one ball of yarn, place another four-stitch cable to close the slit.

You might want similar slits on a poncho, for an armhole, or as a pocket opening. The principle will be the same. The neck opening of Facet (page 117) is worked in exactly the same way, but since the sweater is worked side to center, the neck slit is horizontal.

# Forty-Five°

Named after the forty-five-degree angle of its miters, this jacket is not built entirely of repeated shapes like its neighbors in this chapter. Instead, multiple mitered squares are placed strategically, to define the side slits and add interest to each lapel. A modified rectangular version of the mitered square makes the back as interesting as the front, while a much larger mitered square is folded to form a dolman in each armhole, allowing the main pieces of the sweater to remain rectangular and easy to knit in moss stitch.

## FINISHED MEASUREMENTS

43 (47, 51, 55, 59) (63, 67, 71, 75)" [109 (119.5, 129.5, 100.5, 150) (160, 170, 180.5, 190.5) cm] chest, with fronts overlapped

*Note: This piece is intended to be worn with approximately 12–14" (30.5–35.5 cm) positive ease.*

## YARN

Hudson + West Forge [70% US Merino/30% US Corriedale; 235 yards (215 m)/3½ ounces (100 g)]: 8 (8, 9, 10, 10) (11, 11, 12, 13) skeins Gold Leaf

## NEEDLES

One pair straight needles, size US 6 (4 mm)

Four double-pointed needles, size US 6 (4 mm) (optional)

Change needle size if necessary to obtain correct gauge.

## NOTIONS

Removable stitch markers

Crochet hook size US 6 (4 mm) (optional)

## GAUGE

21 sts and 32 rows = 4" (10cm) in Moss Stitch

## PATTERN STITCH

### MOSS STITCH

(odd number of sts; 4-row repeat)
**Row 1 (RS).** K1, *p1, k1; repeat from * to end.
**Rows 2 and 3:** P1, *p1, k1; repeat from * to end.
**Row 4:** Repeat Row 1.
Repeat Rows 1–4 for pattern.

## SPECIAL TECHNIQUE

### REVERSE SINGLE CROCHET (OPTIONAL)

Make a slipknot and place on hook. Working from left to right, *insert hook into next st along edge, yo hook, pull through to RS—2 loops on hook. Yo hook, draw through both loops—1 loop on hook. Repeat from * to end. Fasten off.

## PATTERN NOTES

The Back and Fronts of this coat are worked from the bottom up in pieces. Mitered inserts are picked up and worked on the lower sides, upper Back, and Front lapels. The Sleeves are picked up from the armhole edges and worked back and forth in rows to the cuffs. A mitered gusset is picked up in the Front underarm and worked outward, then sewn to the Back underarm.

## BACK

### LOWER BACK PANEL

Using Long-Tail Cast-On (see Special Techniques, page 221), CO 61 (71, 81, 81, 91) (101, 103, 115, 125) sts.
Purl 1 row.
Begin Moss st; work even until piece measures 5 (5, 5, 6, 6) (6, 6¾, 6¾, 6¾)" [12.5 (12.5, 12.5, 15, 15) (15, 17, 17, 17) cm] from the beginning, ending with a WS row.

### CO FOR BACK BODY

**Next Row (RS):** Using Cable Cast-On (see Special Techniques, page 221), CO 26 (26, 26, 32, 32) (32, 36, 36, 36) sts, work in pattern across CO sts (beginning with next pattern row after last row worked), work in pattern to end—87 (97, 107, 113, 123) (133, 139, 151, 161) sts.
Repeat last row once more—113 (123, 133, 145, 155) (165, 175, 187, 197) sts.
Work even until piece measures 18¼ (18¾, 19, 18¾, 19) (19¼, 19¼, 19¾, 20¼)" [46.5 (47.5, 48.5, 47.5, 48.5) (49, 49, 50, 51.5) cm] from the beginning (measured at center), ending with a WS row.

### SHAPE NECK OPENING

**Next Row (RS):** Work 35 (40, 45, 50, 55) (60, 64, 70, 75) sts, join a second ball of yarn, BO 43 (43, 43, 45, 45) (45, 47, 47, 47) sts, work to end—35 (40, 45, 50, 55) (60, 64, 70, 75) sts remain each side. Working both sides at the same time, work even for 8¼ (8¼, 8¼, 8½, 8½) (8½, 9, 9, 9)" [21 (21, 21, 21.5, 21.5) (21.5, 23, 23, 23) cm] from BO row, ending with a RS row.
BO all sts in pattern.

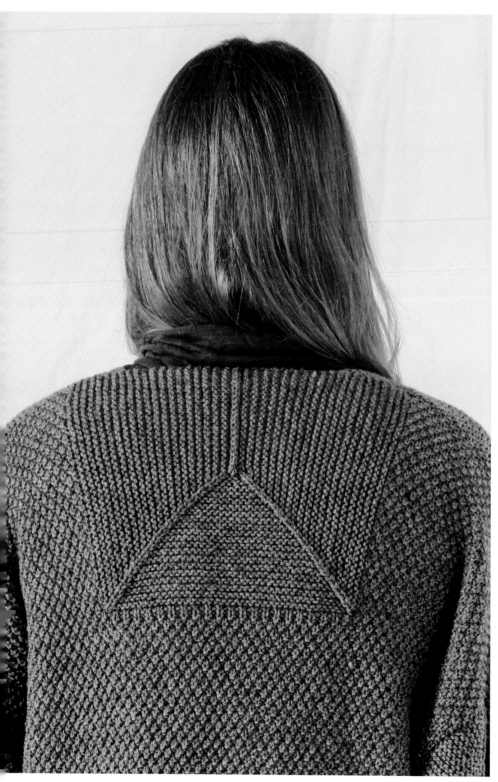

## LOWER BACK INSERT

*Note: Inserts are worked in lower Back corners. You may find it easier to work inserts with 3 dpns—one needle for each pick-up edge and one working needle.*

With RS facing, and beginning at original Back CO edge, pick up and knit 26 (26, 26, 32, 32) (32, 36, 36, 36) sts along right edge of lower Back panel to inside corner (see schematic), 1 st in corner (place removable marker on this corner st), then 26 (26, 26, 32, 32) (32, 36, 36, 36) sts along second CO edge to outside edge—53 (53, 53, 65, 65) (65, 73, 73, 73 sts. Purl 1 row.

**Row 1 (RS):** Knit to 1 st before marked st, s2kp2, knit to end—2 sts decreased.

**Row 2:** Knit to marked st, p1, knit to end.

Repeat Rows 1 and 2 until 3 sts remain.

**Next Row (RS):** S2kp2—1 st remains.

Fasten off.

Repeat for second insert, beginning at CO edge for Back body panel.

## NECK INSERT

*Note: You may find it easier to work insert with 4 dpns—one needle for each pick-up edge and one working needle.*

With RS of Back facing, and beginning at right neck edge, pick up and knit 43 (43, 43, 45, 45) (45, 47, 47, 47) sts along right side of opening to corner, 1 st in corner (place removable marker on this corner st), 42 (42, 42, 44, 44) (44, 46, 46, 46) sts from BO sts to corner, 1 st in corner (place removable marker on this corner st), then 42 (42, 42, 44, 44) (44, 46, 46, 46) sts to top of neck opening—130 (130, 130, 136, 136) (136, 142, 142, 142) sts. Purl 1 row.

**Row 1 (RS):** [Knit to 1 st before marked st, s2kp2] twice, knit to end—4 sts decreased.

**Row 2:** [Knit to marked st, p1] twice, knit to end.

Repeat Rows 1 and 2 until 0 sts remain between marked sts; remove markers—23 (23, 23, 24, 24) (24, 25, 25, 25) sts remain each side.

Divide halves of insert onto 2 needles. With WSs of sides together (seam will be on RS), use 3-Needle Bind-Off (see Special Techniques, page 222) to BO all sts.

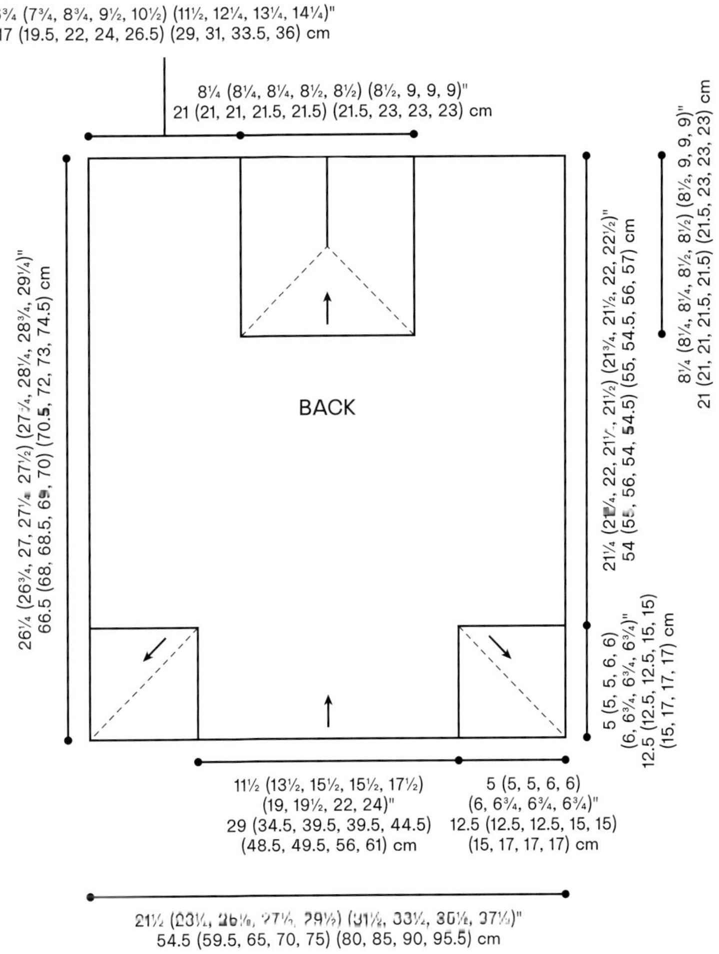
6¾ (7¾, 8¾, 9½, 10½) (11½, 12¼, 13¼, 14¼)"
17 (19.5, 22, 24, 26.5) (29, 31, 33.5, 36) cm
8¼ (8¼, 8¼, 8½, 8½) (8½, 9, 9, 9)"
21 (21, 21, 21.5, 21.5) (21.5, 23, 23, 23) cm
BACK
26¼ (26¾, 27, 27¼, 27½) (27¾, 28¼, 28¾, 29¼)"
66.5 (68, 68.5, 69, 70) (70.5, 72, 73, 74.5) cm
21¼ (21¾, 22, 21½, 21½) (21¾, 21½, 22, 22½)"
54 (55, 56, 54, 54.5) (55, 54.5, 56, 57) cm
8¼ (8¼, 8¼, 8½, 8½) (8½, 9, 9, 9)"
21 (21, 21, 21.5, 21.5) (21.5, 23, 23, 23) cm
5 (5, 5, 6, 6)
(6, 6¾, 6¾, 6¾)"
12.5 (12.5, 12.5, 15, 15)
(15, 17, 17, 17) cm
11½ (13½, 15½, 15½, 17½)
(19, 19½, 22, 24)"
29 (34.5, 39.5, 39.5, 44.5)
(48.5, 49.5, 56, 61) cm
5 (5, 5, 6, 6)
(6, 6¾, 6¾, 6¾)"
12.5 (12.5, 12.5, 15, 15)
(15, 17, 17, 17) cm
21½ (23½, 25½, 27½, 29½) (31½, 33½, 35½, 37½)"
54.5 (59.5, 65, 70, 75) (80, 85, 90, 95.5) cm

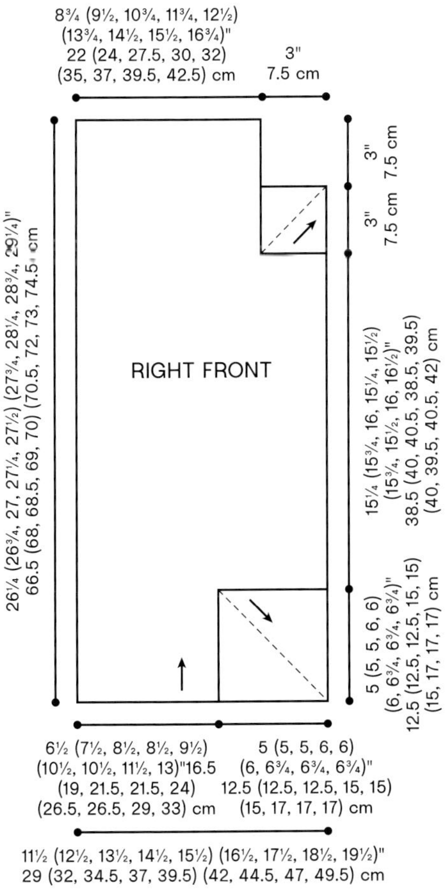
8¾ (9½, 10¾, 11¾, 12½)
(13¾, 14½, 15½, 16¾)"
22 (24, 27.5, 30, 32)
(35, 37, 39.5, 42.5) cm
3"
7.5 cm
RIGHT FRONT
26¼ (26¾, 27, 27¼, 27½) (27¾, 28¼, 28¾, 29¼)"
66.5 (68, 68.5, 69, 70) (70.5, 72, 73, 74.5) cm
3" 7.5 cm
3" 7.5 cm
15¼ (15¾, 16, 15¼, 15½)
(15¾, 15½, 16, 16½)"
38.5 (40, 40.5, 38.5, 39.5)
(40, 39.5, 40.5, 42) cm
5 (5, 5, 6, 6)
(6, 6¾, 6¾, 6¾)"
12.5 (12.5, 12.5, 15, 15)
(15, 17, 17, 17) cm
6½ (7½, 8½, 8½, 9½)
(10½, 10½, 11½, 13)"16.5
(19, 21.5, 21.5, 24)
(26.5, 26.5, 29, 33) cm
5 (5, 5, 6, 6)
(6, 6¾, 6¾, 6¾)"
12.5 (12.5, 12.5, 15, 15)
(15, 17, 17, 17) cm
11½ (12½, 13½, 14½, 15½) (16½, 17½, 18½, 19½)"
29 (32, 34.5, 37, 39.5) (42, 44.5, 47, 49.5) cm

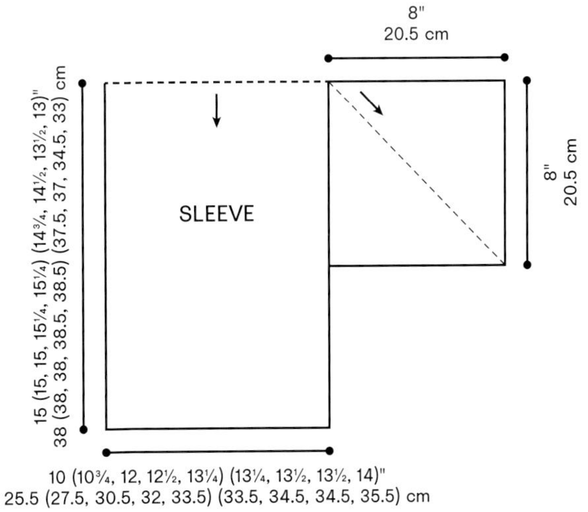
8"
20.5 cm
SLEEVE
15 (15, 15, 15¼, 15¼) (14¾, 14½, 13½, 13)"
38 (38, 38, 38.5, 38.5) (37.5, 37, 34.5, 33) cm
8"
20.5 cm
10 (10¾, 12, 12½, 13¼) (13¼, 13½, 13½, 14)"
25.5 (27.5, 30.5, 32, 33.5) (33.5, 34.5, 34.5, 35.5) cm

## RIGHT FRONT

Using Long-Tail Cast-On, CO 35 (39, 45, 45, 49) (55, 55, 61, 67) sts.
Purl 1 row.
Begin Moss st; work even until piece measures 5 (5, 5, 6, 6) (6, 6¾, 6¾, 6¾)" [12.5 (12.5, 12.5, 15, 15) (15, 17, 17, 17) cm] from the beginning (measured along long edge), ending with a RS row.

### CO FOR FRONT BODY

**Next Row (WS):** Using Cable Cast-On, CO 26 (26, 26, 32, 32) (32, 36, 36, 36) sts, work in pattern across CO sts (beginning with next pattern row after last row worked), work in pattern to end—61 (65, 71, 77, 81) (87, 91, 97, 103) sts.
Work even until piece measures 20¼ (20¾, 21, 21¼, 21½) (21¾, 22¼, 22¾, 23¼)" [51.5 (52.5, 53.5, 54, 54.5) (55, 56.5, 58, 59) cm] from the beginning (measured along long edge), ending with a WS row.
**Lapel BO Row (RS):** BO 15 sts, work to end—46 (50, 56, 62, 66) (72, 76, 82, 88) sts remain.
Work even for 6" (15 cm) from BO row, ending with a RS row.
BO all sts in pattern.

### LOWER FRONT INSERT

Work as for Lower Back Insert.

### LAPEL INSERT

Place removable marker 3" (7.5 cm) up from corner above Lapel BO Row. With WS facing (lapel will be folded back so WS of lapel is facing the RS), and beginning at marker, pick up and knit 15 sts to corner, 1 st in corner (place removable marker on this corner st), then 15 sts to edge—31 sts.
Purl 1 row.
**Row 1 (RS):** Knit to 1 st before marked st, s2kp2, knit to end—2 sts decreased.
**Row 2:** Knit to marked st, p1, knit to end.
Repeat Rows 1 and 2 until 3 sts remain.
**Next Row (RS):** S2kp2—1 st remains.
Fasten off.

## LEFT FRONT

Using Long-Tail Cast-On, CO 35 (39, 45, 45, 49) (55, 55, 61, 67) sts.
Purl 1 row.
Begin Moss st; work even until piece measures 5 (5, 5, 6, 6) (6, 6¾, 6¾, 6¾)" [12.5 (12.5, 12.5, 15, 15) (15, 17, 17, 17) cm] from the beginning (measured along long edge), ending with a WS row.

### CO FOR FRONT BODY

**Next Row (RS):** Using Cable Cast-On, CO 26 (26, 26, 32, 32) (32, 36, 36, 36) sts, work in pattern across CO sts (beginning with next pattern row after last row worked), work in pattern to end—61 (65, 71, 77, 81) (87, 91, 97, 103) sts.
Work even until piece measures 20¼ (20¾, 21, 21¼, 21½) (21¾, 22¼, 22¾, 23¼)" [51.5 (52.5, 53.5, 54, 54.5) (55, 56.5, 58, 59) cm] from the beginning (measured along long edge), ending with a RS row.
**Lapel BO Row (WS):** BO 15 sts, work to end—46 (50, 56, 62, 66) (72, 76, 82, 88) sts remain.
Work even for 6" (15 cm) from BO row, ending with a RS row.
BO all sts in pattern.

### LOWER FRONT INSERT

Work as for Lower Back Insert.

### LAPEL INSERT

Place removable marker 3" (7.5 cm) up from corner above Lapel BO Row. With WS facing (lapel will be folded back so WS of lapel is facing the RS), and beginning at Front edge, pick up and knit 15 sts to corner, 1 st in corner (place removable marker on this corner st), then 15 sts to marker—31 sts.
Purl 1 row.
**Row 1 (RS):** Knit to 1 st before marked st, s2kp2, knit to end—2 sts decreased.
**Row 2:** Knit to marked st, p1, knit to end.
Repeat Rows 1 and 2 until 3 sts remain.
**Next Row (RS):** S2kp2—1 st remains.
Fasten off.
Block pieces as desired. Sew shoulder seams, sewing for the full width of the front shoulder, leaving 4 (4½, 4, 4½, 4½) (5, 4, 4½, 4)" [10 (11.5, 10, 11.5, 11.5) (12.5, 10, 11.5, 10) cm] unsewn at Back neck, between shoulder seams. *Note: For added stability across Back neck, use crochet hook to work 1 row Reverse Single Crochet across Back neck sts (optional).*

## SLEEVES

Place removable markers 5 (5½, 6, 6¼, 6½) (6½, 6¾, 6¾, 7)" [12.5 (14, 15, 16, 16.5) (16.5, 17, 17, 18) cm] down from shoulder seams on Fronts and Back. With RS facing, pick up and knit 53 (57, 63, 65, 69) (69, 71, 71, 73) sts between markers. Do not join; work back and forth in rows.
Purl 1 row.
Begin Moss st; work even until piece measures 15 (15, 15, 15, 15) (14½, 14½, 13½, 13)" [38 (38, 38, 38, 38) (37, 37, 34.5, 33 cm] from pick-up row, ending with a RS row.
BO all sts.

## UNDERARM GUSSET

Place removable markers 9" (23 cm) down from underarm on Fronts and Sleeves. *Note: This is 1" (2.5 cm) more than width of gusset, which prevents gusset from sagging.* With RS of piece facing, beginning at first marker, pick up and knit 43 sts from marker to underarm, 1 st at underarm (place removable marker on this st), then 43 sts from underarm to second marker.
Purl 1 row.
**Row 1 (RS):** Knit to 1 st before marked st, s3kp2, knit to end—2 sts decreased.
**Row 2:** Knit to marked st, p1, knit to end.
Repeat Rows 1 and 2 until 3 sts remain.
**Next Row (RS):** S2kp2—1 st remains.
Fasten off.

## FINISHING

Sew free edges of underarm gusset to Back and back edge of Sleeve. Sew Sleeve seams; sew side seams to top of inserts, leaving edges of inserts unsewn. Block as desired.

# DESIGN YOUR OWN

## DESIGNING FORTY-FIVE°

The concept of using mitered squares as design details started with picturing a mitered garter stitch block incorporated into a lapel. The idea was a bit nebulous in my mind. I couldn't quite nail it down, or figure out how it would really work, until I started sketching. Once I saw how a small mitered square could become part of a simplified lapel, I realized that my work had just begun. How could I repeat the mitered square detail elsewhere in the jacket? My next step was to place larger versions in the lower side corners of the fronts and back. In those locations the mitered squares not only provided interest, they launched the idea of adding side slits, defined how high the split would be, and acted as a lovely finished edge. Since I was still keeping the main sweater pieces as rectangles in this chapter, I already needed a way to make the upper arm larger. Adding a square folded along its diagonal was a good solution for that

(as in Patch, page 87), so why not make it a mitered square? I placed a fairly huge mitered square in each underarm, creating a dolman silhouette. That's eight mitered squares incorporated so far. The only lonely looking area was the upper back. I decided that something mitered should define the width of the back neck and add a focal point at the same time. A simple mitered square, however, was not going to work the way I wanted it to because of its inherent asymmetry. The location smack in the center of the back called for symmetry, so a double miter was in order.

## SCHEMATICS AS DESIGN TOOLS

If I haven't said this already, and even if I have, a schematic, one that is drawn to scale, is a really useful and important design tool. I now draw schematics on my computer. My favorite program, EazyDraw, makes it simple to set up a grid and a thicker line every ten squares,

making counting by tens a breeze. In the past, I drew schematics on graph paper and ten squares to the inch was my favorite, for the same reason. Draw your sweater pieces out with one square representing one inch. If you work in centimeters, you might use one square equals one centimeter or one square equals two centimeters. Representing every detail of your sweater to scale—armholes, shoulder width, neckline slope, pockets, etc.—will enable you to visualize how all of the details will work together, before any instructions are written or any knitting started. While I was planning Forty-Five°, I played around with different sizes for each of the mitered square details to find the proportions I liked best. Drawing in all of the details brings up questions you might not have thought of, too. While placing the double mitered detail on the upper back of my sample schematic, I realized that it could define the width of the back neck, that the miter should definitely not be narrower than the back neck, and while it could be wider, I liked the idea of synchronicity.

# Pyramid

Strangely satisfying to knit, highly dimensional pyramids are knit onto a flat scarf, already enhanced with slipped-stitch ribs and garter ridges knit in to act as guides. A good quality in a scarf, the wrong side—let's call it the calmer side—also looks good facing outward to the public, with its garter ridges and softly bulging pillows of stockinette.

**DIMENSIONS**
8½" (21.5 cm) wide × 50" (127 cm) long

**YARN**
Neighborhood Fiber Co. Capital Luxury Sport [70% merino wool/20% cashmere/10% nylon; 360 yards (329 m)/4 ounces (114 g)]: 3 skeins Charles Centre

**NEEDLES**
One pair straight needles, size US 2 (2.75 mm)

Five double-pointed needles, size US 2 (2.75 mm)

Change needle size if necessary to obtain correct gauge.

**NOTIONS**
Stitch marker

Wool fleece, yarn scraps, or fiber fill for stuffing

**GAUGE**
28 sts and 36 rows = 4" (10 cm) in St st

## PATTERN STITCH

### GRID PATTERN (SEE CHART)

*Note: All slipped sts should be slipped purlwise wyib.*
(multiple of 19 sts + 2; 28-row repeat)
**Row 1 (RS):** K2, *p1, k1, p1, k11, p1, k1, p1, k2; repeat from * to end.
**Row 2:** *K3, p1, k13, p1, k1; repeat from * to last 2 sts, k2.
**Row 3:** K2, *p1, slip 1, p1, k11, p1, slip 1, p1, k2; repeat from * to end.
**Row 4:** Repeat Row 2.
**Row 5:** K2, *p1, slip 1, p13, slip 1, p1, k2; repeat from * to end.
**Row 6:** Repeat Row 2.
**Rows 7–24:** Repeat Rows 5 and 6.
**Rows 25–28:** Repeat Rows 3 and 4 twice.
Repeat Rows 3–28 for pattern.

## PATTERN NOTES

The Matrix of this scarf is worked first and forms a base on which to work the Pyramids, which are worked one at a time. Stitches are picked up from around the purl rectangle in the center of each repeat, then the Pyramid is worked in the round to the tip; stuffing is added before working the final round and closing up the top.

## MATRIX

Using straight needles and Long-Tail Cast-On (see Special Techniques, page 221), CO 59 sts.
Begin Grid Pattern; work Rows 1–28 once, then work Rows 3–28 eighteen more times, or to desired length, then work Rows 3–27 once more.
BO all sts knitwise.
Steam or wet-block.

## PYRAMIDS

With RS of Matrix facing, using dpns, pick up and knit around all 4 sides of 13-st, 21-row rev St st rectangle in each repeat of Grid Pattern as follows:
**Needle 1:** Pick up and knit 11 sts in bottom "U" loops of lowest row of rev St st rectangle, working from the bottom up (see pink sts on chart).
**Needle 2:** Pick up and knit 11 sts into column of slipped sts on left side of rectangle (1 st in each slipped st; see blue sts on chart), working from left to right into each slipped st.
**Needle 3:** Pick up and knit 11 sts into top loops of highest row in rev St st rectangle, working from the top down.
**Needle 4:** Pick up and knit 11 sts into column of slipped sts on right side of rectangle (1 st in each slipped st), working from right to left into each slipped st (from the outside in)—44 sts. Join for working in the rnd; pm for beginning of rnd.
**Rounds 1 and 2:** Knit.
**Round 3:** *K2tog, k7, ssk; repeat from * to end—36 sts remain.
**Rounds 4 and 5:** Knit.
**Round 6:** *K2tog, k5, ssk; repeat from * to end—28 sts remain.
**Rounds 7 and 8:** Knit.
**Round 9:** *K2tog, k3, ssk; repeat from * to end—20 sts remain.
**Rounds 10 and 11:** Knit.
**Round 12:** *K2tog, k1, ssk; repeat from * to end—12 sts remain.
**Rounds 13 and 14:** Knit.
Softly stuff pyramid with wool fleece, yarn scraps, or fiberfill.
**Round 15** *S2kp2; repeat from * to end—4 sts remain.
Cut yarn, leaving a long tail. Thread tail through remaining sts, pull tight, and fasten off.
Repeat for remainder of Scarf.

## FINISHING

Block as desired.

## Grid Pattern

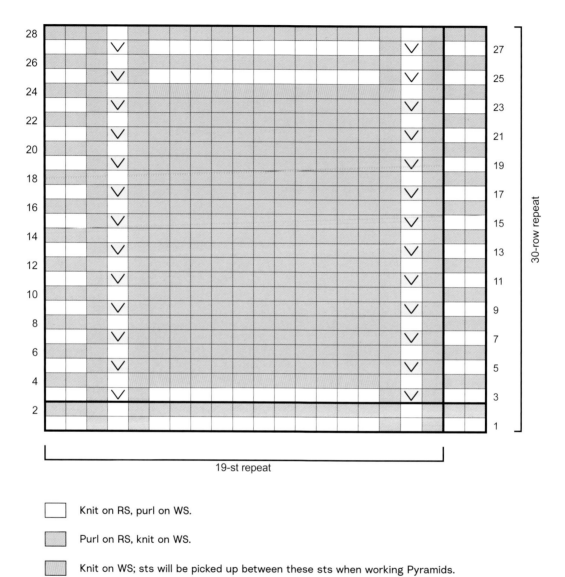

Knit on RS, purl on WS.

Purl on RS, knit on WS.

Knit on WS; sts will be picked up between these sts when working Pyramids.

∨ Slip 1 wyib on RS.

∨ Slip 1 wyib on RS; sts will be picked up into these sts when working Pyramids.

# DESIGN YOUR OWN

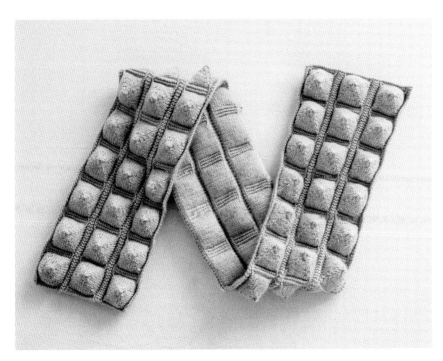

## DESIGNING PYRAMID

Among the goodies on my Pinterest board ideas for this book was a three-dimensional scarf, created in some sort of high-tech fabric, pyramids protruding from its surface like a highly enlarged view of an abrasive surface seen through a microscope. I had to make a knitted version. I knew how to go about knitting the pyramids because, years ago, I knit a stellated dodecahedron for a Christmas tree topper/baby toy. (You can see that one up on the interwebs, on Berroco's site). I thought that it would be efficient to knit the pyramids onto a scarf, which would act as the base. The tricky part, it seemed to me, was creating an intuitive way to pick up stitches, one that wouldn't drive me and other knitters insane. I thought back to all of the guidelines and guide stitches introduced in Chapter 3, which is all about smocking and pleating. I remembered the precisely placed purl stitches to guide smocking for Floret (page 59) and Multiflora (page

63), as well as the horizontal lines of garter stitch becoming guidelines for Folded Headband (page 55) and Smocked (page 67), which also has vertical fold lines. When it came time to figure out how to make Pyramid in a way that was not difficult to knit and was also fairly easy to describe, I reached for my old friends, knit guides. Garter ridges act both as stitches to pick up into and decoration. Slipped stitches create vertical lines that are also easy to pick up into. The combination of garter, slipped stitches, and reverse stockinette makes an easy-to-knit scarf that serves as the base for the pyramids. At one point I considered placing pyramids sporadically across the scarf, corners filled with protrusions while other squares left flat. In the end, I loved the look of the grid filled with pyramids, and I knit one into every spot available.

## STELLATED (POINTY) SHAPES

Most of the time, when I'm designing with geometric shapes, I'm knitting in the round, from the outside in. And most of the time, I want the shapes to lie flat, so I spend a bit of time with the math. How many rounds should it take to get to the center of the square or octagon or hexagon? How many decreases will it take to eliminate the number of stitches I need to get rid of for each section of my shape? From there I can figure out how often I need to make decreases (these are usually paired decreases). See Polly (page 111) for some examples. While this is a great starting point, I've found I can't quite trust the math, so spending time to make a knit sample is a good idea. Now that you've perfected a flat polygon, you can make it pointy, or as mathematicians say, stellated. Start adding plain rounds between your decrease rounds. If the decreases are worked every other round for a flat shape, try working the same decreases every third round. If that's not pointy enough, add more plain rounds between the decrease rounds.

# Polly

A miracle due to the flexibility of knitting, four different polygons combine to create this rug. Octagons, hexagons, half hexagons, and pentagons are each knit separately in a pale, earthy palette and sewn together later. The large yarn and needles make the work go quickly. The finished rug is perfect for small, cozy spaces or as an accent in a larger context. In the bedroom, you can slip out of the covers in the morning and land on this warm wool rug or stay under the covers contemplating the radiating ribs that look like the fold lines of origami.

## FINISHED MEASUREMENTS

Approximately 3" (3 m) wide × 4½" (1.5 m) long

## YARN

Halcyon Yarn Rug Wool [100% wool; 65 yards (59 m)/3½ ounces (100 g)]: 7 skeins #1310 (A), 3 skeins each #1280 (B) and #1300 (C), and 2 skeins #1910 (D)

## NEEDLES

Needle(s) in preferred style for small-circumference circular knitting, size US 13 (9 mm)

Change needle size if necessary to obtain correct gauge.

## NOTIONS

Stitch markers

## GAUGE

10 sts and 12½ rows = 4" (10 cm) in St st

## PATTERN STITCHES

### OCTAGON PATTERN (SEE CHART)

(multiple of 14 sts; decreases to multiple of 1 st; 22 rnds)
**Rnd 1:** *K13, p1; repeat from * to end.
**Rnd 2:** *LT, k9, RT, p1-tbl; repeat from * to end.
**Rnd 3:** *K1, LT, k7, RT, k1, p1-tbl; repeat from * to end.
**Rnd 4:** *K2tog, LT, k5, RT, ssk, p1-tbl; repeat from * to end—2 sts decreased.
**Rnd 5:** *K2, LT, k3, RT, k2, p1-tbl; repeat from * to end.
**Rnd 6:** *K3, LT, k1, RT, k3, p1-tbl; repeat from * to end.
**Rnd 7:** *K2tog, k3, p1-tbl, k3, ssk, p1-tbl; repeat from * to end—2 sts decreased.
**Rnds 8 and 9:** *K4, p1-tbl; repeat from * to end.
**Rnd 10:** *K2tog, k2, p1-tbl, k2, ssk, p1-tbl; repeat from * to end—2 sts decreased.
**Rnds 11 and 12:** *K3, p1-tbl; repeat from * to end.
**Rnd 13:** *K2tog, k1, p1-tbl, k1, ssk, p1-tbl—2 sts decreased.
**Rnds 14 and 15:** *K2, p1-tbl; repeat from * to end.
**Rnd 16:** *K2tog, p1-tbl, ssk, p1-tbl; repeat from * to end—2 sts decreased.
**Rnds 17 and 18:** *K1, p1-tbl; repeat from * to end.
**Rnd 19:** *S2kp2, p1-tbl; repeat from * to end—2 sts decreased.
**Rnds 20 and 21:** *K1, p1-tbl; repeat from * to end.
**Rnd 22:** *Ssk; repeat from * to end—1 st decreased.

### HEXAGON PATTERN (SEE CHART)

(multiple of 14 sts; decreases to multiple of 2 sts; 18 rnds)

**Rnd 1:** *K13, p1; repeat from * to end.
**Rnd 2:** *K13, p1-tbl; repeat from * to end.
**Rnd 3:** *K2tog, k9, ssk, p1-tbl; repeat from * to end—2 sts decreased.
**Rnds 4 and 5:** *K11, p1-tbl; repeat from * to end.
**Rnd 6:** *K2tog, k7, ssk, p1-tbl; repeat from * to end—2 sts decreased.
**Rnds 7 and 8:** *K9, p1-tbl; repeat from * to end.
**Rnd 9:** *K2tog, k5, ssk, p1-tbl; repeat from * to end—2 sts decreased.
**Rnds 10 and 11:** *K7, p1-tbl; repeat from * to end.
**Rnd 12:** *K2tog, k3, ssk, p1-tbl; repeat from * to end—2 sts decreased.
**Rnds 13 and 14:** *K5, p1-tbl; repeat from * to end.
**Rnd 15:** *K2tog, k1, ssk, p1-tbl; repeat from * to end—2 sts decreased.
**Rnds 16 and 17:** *K3, p1-tbl; repeat from * to end.
**Rnd 18:** *S2kp2, p1-tbl; repeat from * to end—2 sts decreased.

### PENTAGON PATTERN (SEE CHART)

(multiple of 14 sts; decreases to multiple of 2 sts; 12 rnds)
**Rnd 1:** *K13, p1; repeat from * to end.
**Rnd 2:** *K2tog, k9, ssk, p1-tbl; repeat from * to end—2 sts decreased.
**Rnd 3:** *K11, p1-tbl; repeat from * to end.
**Rnd 4:** *K2tog, k7, ssk, p1-tbl; repeat from * to end—2 sts decreased.
**Rnd 5:** *K9, p1-tbl; repeat from * to end.
**Rnd 6:** *K2tog, k5, ssk, p1-tbl; repeat from * to end—2 sts decreased.
**Rnd 7:** *K7, p1-tbl; repeat from * to end.
**Rnd 8:** *K2tog, k3, ssk, p1-tbl; repeat from * to end—2 sts decreased.
**Rnd 9:** *K5, p1-tbl; repeat from * to end.
**Rnd 10:** *K2tog, k1, ssk, p1-tbl; repeat

from * to end—2 sts decreased.
**Rnd 11:** *K3, p1-tbl; repeat from * to end.
**Rnd 12:** *S2kp2, p1-tbl; repeat from * to end—2 sts decreased.

### HALF HEXAGON PATTERN (SEE CHART)

(multiple of 14 sts + 15; decreases to multiple of 2 sts + 3; 18 rnds)
**Setup Row (WS):** P1, [p13, k1] twice, p14.
**Row 1:** K1, [k13, p1-tbl] twice, k14.
**Row 2:** P1, [ssp, p9, p2tog, k1-tbl] twice, ssp, k9, p2tog, p1—6 sts decreased.
**Row 3:** K1, [k11, p1-tbl] twice, k12.
**Row 4:** P1, [p11, k1-tbl] twice, p12.
**Row 5:** K1, [k2tog, k7, ssk, p1-tbl] twice, k2tog, k7, ssk, k1—6 sts decreased.
**Row 6:** P1, [p9, k1-tbl] twice, p10.
**Row 7:** K1, [k9, p1-tbl] twice, k10.
**Row 8:** P1, [ssp, p5, p2tog, k1-tbl] twice, ssp, k5, p2tog, p1—6 sts decreased.
**Row 9:** K1, [k7, p1-tbl] twice, k8.
**Row 10:** P1, [p7, k1-tbl] twice, p8.
**Row 11:** K1, [k2tog, k3, ssk, p1-tbl] twice, k2tog, k3, ssk, k1—6 sts decreased.
**Row 12:** P1, [p5, k1-tbl] twice, p6.
**Row 13:** K1, [k5, p1-tbl] twice, k6.
**Row 14:** P1, [ssp, p1, p2tog, k1-tbl] twice, ssp, k1, p2tog, p1—6 sts decreased.
**Row 15:** K1, [k3, p1-tbl] twice, k4.

**Row 16:** P1, [p3, k1-tbl] twice, p4.
**Row 19:** K1, [s2kp2, p1-tbl] twice, s2kp2, k1—6 sts decreased.

### PATTERN NOTES

Each piece is worked separately and sewn together to make the rug. Mathematically, these geometric pieces do not fit perfectly together, but it works in knit fabric. Each side of each piece has 14 stitches, which makes it easier to sew the pieces together.

Most of the outside edge of the Rug is a CO edge. The exceptions are the Half Hexagons, where the single knit st along the edge forms the outside border. This works fine for the very heavy rug yarn. No additional finishing is required.

### OCTAGON (MAKE 5)

Using A and Long-Tail Cast-On (see Special Techniques, page 221), CO 112 sts. Join for working in the rnd, being careful not to twist sts; pm for beginning of rnd.
Begin Octagon Pattern, working pattern from text or chart. *Note: Change to needle(s) in preferred style for small-circumference circular knitting when necessary for number of sts on needle.*

You may find it helpful to place a marker at the end of each repeat.
Work Rnds 1–22 of pattern—8 sts remain after Rnd 22.
Cut yarn, leaving a long tail. Thread tail through remaining sts, pull tight, and fasten off.

### HEXAGON (MAKE 4)

Using B and Long-Tail Cast-On, CO 84 sts. Join for working in the rnd, being careful not to twist sts; pm for beginning of rnd.
Begin Hexagon Pattern, working pattern from text or chart. Work Rnds 1–18 of pattern—12 sts remain after Rnd 18.
Cut yarn, leaving a long tail. Thread tail through remaining sts, pull tight, and fasten off.

### INTERNAL PENTAGON (MAKE 4)

Using D and Long-Tail Cast-On, CO 70 sts. Join for working in the rnd, being careful not to twist sts; pm for beginning of rnd.
Begin Pentagon Pattern, working pattern from text or chart. Work Rnds 1–12 of pattern—10 sts remain after Rnd 12.
Cut yarn, leaving a long tail. Thread tail through remaining sts, pull tight, and fasten off.

### EXTERNAL PENTAGON (MAKE 2)

Using C, work as for Internal Pentagon.

### HALF HEXAGON (MAKE 4)

Using C and Long-Tail Cast-On, CO 43 sts. Do not join; work back and forth.
Begin Half Hexagon Pattern, working pattern from text or chart. Work Setup Row (beginning on WS row), then Rnds 1–17 of pattern—7 sts remain after Rnd 17.
Cut yarn, leaving a long tail. Thread tail through remaining sts, pull tight, and fasten off.

## Octagon Pattern

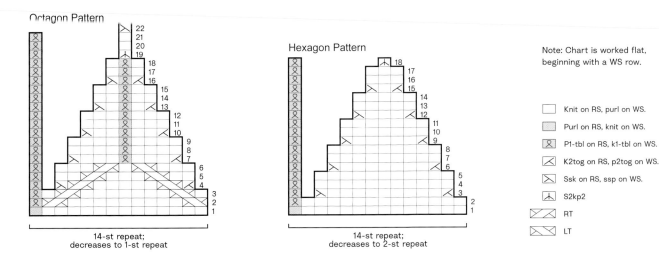

14-st repeat;
decreases to 1-st repeat

## Hexagon Pattern

14-st repeat;
decreases to 2-st repeat

Note: Chart is worked flat, beginning with a WS row.

☐ Knit on RS, purl on WS.

▨ Purl on RS, knit on WS.

▧ P1-tbl on RS, k1-tbl on WS.

◿ K2tog on RS, p2tog on WS.

◺ Ssk on RS, ssp on WS.

⊼ S2kp2

▧ RT

▧ LT

## Pentagon Pattern

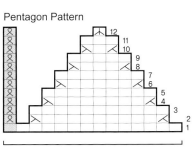

14-st repeat;
decreases to 2-st repeat

## Half Hexagon Pattern

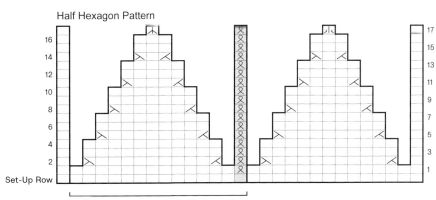

Set-Up Row

14-st repeat; decreases to 2-st repeat
work twice

## FINISHING

Block all pieces as desired. With RSs of 2 pieces facing, working from right to left, and following placement on Schematic, sew pieces together by threading tapestry needle through the 2 legs of a CO st on the first piece, just behind the rope edge of the CO, then through the 2 legs of the matching CO st on the opposite piece. This will give you a seam that is invisible on the RS. Alternatively, you may work the seam with the WSs of the pieces facing, threading tapestry needle through the 2 legs of the first purl bump directly below the rope edge of the CO.

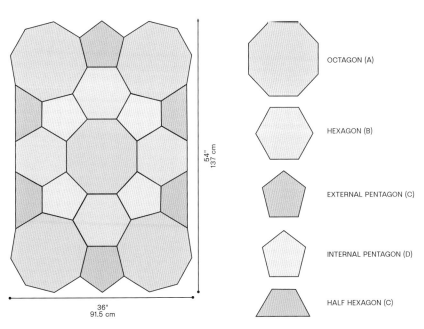

54"
137 cm

36"
91.5 cm

OCTAGON (A)

HEXAGON (B)

EXTERNAL PENTAGON (C)

INTERNAL PENTAGON (D)

HALF HEXAGON (C)

# DESIGN YOUR OWN

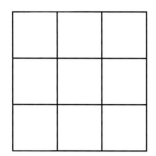
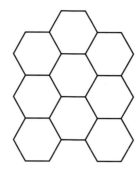
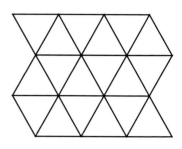

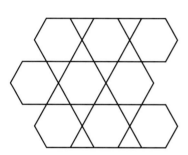
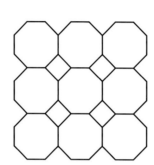
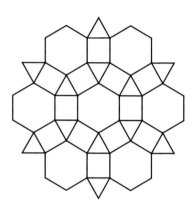

### DESIGNING POLLY

Some of you are already shaking your heads. These shapes should not fit together—they should not lie flat. Indeed, if they were made of stiffer stuff, they would not fit together so well. How lucky are we to work in a more fluid medium. Knitted fabric stretches and condenses enough to accommodate the small gaps and overlaps that would otherwise be a problem, especially after a good soak or steam blocking. With the drawing program on my Mac (I use EazyDraw), it's easy to make polygons with any number of sides—triangles, pentagons, octagons, etc. I drew up a variety of polygons all with the same length sides, so they would match up, and started to play with fitting the various shapes together.

I was well aware that the fit would not be perfect, but I placed the shapes next to each other to see how close I could get and came up with the placement I used for Polly. Deciding on the very subtle collection of colors was fun, since the yarn line had many shades to choose from. I used my computer again to determine which shades I wanted, and where. After knitting a few swatches in a DK-weight yarn, I was convinced that my idea would work and dug into knitting with the significantly heavier rug yarn.

### ABOUT TILING

Among the regular (that is, equal-sided) geometric shapes, squares, triangles, and hexagons will fit a flat surface perfectly when set down in multiples. This is called tiling (top row above). Sometimes two or more regular polygons can also tile, which is called semi-regular tiling. Octagons and squares fit together in this way. Other self-tiling combinations include hexagons with triangles and hexagons, squares, and triangles, but there are many more (bottom row above).

# Facet

A geometric puff at the base of each sleeve is the primary focus of this otherwise rectangular T-shaped pullover. The spiky puff is made from three hexagons knit one upon the other. Although it's not a crystal formation found in nature, the puffs appeared to me to be gem-like. Each is worked in the round and each is picked up along the edges of the previous hexagon. The rest of the pullover is kept simple with a few special details. Knit from sleeve to center, with a split for the neckline, a Russian graft zips the two halves together with a decorative zig-zag.

## FINISHED MEASUREMENTS
32 (36, 40, 44, 48) (52, 56, 60, 64)" [81.5 (91.5, 101.5, 112, 122) (132, 142, 152.5, 162.5) cm] *Note: This piece is intended to be worn with approximately 2–4" (5–10 cm) positive ease.*

## YARN
Blue Sky Fibers Eco-Cashmere [50% recycled cashmere/50% virgin cashmere; 164 yards (150 m)/1¾ ounces (50 g)]: 8 (8, 9, 10, 11) (12, 13, 14, 15) skeins #1801 Arctic Shadow

## NEEDLES
One 32" (80 cm) or longer circular needle, size US 6 (4 mm)

Two spare 24" (60 cm) or longer circular needles, size US 6 (4 mm) or one or two sizes smaller

Needle(s) in preferred style for small-circumference circular knitting, size US 6 (4 mm)

Change needle size if necessary to obtain correct gauge.

## NOTIONS
Stitch markers

Crochet hook size US F-5 (3.75 mm) or one or two sizes smaller

## GAUGE
21 sts and 30 rows = 4" (10 cm) in St st

## SPECIAL TECHNIQUE
### RUSSIAN GRAFTING
This technique joins two pieces together without using any yarn and creates a decorative zigzag seam on the RS. Place sts to be grafted on separate needles, with WSs together. Using a crochet hook, work as follows:
1. Insert hook into first st on back needle knitwise, dropping st from needle—1 st on hook.
2. Insert hook into first st on front needle knitwise, dropping st from needle—2 sts on hook.
3. Draw first st on hook through second st—1 st remains.
4. Insert hook into first st on back needle knitwise, dropping st from needle, then draw first st on hook through second st—1 st on hook.
5. Insert hook into first st on front needle knitwise, dropping st from needle, then draw first st on hook through second st—1 st on hook.
Repeat Steps 4 and 5 until 1 st remains on hook; fasten off.

## PATTERN NOTES
This pullover is worked in pieces, then grafted and sewn together. The hexagonal Sleeve Bubbles are worked first, and joined together by picking up stitches. The cuffs are picked up from one edge of the Bubble, then worked down in the round, and the bind-off edge is sewn to the wrong side. Each Sleeve/Body is picked up from the remaining edge of one Bubble; the Sleeve is worked in the round to the armhole, where stitches are cast on for the Front and Back Body, and the piece is worked to the center. The pieces are joined at the center using Russian Grafting for a decorative seam, and a bottom hem is picked up and worked in the round, then finished as for the cuffs.

## SLEEVE BUBBLE (MAKE 2)
### HEXAGON 1
Using needle(s) in preferred style for small-circumference circular knitting and Long-Tail Cast-On (see Special Techniques, page 221), CO 126 (126, 138, 138, 150) (162, 162, 174, 174) sts. Join for working in the rnd, being careful not to twist sts; pm for beginning of rnd.
**Setup Rnd:** *K20 (20, 22, 22, 24) (26, 26, 28, 28), p1, pm; repeat from * to end, omitting final pm (beginning-of-rnd marker is here).
Continue to knit the knit sts and purl the purl sts as they face you.
**Decrease Rnd:** *K2tog, knit to 3 sts before marker, ssk, p1; repeat from * to end—12 sts decreased.
Repeat Decrease Rnd every 3 rnds 8 (8, 9, 9, 10) (11, 11, 12, 12) more times—18 sts remain.
Work 2 rnds even. Cut yarn, leaving a long tail. Thread tail through remaining sts, pull tight, and fasten off.

### HEXAGON 2
Using needle(s) in preferred style for small-circumference circular knitting and Long-Tail Cast-On, CO 84 (84, 92, 92, 100) (108, 108, 116, 116) sts, then with RS of Hexagon facing, pick up and knit 21 (21, 23, 23, 25) (27, 27, 29, 29) sts along sides A and B of Hexagon 1 (see diagram)—126 (126, 138, 138, 150) (162, 162, 174, 174) sts. Join for working in the rnd, being careful not to twist sts; pm for beginning of rnd. Complete as for Hexagon 1.

## HEXAGON 3

*Note: When picking up sts from Hexagons 1 and 2, alternate picking up 1 st with the working yarn, then 1 st with the tail yarn across all picked-up sts; this will ensure that both ends are available when you need to CO sts for the fourth side. Be sure to begin with a long enough tail to work around the entire Hexagon.*
Using needle(s) in preferred style for small-circumference circular knitting, CO 21 (21, 23, 23, 25) (27, 27, 29, 29) sts, then with RS of Hexagon 2 facing, and alternating between working yarn and tail yarn, pick up and knit 21 (21, 23, 23, 25) (27, 27, 29, 29) sts each along sides C and D of Hexagon 2, CO 21 (21, 23, 23, 25) (27, 27, 29, 29) sts, then with RS of Hexagon 1 facing, and alternating between working yarn and tail yarn, pick up and knit 21 (21, 23, 23, 25) (27, 27, 29, 29) sts each along sides E and F of Hexagons 1 and 2—126 (126, 138, 138, 150) (162, 162, 174, 174) sts. Join for working in the rnd, being careful not to twist sts; pm for beginning of rnd.
Complete as for Hexagon 1.

## SLEEVE CUFF

With RS of Sleeve Bubble facing, using needle(s) in preferred style for small-circumference circular knitting, and beginning between two Hexagons, pick up and knit 22 (22, 24, 24, 26) (28, 28, 30, 30) sts evenly along bottom edge of each Hexagon—66 (66, 72, 72, 78) (84, 84, 90, 90) sts. Join for working in the rnd; pm for beginning of rnd.
Begin rev St st (purl every rnd); work even for 2" (5 cm).
Fold live sts to WS and loosely sew live sts to pick-up ridge. *Note: If you prefer, you may BO all sts, then sew BO edge to pick-up ridge.*

## LEFT SLEEVE/BODY

With RS of Sleeve Bubble facing, using needle(s) in preferred style for small-circumference circular knitting, and beginning between two Hexagons, pick up and knit 66 (66, 72, 78, 84) (92, 98, 102, 104) evenly around Hexagons, approximately 22 (22, 24, 26, 28) (31, 33, 34, 35) sts along top edge of each Hexagon. Join for working in the rnd; place marker for beginning of rnd.

Begin St st (knit every rnd); work even for 5" (12.5 cm).

Change to circular needle if necessary.

**Next Row (RS):** Using Cable Cast-On (see Special Techniques, page 221), CO 77 (80, 79, 76, 75) (72, 72, 72, 74) sts, knit across these sts, knit to end of Sleeve, remove marker; turn—143 (146, 151, 154, 159) (164, 170, 174, 178) sts.

**Next Row (WS):** Using Cable Cast-On, CO 77 (80, 79, 76, 75) (72, 72, 72, 74) sts, purl across these sts, purl to end—220 (226, 230, 230, 234) (236, 242, 246, 252) sts. Continuing in St st, work even until piece measures 3 (4, 5, 5½, 6½) (7½, 8, 9, 10)" [7.5 (10, 12.5, 14, 16.5) (19, 20.5, 23, 25.5 cm] from Body CO, ending with a WS row.

### DIVIDE FOR NECK

**Division Row (RS):** K107 (110, 112, 112, 114) (115, 118, 120, 123), slip 3 sts to cable needle and hold to front, k3, join a second ball of yarn, k3 from cable needle, knit to end—107 (110, 112, 112, 114) (115, 118, 120, 123) sts each side. Working both sides at the same time, work even until piece measures 5 (5, 5, 5½, 5½) (5½, 6, 6, 6)" [12.5 (12.5, 12.5, 14, 14) (14, 15, 15, 15) cm] from Division Row, ending with a WS row. Transfer sts to two spare needles.

### RIGHT SLEEVE/BODY

Work as for Left Sleeve/Body to neck division, ending with a WS row.

### DIVIDE FOR NECK

**Division Row (RS):** K107 (110, 112, 112, 114) (115, 118, 120, 123), slip 3 sts to cable needle and hold to back, k3, join a second ball of yarn, k3 from cable needle, knit to end—107 (110, 112, 112, 114) (115, 118, 120, 123) sts each side. Working both sides at the same time, work even until piece measures 5 (5, 5, 5½, 5½) (5½, 6, 6, 6)" [12.5 (12.5, 12.5, 14, 14) (14, 15, 15, 15) cm] from Division Row, ending with a WS row. Join Right and Left Front sts using Russian Grafting. Repeat for Back sts.

### FINISHING

Block pieces as desired.
Sew side seams.

### BOTTOM HEM

With RS facing, using circular needle and beginning at side seam, pick up and knit 168 (188, 212, 232, 252) (272, 296, 316, 336) sts around bottom edge [42 (47, 53, 58, 63) (68, 74, 79, 84) sts per quarter]. Join for working in the rnd. Begin rev St st; work even for 2" (5 cm). BO all sts. Fold live sts to WS and loosely sew live sts to pick-up ridge. *Note: If you prefer, you may BO all sts, then sew BO edge to pick-up ridge.*

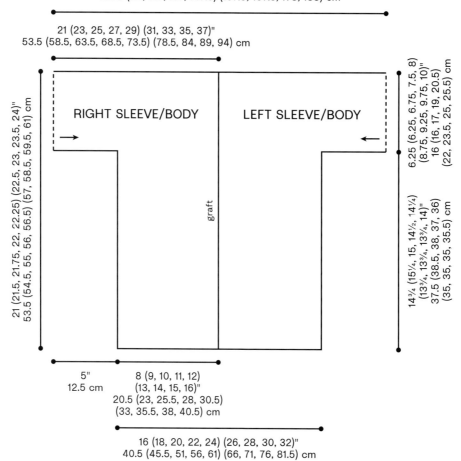

42 (46, 50, 54, 58) (62, 66, 70, 74)"
106.5 (117, 127, 137, 147.5) (157.5, 167.5, 178, 188) cm

21 (23, 25, 27, 29) (31, 33, 35, 37)"
53.5 (58.5, 63.5, 68.5, 73.5) (78.5, 84, 89, 94) cm

RIGHT SLEEVE/BODY

LEFT SLEEVE/BODY

graft

6.25 (6.25, 6.75, 7.5, 8)"
(8.75, 9.25, 9.75, 10)"
16 (16, 17, 19, 20.5)
(22, 23.5, 25, 25.5) cm

21 (21.5, 21.75, 22, 22.25) (22.5, 23, 23.5, 24)" cm
53.5 (54.5, 55, 56, 56.5) (57, 58.5, 59.5, 61) cm

14¾ (15¼, 15, 14½, 14¼)"
(13¾, 13¾, 13¾, 14)"
37.5 (38.5, 38, 37, 36)
(35, 35, 35, 35.5) cm

5"
12.5 cm

8 (9, 10, 11, 12)
(13, 14, 15, 16)"
20.5 (23, 25.5, 28, 30.5)
(33, 35.5, 38, 40.5) cm

16 (18, 20, 22, 24) (26, 28, 30, 32)"
40.5 (45.5, 51, 56, 61) (66, 71, 76, 81.5) cm

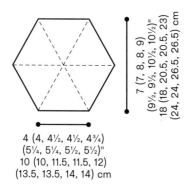

7 (7, 8, 8, 9)
(9½, 9½, 10½, 10½)"
18 (18, 20.5, 20.5, 23
(24, 24, 26.5, 26.5) cm

4 (4, 4½, 4½, 4¾)
(5¼, 5¼, 5½, 5½)"
10 (10, 11.5, 11.5, 12)
(13.5, 13.5, 14, 14) cm

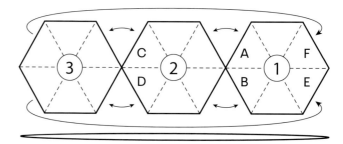

12 (12, 13½, 13½, 14¼) (15¾, 15¾, 16½, 16½)"
30.5 (30.5, 34.5, 34.5, 36) (40, 40, 42, 42) cm

# DESIGN YOUR OWN

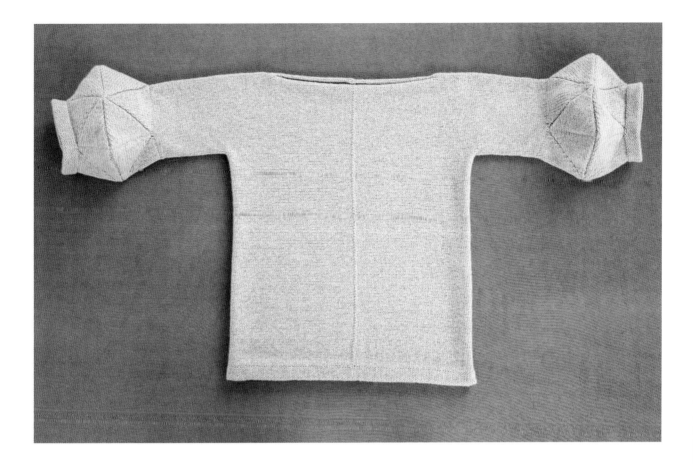

### DESIGNING FACET'S HEXAGONS

Wanting to take advantage of work already done, I used the hexagon from Polly (page 111) to construct the spiky puff that begins each sleeve. Don't be afraid to reuse ideas or instructions for the tricky bits—it's not cheating! I think of the elements I use over and over as my design vocabulary. The hexagon has been an important element in my design vocabulary ever since I wrote *Knitting Nature*, which explored knitting garments from shapes found in nature, among them hexagons. I return to them again and again, refining my instructions occasionally. Row gauge can sometimes make reusing hexagon

instructions tricky—the frequency of decreases that work for one yarn might not be exactly right for a different yarn, if the row to stitch ratio is different. Adding a one-stitch column of reverse stockinette between each of the six stockinette triangles acts as a buffer. It behaves like rib, which can be stretched or compressed easily, especially when blocked and because of that, one pattern can work for a larger variety of yarns.

### DESIGN LESSON: 3-D FORMS

In the Design Your Own section of the rug Polly, I looked at tiling and how some shapes fit together to form a

flat surface. Here I am thinking about the opposite—wanting to make three-dimensional shapes. I can think of three ways to combine polygons into rounded structures:
1. Put the points of polygons together, like I did for Facet. Instead of nestling the sides of adjacent hexagons together in a perfect flat fit, the hexagons are attached point to point, making a three-dimensional, spiky protrusion.
2. Use multiples of a shape that does not tile, like pentagons (soccer balls are made mostly of pentagons).
3. Add extra rows between the decrease rows, causing the center of each polygon to stick out, like the four-sided projections of Pyramid (page 107).

# Octagram

Plucking the octagonal motif from Polly (page 111), this pillow's front and back are identical. Easy twisted stitches and ribs act as lines, drawing the snowflake-like pattern while defining the eight segments. The band of garter stitch provides thickness to the pillow cover and is knit on, joining the front and back along the way.

## FINISHED MEASUREMENTS

Approximately 14" (35.5 cm) diameter × 5"(12.5 cm) deep, before stuffing

Note: Stretches to fit 16" (40.5 cm) round pillow form

## YARN

Harrisville Designs Turbine [100% pure virgin wool; 110 yards (100 m)/3½ ounces (100 g)]: 3 skeins Meadows

## NEEDLES

Two 24" (60 cm) circular needles, size US 13 (9 mm)

Needle(s) in preferred style for small-circumference circular knitting, size US 13 (9 mm)

Three double-pointed needles, size US 13 (9 mm), for Side Panel

Change needle size if necessary to obtain correct gauge.

## NOTIONS

Stitch markers

16" (40.5 cm) round pillow form

## GAUGE

10 sts and 12½ rows = 4" (10 cm) in St st

## STITCH PATTERN

### OCTAGON PATTERN (SEE CHART)

(multiple of 14 sts; decreases to multiple of 1 st; 22 rnds)

**Rnd 1:** *K13, p1; repeat from * to end.
**Rnd 2:** *LT, k9, RT, p1-tbl; repeat from * to end.
**Rnd 3:** *K1, LT, k7, RT, k1, p1-tbl; repeat from * to end.
**Rnd 4:** *K2tog, LT, k5, RT, ssk, p1-tbl; repeat from * to end—2 sts decreased.
**Rnd 5:** *K2, LT, k3, RT, k2, p1-tbl; repeat from * to end.
**Rnd 6:** *K3, LT, k1, RT, k3, p1-tbl; repeat from * to end.
**Rnd 7:** *K2tog, k3, p1-tbl, k3, ssk, p1-tbl; repeat from * to end—2 sts decreased.
**Rnds 8 and 9:** *K4, p1-tbl; repeat from * to end.
**Rnd 10:** *K2tog, k2, p1-tbl, k2, ssk, p1-tbl; repeat from * to end—2 sts decreased.
**Rnds 11 and 12:** *K3, p1-tbl; repeat from * to end.
**Rnd 13:** *K2tog, k1, p1-tbl, k1, ssk, p1-tbl; repeat from * to end—2 sts decreased.
**Rnds 14 and 15:** *K2, p1-tbl; repeat from * to end.
**Rnd 16:** *K2tog, p1-tbl, ssk, p1-tbl; repeat from * to end—2 sts decreased.
**Rnds 17 and 18:** *K1, p1-tbl; repeat from * to end.
**Rnd 19:** *S2kp2, p1-tbl; repeat from * to end—2 sts decreased.
**Rnds 20 and 21:** *K1, p1-tbl; repeat from * to end.
**Rnd 22:** *Ssk; repeat from * to end—1 st decreased.

## PATTERN NOTE

The front and back Octagons are knit separately, then joined together while knitting the Side Panel. The piece is stuffed, then the live stitches of the Side Panel are grafted to the cast-on edge. If you prefer, you may bind off the stitches, then sew the two ends together.

## OCTAGON (MAKE 2)

Using Long-Tail Cast-On (see Special Techniques, page 221), CO 112 sts. Join for working in the rnd, being careful not to twist sts; pm for beginning of rnd. Begin Octagon Pattern, working pattern from text or chart. Note: Change to needle(s) in preferred style for small-circumference circular knitting when necessary for number of sts on needle. You may find it helpful to place a marker at the end of each repeat.
Work Rnds 1–22 of pattern—8 sts remain after Rnd 22.
Cut yarn, leaving a long tail. Thread tail through remaining sts, pull tight, and fasten off.

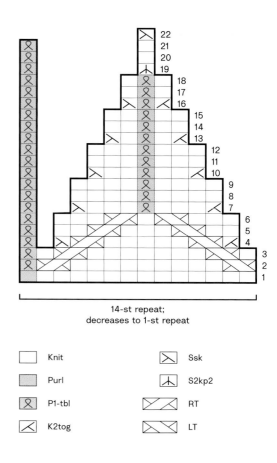

14-st repeat;
decreases to 1-st repeat

| | |
|---|---|
| ☐ Knit | ⟋ Ssk |
| ▨ Purl | ⟑ S2kp2 |
| ⟊ P1-tbl | ⧄ RT |
| ⟍ K2tog | ⧅ LT |

## SIDE PANEL

With WS of one Octagon facing, using a circular needle and beginning at a purl column between 2 motifs, pick up and knit 112 sts around Octagon, turn to RS; using same strand of yarn and Cable Cast-On (see Special Techniques, page 221), CO 9 sts onto dpn. Cut yarn. With WS of second Octagon facing, using second circular needle and beginning at a purl column between 2 motifs, pick up and knit 112 sts around second Octagon; using second dpn and yarn attached to second Octagon, knit across 8 sts on first dpn, ssk (last st on dpn together with first picked-up st from first Octagon), turn.

**All Rows:** K7, ssk (last st on dpn together with 1 picked-up st from Octagon), turn. Continue in this manner until you have a 3" (7.5 cm) opening left in the Side Panel. Stuff pillow. Continue until all sts on both Octagons have been worked—9 sts remain.

## FINISHING

Graft live sts on needle to CO edge (see Special Techniques, page 221). *Note: If you prefer, you may BO the sts, then sew CO and BO edges together.*

# DESIGN YOUR OWN

### DESIGNING OCTAGRAM

Borrowing from the multi-polygonal rug Polly (page 111), I copied the octagon instructions directly to make this pillow. The yarn is even the same gauge. Lucky for me, the piece is 14" (40.5 cm) across, and it's easy to find that same size circular pillow inserts. One octagon each for front and back made obvious sense, but how should they be joined? I tried to picture this as a knife-edge pillow and it seemed too skimpy—too much work for too little impact. It would have to be a box pillow, a round pillow with deep sides. I folded some swatches I had on hand and experimented with the depth of the side piece between the octagons until I found the depth I liked best. Looking at some box pillows online, I especially like the ones with some kind of element defining the edges where the band circling the pillow meets both the top and the bottom. I contemplated using an applied I-cord edge to look like piping. Trying to keep things pared down, though, I didn't want to add that much complexity or extra thickness. I decided that I would get enough of an edge if I picked up all around the octagon with the wrong side facing, instead of the right side. So in place of a smooth seam where the top and bottom meet the band, I would get an exposed seam. The edge of the octagon would show. The band was knit and attached to the picked-up stitches at the end of every row. I tested slipping the first stitch of every row as you normally would when using this technique, but for this pillow, I liked the look better when the first stitch was not slipped.

### QUESTION TRADITION

Okay, this is pretty cheesy, but the following story illustrates a point I want to make. Years ago I saw this quip in a magazine, maybe *TV Guide* (who else remembers that weekly must-have?). A woman was preparing a big ham to go in the oven by cutting a chunk off one end before placing it in the pan. When her neighbor wondered why she did that, the woman replied that cutting the end off the ham was what her mother always did, so she always did it, too, never thinking to question why. Later that week, the woman got a chance to ask her mother why she always cut the end off the ham before placing it in the oven. Her mom said, "Oh, I didn't have a roasting pan big enough, so I cut the ham to fit in my pan." This is all to say that it is good to question techniques, like cutting off the end of your ham, folding your towels in thirds (to fit my mom's shelves), or slipping the first stitch (mentioned in the last section). Maybe the details of the technique work great in many circumstances but aren't the solution you want for your yarn and pattern. Question the "right" way. Question tradition.

# CHAPTER 5

# HONE

In this chapter, still primarily inhabited by rectangles, the addition of traditional shaping techniques helps attain a more precise fit. Shaping carves away excess fabric, while inserts and short rows fill in where more is needed and add extra decorative elements.

# Dickey

Worn under a coat or as you might wear a cowl, this squishy, soft dickey warms your shoulders, keeps your neck cozy, and protects your neckline from chilly breezes.

**FINISHED MEASUREMENTS**

15½" (39.5 cm) shoulder width

12" (30.5 cm) front length to high shoulder

6" (15 cm) back length to high shoulder

**YARN**

Purl Soho Flax Down [43% baby alpaca/42% extra fine merino wool/15% linen; 219 yards (200 m)/3½ ounces (100 g)]: 2 skeins 1260 Rose Granite

**NEEDLES**

One pair straight needles, size US 4 (3.5 mm)

One needle in any style, size US 6 (4 mm), for binding off

Change needle size if necessary to obtain correct gauge.

**NOTIONS**

Removable stitch markers

**GAUGE**

17 sts and 50 rows = 4" (10 cm) in Brioche Stitch

## SPECIAL ABBREVIATIONS

**Yf sl1yo:** (Slip next st purlwise while creating a yo.) Bring yarn to front, slip next st purlwise; leave yarn in front, ready to work the following st. When you knit the following st, the yarn will drape over the needle to create the yo. The slipped st and its accompanying yo should be counted as 1 st.

**Brk1:** Knit the next st and its accompanying yo together.

**Brk2tog:** With yarn in front, knit 3 loops together (a single st and the following slipped st and its accompanying yo)—1 st decreased.

**Brsssk:** With yarn in front, slip next st and its accompanying yo together knitwise, slip following single st knitwise (3 loops on right-hand needle), brk1, pass 3 loops over—2 sts decreased.

**Brk3tog:** Brk2tog, return this st to left-hand needle, pass second st on left-hand needle and its accompanying yo over first st—2 sts decreased.

## PATTERN STITCH

### BRIOCHE STITCH

(odd number of sts; 2-row repeat)

**Setup Row (WS):** K1, *yf sl1yo, k1; repeat from * to end.

**Row 1 (RS):** K1, *brk1, yf sl1yo; repeat from * to last 2 sts, brk1, k1.

**Row 2:** K1, *yf sl1yo, brk1; repeat from * to last 2 sts, yf sl1yo, k1.

Repeat Rows 1 and 2 for pattern.

## PATTERN NOTES

Center Front and Back rectangles are worked first, then sewn together to form the turtleneck. Stitches are picked up along each remaining side edge for Right and Left Borders, which are worked outward with shoulder shaping.

## CENTER FRONT

Using smaller needles, CO 39 sts.
Begin Brioche Stitch; work even until piece measures 17" (43 cm) from the beginning, ending with a WS row.
BO all sts in 1×1 rib (without yo's) using larger needle, and working all slipped sts and their accompanying yos as 1 st.

## CENTER BACK

Using smaller needles, CO 39 sts.
Begin Brioche Stitch; work even until piece measures 11" (28 cm) from the beginning, ending with a WS row.
BO all sts knitwise using larger needle, and working all slipped sts and their accompanying yos as 1 st.
With RS of Center Front and Back facing, sew side edges of pieces together for 5" (12.5 cm) down from the BO edge, threading the yarn through the first purl bump at the edge of each piece to create a flat seam.

## RIGHT BORDER

With RS facing, using smaller needles, and beginning at Center Back CO edge, pick up and knit 25 sts along right edge of Center Back, then 54 sts along right edge of Center Front—79 sts.
Begin Brioche Stitch; work 11 rows even.
With RS facing, place removable marker around the 26th st (this should be the knit st closest to the shoulder, where Center Back meets Center Front).
**Decrease Row (RS):** Continuing in established pattern, work to 6 sts before marked st (counting each slipped st and its accompanying yo as 1 st), brsssk, work 7 sts, brk3tog, work to end—4 sts decreased.
Repeat Decrease Row every 12 rows two more times—67 sts remain.
BO all sts in 1×1 Rib using larger needle.

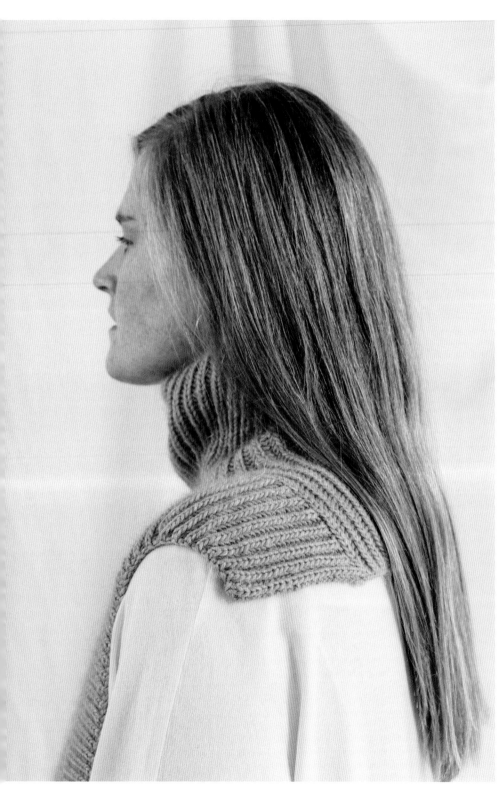

## LEFT BORDER

With RS facing, using smaller needles, and beginning at Center Front CO edge, pick up and knit 54 sts along left edge of the Center Front (as worn) and 25 sts along left edge of the Center Back— 79 sts.

Begin Brioche Stitch; work 11 rows even. With RS facing, Place removable marker around the 55th st (this should be the knit st closest to the shoulder, where Center Back meets Center Front).

**Decrease Row (RS):** Continuing in established pattern, work to 6 sts before marked st (counting each slipped st and its accompanying yo as 1 st), brsssk, work 7 sts, brk3tog, work to end—4 sts decreased.

Repeat Decrease Row every 12 rows two more times—67 sts remain.

BO all sts using larger needle.

## FINISHING

Block to measurements.

# DESIGN YOUR OWN

### DESIGNING DICKEY

Sometimes it's hard for me to keep things simple. I so admire designers who are able to pare designs down to their barest elements. I am always afraid that, in my own designing, plain and simple is not enough. There is that inner voice nagging at me: Shouldn't I add cables or make up a new pattern stitch to ensure this design is worth knitting? Simple, however, can be so beautiful, so calming, so wearable. I quieted those inner doubts and stuck with plain brioche rib, knit in only one color. If you are feeling more maximalist, add two-color brioche, striped brioche, or heck, two-color brioche with stripes. The center panel could also easily be adorned with the many beautiful increase and decrease patterns you see in brioche patterns these days. Cabling brioche ribs would pull the width in a bit, so you'd have to compensate for that, if you wanted to add cabled fanciness.

Although I had to hold myself back, the overall simplicity of this pattern lets the shoulder decreases shine as a beautiful decorative element and the piece is easy to knit. I chose to knit the front and back rectangles as separate pieces, which are seamed at each side of the neck, to avoid the fussiness and little complications that joining them and keeping in pattern would entail.

### TO SHAPE SHOULDERS OR NOT

Sometimes it's difficult to choose between straight shoulders—which are a breeze to knit, make a smooth shoulder line, and create no angst about keeping in pattern—or adding some shoulder shaping, which means sewing a sloped seam and improves fit in several ways. When my goal is writing a pattern that is super simple to knit, like Weave (page 23), Blouse (page 47) or Forty-Five° (page 101), I'll opt for the straight shoulder.

Most often (when not writing a book based on rectangular shapes) I like some shoulder shaping. Without the shaping there is some extra knitted fabric that has to end up somewhere, and it usually makes things a little ruffly below the shoulder, or the extra goes upward, making the shoulder stand up instead of sitting smoothly on the shoulder. Knit fabric is amazing at absorbing the slack, especially if there is a fair amount of weight pulling the sweater downward. In the case of Dickey, there is not much weight to keep the shoulder down, and I think the shoulder of the piece would stand up without the shaping.

# Centrale

Glamorously draped in back and swingy allover, this oversized summer top is made entirely from folded rectangular shapes. Centrale has no shaping—in fact the only shaping at all is a stitch-doubling increase row before the center panel mistake stitch rib begins and later, after the rib is complete, a decrease row restoring the stitch count. This piece might have been included in the purely rectangular Chapter 2, but its extremely close relationship to Lotus, the next pattern in this book, places it here.

## FINISHED MEASUREMENTS
40 (44, 48, 52, 56) (60, 64, 68, 72)" [101.5 (112, 122, 132, 142) (152.5, 162.5, 172.5, 183) cm] chest

*Note: This piece is intended to be worn with approximately 10" (25.5 cm) positive ease.*

## YARN
Shibui Knits Reed [100% linen; 246 yards (225 m)/1¾ ounces (50 g)]: 4 (4, 5, 5, 5) (6, 6, 6, 7) skeins #2004 Ivory

## NEEDLES
One 29" (70 cm) or longer circular needle, size US 4 (3.5 mm)

Change needle size if necessary to obtain correct gauge.

## NOTIONS
Removable stitch markers

Stitch holder or waste yarn

Crochet hook size US E-4 (3.5 mm) (optional; for neck edge)

## GAUGE
24 sts and 32 rows = 4" (10 cm) in St st

## PATTERN STITCH
### SEEDED RIB

(multiple of 4 sts + 7; 2-row repeat)
**Row 1 (RS):** K5, *p1, k3; repeat from * to last 2 sts, k2.
**Row 2:** K3, *p1, k3; repeat from * to last 4 sts, p1, k3.
Repeat Rows 1 and 2 for pattern.

## PATTERN NOTES

The body of this top is worked flat in one piece to the armholes, then Fronts and Back are worked separately. The Back side edges are folded down and sewn to the top of the Fronts. The Center Front Panel is picked up and worked from the Left Front, then sewn to the Right Front. There is no finishing for the armholes and neck. If you prefer a firmer neck edge, you may work crocheted slip stitch around a portion of the neck opening.

## BODY

CO 192 (216, 240, 264, 288) (312, 336, 360, 384) sts.
Begin St st; work even until piece measures 11½ (10¾, 9½, 8, 7¾) (6½, 6½, 6¼, 5¾)" [29 (27.5, 24, 20.5, 19.5) (16.5, 16.5, 16, 14.5) cm] from the beginning, ending with a WS row.

## DIVIDE FOR FRONTS AND BACK

**Division Row (RS):** K36 (42, 48, 54, 60) (66, 72, 78, 84), turn, transferring remaining 156 (174, 192, 210, 228) (246, 264, 282, 300) sts to st holder or waste yarn.

## RIGHT FRONT

Working on 36 (42, 48, 54, 60) (66, 72, 78, 84) Front sts only, work even until piece measures 5½ (5¾, 6¼, 7, 7) (8, 8, 8, 8¼)" [14 (14.5, 16, 18, 18) (20.5, 20.5, 20.5, 21) cm] from Division Row, ending with a WS row.
BO all sts.

## BACK

With RS facing, rejoin yarn to remaining sts. K120 (132, 144, 156, 168) (180, 192, 204, 216), turn, leaving remaining 36 (42, 48, 54, 60) (66, 72, 78, 84) sts on st holder or waste yarn for Left Front. Working on 120 (132, 144, 156, 168) (180, 192, 204, 216) Back sts only, work even until piece measures 5½ (5¾, 6¼, 7, 7) (8, 8, 8, 8¼)" [14 (14.5, 16, 18, 18) (20.5, 20.5, 20.5, 21) cm] from Division Row, ending with a WS row. Place removable markers at beginning and end of row.
Work even until piece measures 6 (7, 8, 9, 10) (11, 12, 13, 14)" [15 (18, 20.5, 23, 25.5) (28, 30.5, 33, 35.5) cm] from markers, ending with a WS row.
BO all sts.

## LEFT FRONT

With RS facing, rejoin yarn to remaining 36 (42, 48, 54, 60) (66, 72, 78, 84) sts. Work even until piece measures 5½ (5¾, 6¼, 7, 7) (8, 8, 8, 8¼)" [14 (14.5, 16, 18, 18) (20.5, 20.5, 20.5, 21) cm] from Division Row, ending with a WS row.
BO all sts.
Block piece to measurements. Fold left side of Back at marker. Align marker with top corner of Left Front; sew side edge of Back (from marker to BO edge) to BO edge of Left Front. Repeat for right side of Back.

## CENTER FRONT PANEL

With RS of Left Front facing, beginning ¾ (¾, 1, 1, 1¾) (2½, 3¼, 4, 5)" [2 (2, 2.5, 2.5, 4.5) (6.5, 8.5, 10, 12.5) cm] above seam at top of Front, pick up and knit 100 (98, 94, 90, 92) (96, 100, 102, 106) sts along side edge of Left Front to bottom edge.

Knit 4 rows.

**Next Row (WS):** K2, *p1-f/b; repeat from * to last 3 sts, k3—195 (191, 183, 175, 179) (187, 195, 199, 207) sts.

Begin Seeded Rib; work even until Front Panel measures 7½" (19 cm) from pick-up row, ending with a WS row.

**Next Row (RS):** K2, *s2kp2, p1; repeat from * to last 5 sts, ssk, k3—100 (98, 94, 90, 92) (96, 100, 102, 106) sts remain.

Knit 4 rows.

BO all sts purlwise.

## FINISHING

Sew to BO edge of Panel to Right Front, beginning ¾ (¾, 1, 1, 1¾) (2½, 3¼, 4, 5)" [2 (2, 2.5, 2.5, 4.5) (6.5, 8.5, 10, 12.5) cm] above Front seam.

*Note: Armhole and neck edges have no finishing. If a firmer neck edge is desired, work a crocheted slip st along neck edge as follows: Beginning at lower right front neck edge, *insert crochet hook into both legs of st along neck edge, draw up a loop and bring it through st on hook; repeat from * around neck edge, ending at lower left front neck edge. Fasten off.*

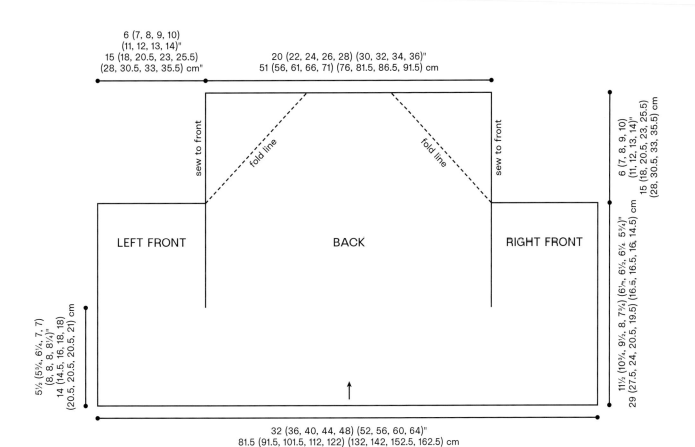

6 (7, 8, 9, 10)
(11, 12, 13, 14)"
15 (18, 20.5, 23, 25.5)
(28, 30.5, 33, 35.5) cm"

20 (22, 24, 26, 28) (30, 32, 34, 36)"
51 (56, 61, 66, 71) (76, 81.5, 86.5, 91.5) cm

6 (7, 8, 9, 10)
(11, 12, 13, 14)"
15 (18, 20.5, 23, 25.5)
(28, 30.5, 33, 35.5) cm

sew to front

fold line

fold line

sew to front

LEFT FRONT

BACK

RIGHT FRONT

5½ (5¾, 6¼, 7, 7)
(8, 8, 8¼)"
14 (14.5, 16, 18, 18)
(20.5, 20.5, 20.5, 21) cm

11½ (10¾, 9½, 8, 7¾) (6½, 6½, 6¼ 5¾)"
29 (27.5, 24, 20.5, 19.5) (16.5, 16.5, 16 14.5) cm

32 (36, 40, 44, 48) (52, 56, 60, 64)"
81.5 (91.5, 101.5, 112, 122) (132, 142, 152.5, 162.5) cm

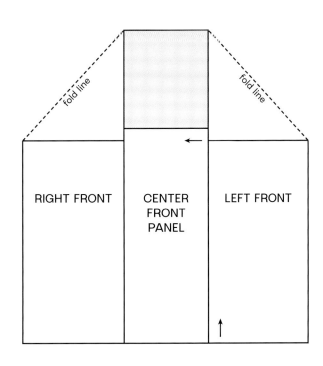

fold line

fold line

RIGHT FRONT

CENTER
FRONT
PANEL

LEFT FRONT

# DESIGN YOUR OWN

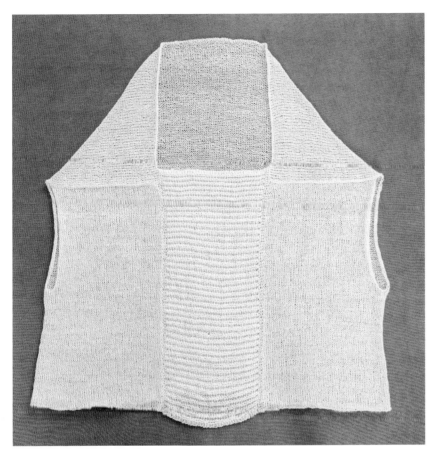

## YARN CHOICES

Maybe even more than with traditional sweater structures, the choice of yarn can entirely change the character of the finished garment with an odd, folded construction. Compare the drapey, fluid quality of Centrale to the more constrained Lotus, the next pattern in this book (page 139). Very similarly folded, Lotus's fabric is not super stretchy like Centrale's. The shoulders are firmer. The fabric does not reveal much about the body underneath it, while Centrale does, despite the sweater being oversized. Everything about Lotus is more solid, more in control. If Centrale were knit in the more stable, less stretchy and fluid yarn, the back neck would not drape as it does. It would most likely be able to fold over to form a wide shawl collar. All to say, it would be a very different sweater.

As always, swatch first to see what your yarn can do. How drapey is it or how stable? While I don't always follow my own advice, making a fabric model (see page 151 for more) can help you plan. Search out a sewing fabric that has similar qualities—a slinky rayon knit to simulate the drape of the yarn used for Centrale, or a medium-weight poly fleece to simulate a more stable knit like that of Lotus.

## CENTRALE

The folded construction of Centrale is a variation of a sweater construction I first saw in fashion magazines a few years back. The back is a tall rectangle, with its upper corners folded down on the diagonal and attached to the front. In the sweater I first noticed, the corners met in the center of the front. Here, I filled the middle of the front with a ribbed panel insert and the back corners fold down to meet the edges of the panel, forming a square neckline. The fabric of Centrale is all about drape. A few key seams stabilize the pullover. First, where the back fold is sewn to the top of the front and then where the central ribbed panel is attached to the stockinette part of the front. With those seams for stability, having side seams felt fussy to me, so I decided that the back and two fronts should be knit in one piece. This folded construction can sometimes be hard to predict. I had assumed that I would want to crochet a slipped stitch across the top of the back, which folds to become the neckline. I am glad I asked our model to try on the pullover before adding any stabilizing crochet. When Emily put it on, the back of the neckline lay gracefully arched and swooped on her upper back, which was totally unpredicted by me. My dress form, lacking full shoulders and arms, had not shown me the true story.

# Lotus

Cropped in length, Lotus is shown off perfectly over a dress or worn with high-waisted trousers. The wedge-shaped center back collar insert is reminiscent of a scallop shell or the expanding petals of a lotus blossom. Front bands are knit in as you go, with garter and slipped stitches, ensuring that the edges will not sag.

**FINISHED MEASUREMENTS**
40 (44, 48, 52, 56) (60, 64, 68, 72)" [101.5 (112, 122, 132, 142) (152.5, 162.5, 172.5, 183 cm], buttoned

*Note: This piece is intended to be worn with approximately 10" (25.5 cm) positive ease.*

**YARN**
Rowan Merino Aria [93% wool/7% polyamide; 92 yards (85 m)/1¾ ounces (50 g)]: 6 (7, 7, 8, 8) (9, 9, 10, 11) balls #043 Ash

**NEEDLES**
One pair straight needles, size US 13 (9 mm)

Change needle size if necessary to obtain correct gauge.

**NOTIONS**
Stitch markers

Removable stitch markers

Five ¾" (19 mm) buttons

**GAUGE**
12 sts and 17 rows = 4" (10 cm) in St st

## PATTERN NOTES

Back, Fronts, and Sleeves are worked separately from the bottom up, then sewn together. The Godet for the Back neck is worked from the top down, then sewn in place.

## BACK

CO 60 (66, 72, 78, 84) (90, 96, 102, 108) sts.
Begin St st; work even until piece measures 15" (38 cm) from the beginning, ending with a WS row. Place removable markers (marker A) at beginning and end of last row.
Work even until piece measures 21 (22, 22½, 23½, 24) (25, 25½, 26½, 27)" [53.5 (56, 57, 59.5, 61) (63.5, 65, 67.5, 68.5) cm] from the beginning, ending with a WS row.

## SPLIT FOR GODET

**Next Row (RS):** K30 (33, 36, 39, 42) (45, 48, 51, 54), join a second ball of yarn, knit to end.

Working both sides at the same time, work even until split measures 4 (4, 4½, 4½, 5) (5, 5½, 5½, 6)" [10 (10, 11.5, 11.5, 12.5) (12.5, 14, 14, 15) cm], ending with a WS row. Place removable markers (marker B) at armhole edge on both sides.
Purl 5 rows.
BO all sts purlwise.

## LEFT FRONT

CO 35 (38, 41, 44, 47) (50, 53, 56, 59) sts.
**Setup Row (WS):** P2, k3, purl to end.
**Row 1 (RS):** Knit.
**Row 2:** Slip 2 sts purlwise wyif, k3, purl to end.
Repeat Rows 1 and 2 until piece measures 15" (38 cm) from the beginning, ending with a WS row. Place marker for buttonhole in Front band on last RS row worked.

## SHAPE UPPER FRONT

BO 5 (6, 6, 7, 7) (8, 8, 8, 9) sts at beginning of next 7 (3, 6, 2, 5) (1, 4, 7, 3)

RS row(s), then 0 (5, 5, 6, 6) (7, 7, 0, 8) sts at beginning of next 0 (4, 1, 5, 2) (6, 3, 0, 4) RS row(s).
Place 4 more removable markers for buttons in Front band, the first 1¾" (4.5 cm) up from bottom edge, and the remaining 3 evenly spaced between the first and the marker placed before shaping upper Front.

## RIGHT FRONT

CO 35 (38, 41, 44, 47) (50, 53, 56, 59) sts.
**Setup Row (WS):** Purl to last 5 sts, k3, p2.
**Row 1 (RS):** Slip 2 sts purlwise wyib, knit to end.
Repeat Rows 1 and 2 until piece measures 15" (38 cm) from the beginning, ending with a RS row, working buttonholes on RS rows opposite markers on Left Front, as follows:
**Buttonhole Row (RS):** Slip 2 sts purlwise wyib, ssk, yo, knit to end.

## SHAPE UPPER FRONT

BO 5 (6, 6, 7, 7) (8, 8, 8, 9) sts at beginning of next 7 (3, 6, 2, 5) (1, 4, 7, 3) WS row(s), then 0 (5, 5, 6, 6) (7, 7, 0, 8) sts at beginning of next 0 (4, 1, 5, 2) (6, 3, 0, 4) WS row(s).

## SLEEVES

CO 35 (37, 37, 41, 43) (45, 47, 49, 51) sts.
Purl 1 row.

### SIZES 48, 52, 56, 60, 64, 68, AND 72 ONLY:

**Row 1 (RS):** K1, k3tog, knit to last 4 sts, sssk, k1—4 sts decreased.
**Row 2:** Purl.
Repeat Rows 1 and 2 - (-, 0, 3, 5) (6, 8, 9, 10) more times— - (-,33, 25, 19) (17, 11, 9, 7) sts remain.

## FINISHING

Lightly block pieces. *Note: When sewing pieces together, to avoid bulky seams, take only half of each edge st into the seam instead of one full st.*

Fold BO edge of Back to RS at marker B and use additional removable markers to hold both layers together at outside edge only. Fold upper corners of Back to WS at marker A on side edges. Sew side edge of each side of Back (between marker A and marker B) to sloped upper Fronts, beginning at outer edge and ending before Front bands, sewing both layers at top Back edge into seam. Place removable markers 9 (9½, 9¼, 9¼, 9) (9¼, 9¼, 9½, 9¾)" [23 (24, 23.5, 23.5, 23) (23.5, 23.5, 24, 25) cm] down from upper front seam on front and back. Sew in sleeves between markers. Sew side seams.

## LOTUS GODET

Cast on 27 sts.
Knit one row.
**Setup Row (WS):** P2, [k5, p2] 4 times, p1.
**Row 1 (RS):** K2, [p5, k1] 4 times, k1.
**Row 2:** P2, [k5, p1] 4 times, p1.
**Row 3:** K1, [ssk, p4] twice, k1, [p4, k2tog] twice, k1—23 sts remain.
**Rows 4 and 6:** P2, [k4, p1] 4 times, p1.
**Row 5:** K2, [p4, k1] 4 times, k1.
**Row 7:** K1, [ssk, p3] twice, k1, [p3, k2tog] twice, k1—19 sts remain.
**Rows 8 and 10:** P2, [k3, p1] 4 times, p1.
**Row 9:** K2, [p3, k1] 4 times, k1.
**Row 11:** K1, [ssk, p2] twice, k1, [p2, k2tog] twice, k1—15 sts remain.
**Rows 12 and 14:** P2, [k2, p1] 4 times, p1.
**Row 13:** K2, [p2, k1] 4 times, k1.
**Row 15:** K1, [ssk, p1] twice, k1, [p1, k2tog] twice, k1—11 sts remain.
**Row 16:** P2, [k1, p1] 4 times, p1.
**Row 17:** K1, [ssk] twice, k1, [k2tog] twice, k1—7 sts remain.
**Row 18:** Purl.
**Row 19:** K1, s3k2p3—3 sts remain.
BO all sts purlwise.
Block lightly. With WS of back and RS of Godet facing, sew Godet to edges of Back split; RS of Godet will be visible when folded over to RS of Back.

## ALL SIZES:

**Row 1 (RS):** K1, k2tog, knit to last 3 sts, ssk, k1—2 sts decreased.
**Row 2:** Purl.
Repeat Rows 1 and 2 fourteen (15, 13, 9, 6) (5, 2, 1, 0) more time(s)—5 sts remain.
**Next Row (RS):** K1, s2kp2, k1—3 sts remain.
BO all sts.

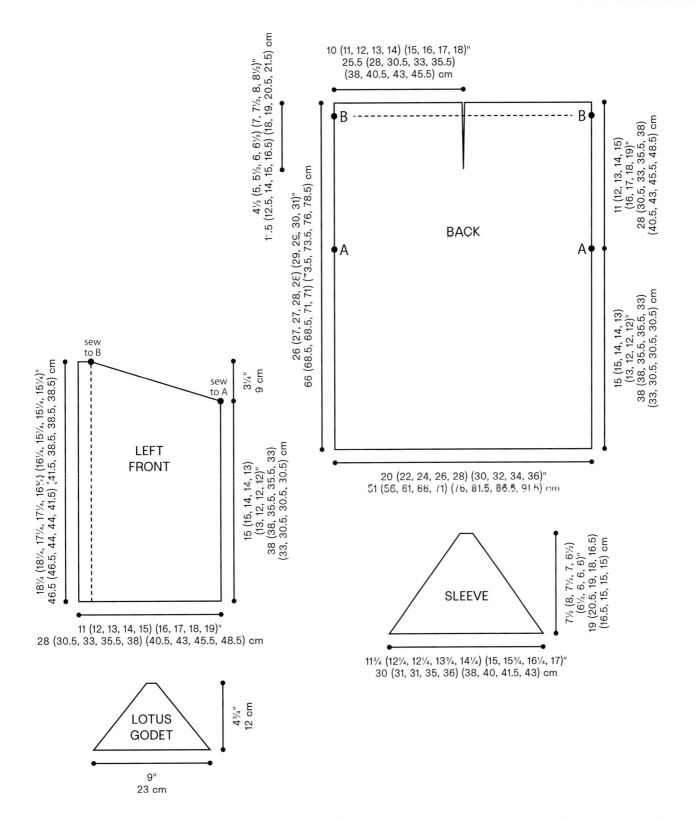

10 (11, 12, 13, 14) (15, 16, 17, 18)"
25.5 (28, 30.5, 33, 35.5)
(38, 40.5, 43, 45.5) cm

4½ (5, 5½, 6, 6½) (7, 7½, 8, 8½)"
11.5 (12.5, 14, 15, 16.5) (18, 19, 20.5, 21.5) cm

BACK

11 (12, 13, 14, 15)
(16, 17, 18, 19)"
28 (30.5, 33, 35.5, 38)
(40.5, 43, 45.5, 48.5) cm

26 (27, 27, 28, 28) (29, 29, 30, 31)"
66 (68.5, 68.5, 71, 71) (73.5, 73.5, 76, 78.5) cm

15 (15, 14, 14, 13)
(13, 12, 12, 12)"
38 (38, 35.5, 35.5, 33)
(33, 30.5, 30.5, 30.5) cm

20 (22, 24, 26, 28) (30, 32, 34, 36)"
51 (56, 61, 66, 71) (76, 81.5, 86.5, 91.5) cm

sew to B

sew to A

3½"
9 cm

LEFT FRONT

18¼ (18¼, 17¼, 17¼, 16½) (16¼, 15¼, 15¼, 15¼)"
46.5 (46.5, 44, 44, 41.5) (41.5, 38.5, 38.5, 38.5) cm

15 (15, 14, 14, 13)
(13, 12, 12, 12)"
38 (38, 35.5, 35.5, 33)
(33, 30.5, 30.5, 30.5) cm

11 (12, 13, 14, 15) (16, 17, 18, 19)"
28 (30.5, 33, 35.5, 38) (40.5, 43, 45.5, 48.5) cm

SLEEVE

7½ (8, 7½, 7, 6½)
(6½, 6, 6, 6)"
19 (20.5, 19, 18, 16.5)
(16.5, 15, 15, 15) cm

11¾ (12¼, 12¼, 13¾, 14¼) (15, 15¾, 16¼, 17)"
30 (31, 31, 35, 36) (38, 40, 41.5, 43) cm

LOTUS GODET

4¾"
12 cm

9"
23 cm

# DESIGN YOUR OWN

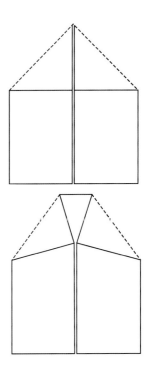

### DESIGNING LOTUS

Lotus is a cousin to Centrale, the previous pattern in this chapter (page 133). Both are based on the idea of folding the top of an extended back to meet the shorter fronts, forming the shoulders and top of the fronts. For Lotus, in order to hone the fit, the upper edge of the fronts is bound off at a shallow angle, leaving a wider back neck opening. The diagrams above illustrate the difference between folding the back over to a straight front and the back neck width you gain if you are folding the same back on to angled fronts. I decided on a barely there sleeve for Lotus, which I felt was in keeping with the cropped length. If you feel differently, it's easy enough to add a longer sleeve by starting with a smaller number of stitches and increasing to the full number in the instructions as you knit the sleeve to your desired length.

The wedge-shaped collar insert is functional as well as decorative. Extra fabric is needed in the back in order to fold back the collar. Without It, the collar wouldn't be able to spread out in the back and would sit tight against the neck, Below, I describe how I used a paper model to decide on several key elements: the angle of the fronts, plus the depth and width of the collar insert.

### MAKE A PAPER MODEL

Sometimes, when I am first questioning the viability of an idea, such as one with an odd construction like Lotus, I make a paper model to prove to myself that the idea will work. While you might experiment with a general idea using any size pieces, I prefer to work with a schematic drawn in scale with one square equaling one inch. Start with the measurements you think might work, based on a similar design or your

knowledge of traditional garments, cut out the pieces, then fold and tape them together. First, you'll learn a lot about how the construction really works. You might find glitches in your logic, realize that you need the pieces to be larger, or come up with clever variations during this process. A paper model helps you figure out if pieces fit together well and gives you a good idea for how an idea will work, but it doesn't reveal much about working with draping elements. For that, you'll want to make a fleece or jersey knit model. For more about that, see the notes at the end of the next pattern, Afloat (page 145).

# Afloat

The drapes and folds of Afloat cascade from each shoulder in both the front and back, extending beyond the remainder of the hemline. A center front panel has both cables and open elements. Full-length raglan sleeves complete the design. At first glance Afloat might appear to be rather complicated, but it isn't. Afloat is two rectangles with a slit for the neck and sleeves sewn to the top. The magic comes when you put it on and let the fabric fall.

## FINISHED MEASUREMENTS

*Note: Garment fits like a poncho with sleeves, so conventional ease measurements don't apply. Choose your size based on your preferred fit at the upper arm.*

12 (13, 14¼, 15, 16) (17, 18¼, 19, 20)" [30.5 (33, 36, 38, 40.5) (43, 46.5, 48.5, 51) cm] Sleeve circumference at upper arm

43 (44, 45, 46, 47) (48, 49, 50, 51)" [109 (112, 114.5, 117, 119.5) (122, 124.5, 127, 129.5) cm] Back width

## YARN

Jill Draper Makes Stuff Ansel [100% American superfine merino wool; 440 yards (402 m)/4 ounces/113 g]: 5 (5, 5, 6, 6) (6, 7, 7, 7) skeins Powder Puff

## NEEDLES

One 29" (70 cm) or longer circular needle, size US 4 (3.5 mm)

Change needle size if necessary to obtain correct gauge.

## NOTIONS

Stitch markers

Removable stitch markers

Cable needle

Stitch holders

## GAUGE

22 sts and 34 rows = 4" (10 cm) in St st

36-st Ornament Cable Pattern = 5" (13 cm) wide

## SPECIAL ABBREVIATIONS

**1/1 LPC (1 over 1 left purl cross):** Slip 1 st to cable needle, hold to front, p1, k1 from cable.

**1/1 RPC (1 over 1 right purl cross):** Slip 1 st to cable needle, hold to back, k1, p1 from cable.

**1/2 LC (1 over 2 left cross):** Slip 1 st to cable needle, hold to front, k2, k1 from cable needle.

**1/2 RC (1 over 2 right cross):** Slip 2 sts to cable needle, hold to back, k1, k2 from cable needle.

**2/1 LC (2 over 1 left cross):** Slip 2 sts to cable needle, hold to front, k2, k1 from cable needle.

**2/1 LPC (2 over 1 left purl cross):** Slip 2 sts to cable needle, hold to front, p1, k2 from cable needle.

**2/1 RC (2 over 1 right cross):** Slip 1 st to cable needle, hold to back, k2, k1 from cable needle.

**2/1 RPC (2 over 1 right purl cross):** Slip 2 sts to cable needle, hold to back, k2, p1 from cable

**2/2 LC (2 over 2 left cross):** Slip 2 sts to cable needle, hold to front, k2, k2 from cable needle.

**2/2 LPC (2 over 2 left purl cross):** Slip 2 sts to cable needle, hold to front, p2, k2 from cable needle.

**2/2 RC (2 over 2 right cross):** Slip 2 sts to cable needle, hold to back, k2, k2 from cable needle.

**2/2 RPC (2 over 2 right purl cross):** Slip 2 sts to cable needle, hold to back, k2, p2 from cable needle.

**2/3 LC (2 over 3 left cross):** Slip 2 sts to cable needle, hold to front, k3, k2 from cable needle.

**2/3 LPC (2 over 3 left purl cross):** Slip 2 sts to cable needle, hold to front, p1, k2, k2 from cable needle.

**2/3 RC (2 over 3 right cross):** Slip 3 sts to cable needle, hold to back, k2, k3 from cable needle.

**2/3 RPC (2 over 3 right purl cross):** Slip 3 sts to cable needle, hold to back, k2, (k2, p1) from cable needle.

**LT (left twist):** Slip 1 stitch knitwise, slip a second stitch knitwise, slip both stitches back to the left-hand needle in their new orientation (just like for the beginning of ssk); knit into the back of the second stitch (approaching from the back), then knit into the back of both stitches and slip both from the needle.

**RT (right twist):** K2tog, leaving the original sts on the left-hand needle, then knit the first st only and slip both sts from needle.

## PATTERN STITCH

### ORNAMENT CABLE PATTERN (SEE CHART)

(panel of 36 sts at beginning; st count varies; 60-row repeat)

**Setup Row (WS):** K2, [p6, p2tog, yo, p7, k2] twice.

**Row 1 (RS):** P2, [k4, 1/2 LC, p1, 1/2 RC, k4, p2] twice.

**Row 2 and all WS Rows:** Knit the knit sts and purl the purl sts as they face you; knit all yos.

**Row 3:** P2, [2/1 LPC, 2/2 LC, p1, 2/2 RC, 2/1 RPC, p2] twice.

**Row 5:** P3, 2/1 LPC, 1/2 LC, p1, 1/2 RC, 2/1 RPC, p4, 2/1 LPC, 1/2 LC, p1, 1/2 RC, 2/1 RPC, p3.

**Row 7:** P1, k1, p2, 2/3 LPC, p1, 2/3 RPC, p2, k2, p2, 2/3 LPC, p1, 2/3 RPC, p2, k1, p1.

**Row 9:** Repeat Row 2.

**Row 11:** P1, 1/1 LC, p2, 2/2 LPC, p1, 2/2 RPC, p2, 1/1 RC, yo, 1/1 LC, p2, 2/2 LPC, p1, 2/2 RPC, p2, 1/1 RC, p1–37 sts.

**Row 13:** P1, [2/1 LC, p2, k3, p1, k3, p2, 2/1 RC, p1] twice.

**Row 15:** P1, [k3, p2, 2/1 LPC, p1, 2/1 RPC, p2, k3, p1] twice.

**Row 17:** P1, [2/2 LC, p2, 1/1 LPC, drop 1 st and unravel down to yo, 1/1 RPC, p2, 2/2 RC, p1] twice–35 sts remain.

**Row 19:** P1, [k4, p3, k2, p3, k4, p1] twice.

**Row 21:** P1, [2/3 LC, p6, 2/3 RC, p1] twice.

**Row 23:** P1, [1/2 LC, 2/1 LC, p4, 2/1 RC, 1/2 RC, p1] twice.

**Row 25:** P1, [2/2 LC, 2/1 LC, p2, 2/1 RC, 2/2 RC, p1] twice.

**Row 27:** P1, [1/2 LC, k4, p2, k4, 1/2 RC, p1] twice.

**Row 29:** P1, [k7, p2, k7, p1] twice.

**Row 31:** P1, [1/2 RC, k4, p2, k4, 1/2 LC, p1] twice.

**Row 33:** P1, 2/2 RC, 2/1 RPC, p2, 2/1 LPC, 2/2 LC, p1] twice.

**Row 35:** P1, 1/2 RC, 2/1 RPC, p4, 2/1 LPC, 1/2 LC, p1] twice.

**Row 37:** P1, [2/3 RPC, p2, k2, p2, 2/3 LPC, p1] twice.

**Row 39:** Repeat Row 2.

**Row 41:** P1, 2/2 RPC, p2, 1/1 RC, yo, 1/1 LC, p2, 2/2 LPC, p1] twice–37 sts.

**Row 43:** P1, k3, p2, 2/1 RC, p1, 2/1 LC, p2, k3, p1] twice.

**Row 45:** P1, 2/1 RPC, p2, k3, p1, k3, p2, 2/1 LPC, p1] twice.

**Row 47:** P1, 1/1 RPC, p2, 2/2 RC, p1, 2/2 LC, p2, 1/1 LPC, drop 1 st and unravel down to yo, 1/1 RPC, p2, 2/2 RC, p1, 2/2 LC, p2, 1/1 LPC, p1–36 sts remain.

**Row 49:** Repeat Row 2.

**Row 51:** P4, 2/3 RC, p1, 2/3 LC, p6, 2/3 RC, p1, 2/3 LC, p4.

**Row 53:** P3, 2/1 RC, 1/2 RC, p1, 1/2 LC, 2/1 LC, p4, 2/1 RC, 1/2 RC, p1, 1/2 LC, 2/1 LC, p3.

**Row 55:** P2, [2/1 RC, 2/2 RC, p1, 2/2 LC, 2/1, LC, p2] twice.

**Row 57:** P2, [k4, 1/2 RC, p1, 1/2 LC, k4, p2] twice.

**Rows 59 and 60:** Repeat Row 2.
Repeat Rows 1–60 for pattern.

# Ornament Cable Pattern

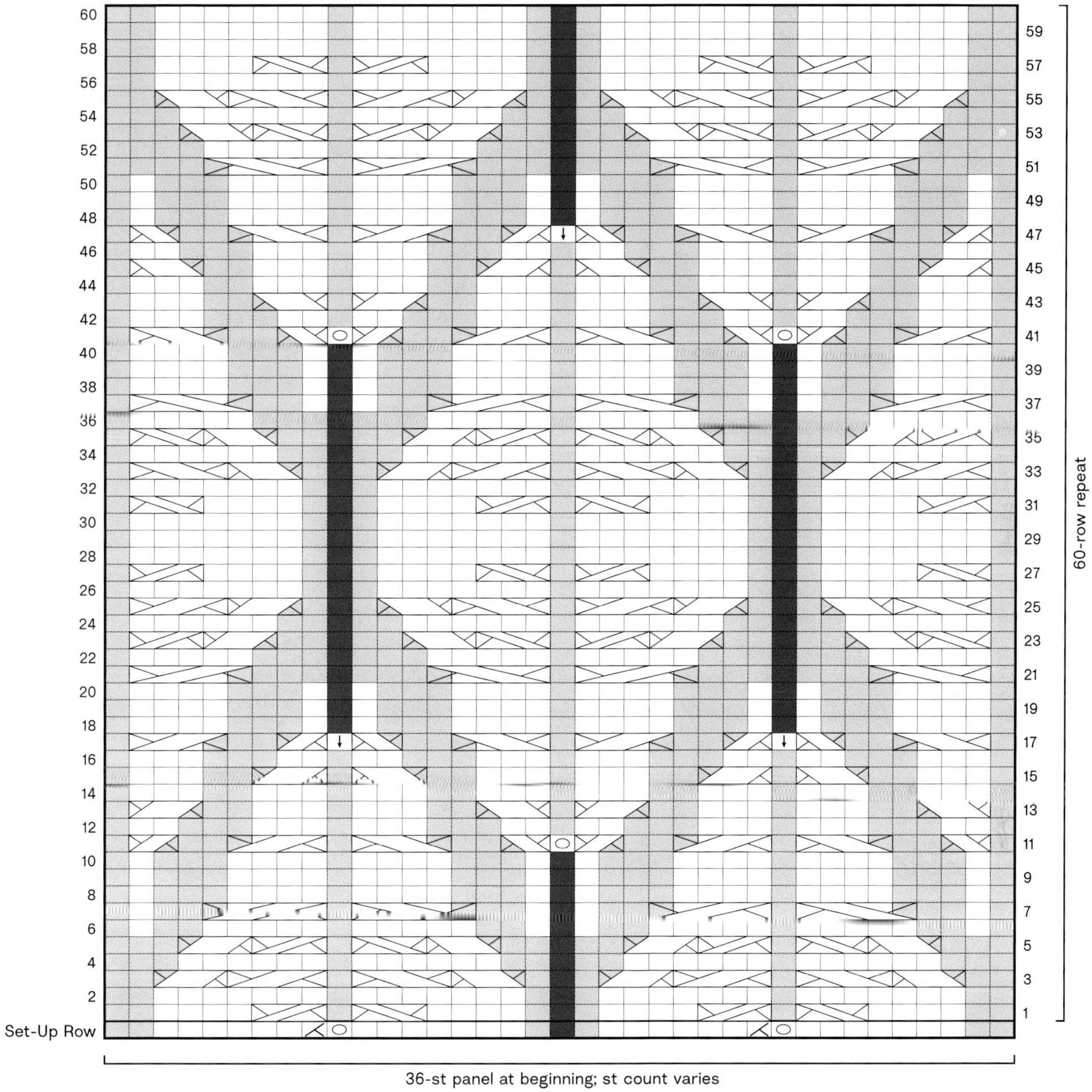

Chart row numbers (left side, bottom to top): 60, 58, 56, 54, 52, 50, 48, 46, 44, 42, 40, 38, 36, 34, 32, 30, 28, 26, 24, 22, 20, 18, 16, 14, 12, 10, 8, 6, 4, 2

Chart row numbers (right side, bottom to top): 59, 57, 55, 53, 51, 49, 47, 45, 43, 41, 39, 37, 35, 33, 31, 29, 27, 25, 23, 21, 19, 17, 15, 13, 11, 9, 7, 5, 3, 1

Set-Up Row

60-row repeat

36-st panel at beginning; st count varies

| | | | | |
|---|---|---|---|---|
| ☐ Knit on RS, purl on WS. | ⬓ LT | ⬓ 2/1 LC | ⬓ 2/2 LPC |
| ▨ Purl on RS, knit on WS. | ⬓ RT | ⬓ 2/1 RC | ⬓ 2/2 RPC |
| ⊙ Yo | ⬓ 1/1 LPC | ⬓ 2/1 LPC | ⬓ 2/3 LC |
| ⟋ P2tog on WS. | ⬓ 1/1 RPC | ⬓ 2/1 RPC | ⬓ 2/3 RC |
| ↓ Drop st, unravelling it down to yo. | ⬓ 1/2 LC | ⬓ OR ⬓ 2/2 LC | ⬓ 2/3 LPC |
| ⬛ No stitch | ⬓ 1/2 RC | ⬓ OR ⬓ 2/2 RC | ⬓ 2/3 RPC |

## PATTERN NOTES

The Front and Back are worked separately, then joined along a portion of the top edge using 3-Needle Bind-Off (see Special Techniques, page 222). The Sleeves are worked flat, the side seams are sewn together, then the Sleeves are sewn into the armholes. No further finishing is required.

The Front has a cable panel and the Back is plain. If you would like the Front to be plain, work two Backs. If you'd like the Back to have a cable pattern, work two Fronts.

To make the pullover longer when worn, you will need to work the front and back to a longer length, and add stitches to the cast ons; add length and width in equal measure. Remember, you'll need more yarn if you make the sweater longer.

## FRONT

Using Long-Tail Cast-On (see Special Techniques, page 221), CO 246 (250, 256, 262, 268) (272, 278, 284, 290) sts.
**Setup Row 1 (RS):** K105 (107, 110, 113, 116) (118, 121, 124, 127) sts, pm, k36, pm, knit to end.
**Setup Row 2:** Knit to marker, sm, work Cable Pattern Setup Row to marker (working pattern from text or chart), sm, knit to end.
**Row 1:** Knit to marker, sm, work Row 1 of Cable Pattern to marker, sm, knit to end.
**Rows 2–4:** Knit to marker, sm, work in pattern to marker, sm, knit to end.
**Row 5:** Knit to marker, sm, work to marker, sm, knit to end.
**Row 6:** K3, purl to 3 sts before marker, k3, sm, work to marker, k3, purl to last 3 sts, k3.
Repeat Rows 5 and 6 until piece measures approximately 17 (17½, 18, 18½, 19) (19½, 20, 20½, 21)" [43 (44.5, 45.5, 47, 48.5) (49.5, 51, 52, 53.5) cm] from the beginning, ending with a RS row.
Repeat Row 2 five times.
**Next Row (RS):** Place removable marker 42 (40, 39, 39, 39) (37, 36, 36, 35) sts in from each edge. Knit to removable marker, remove marker and transfer 42 (40, 39, 39, 39) (37, 36, 36, 35) sts just worked to st holder or waste yarn, BO sts in pattern to next removable marker, dropping sts in Cable pattern if indicated, knit to end and transfer last 42 (40, 39,

39, 39) (37, 36, 36, 35) sts to st holder or waste yarn. Cut yarn, leaving a 2' (61 cm) tail.

## BACK

Using Long-Tail Cast-On, CO 236 (242, 248, 254, 258) (264, 270, 276, 280) sts. Knit 6 rows.
**Row 1 (RS):** Knit.
**Row 2:** K3, purl to last 3 sts, k3.
Repeat Rows 1 and 2 until piece measures approximately 17 (17½, 18, 18½, 19) (19½, 20, 20½, 21)" [43 (44.5, 45.5, 47, 48.5) (49.5, 51, 52, 53.5) cm] from the beginning, ending with a RS row.
Knit 5 rows.
**Next Row (RS):** K42 (40, 39, 39, 39) (37, 36, 36, 35) and just worked to st holder or waste yarn, BO 152 (162, 170, 176, 180) (190, 198, 204, 210) sts, knit to end and transfer last 42 (40, 39, 39, 39) (37, 36, 36, 35) sts to st holder or waste yarn. Cut yarn, leaving a 2' (61 cm) tail.

## SLEEVES

Using Long-Tail Cast-On, CO 50 (52, 56, 58, 60) (64, 66, 68, 72) sts.
Knit 6 rows. Knit 1 row. Purl 1 row.

## SHAPE SLEEVE

**Increase Row (RS):** K2, M1L, knit to last 2 sts, M1R, k2—2 sts increased.
Continuing in St st, repeat Increase Row every 10 (8, 8, 8, 6) (6, 6, 4, 4) rows 4 (5, 8, 11, 5) (10, 16, 5, 8) more times, then every 12 (10, 10, 0, 8) (8, 0, 6, 6) rows 3 (4, 2, 0, 8) (4, 0, 12, 10) more times—66 (72, 78, 82, 88) (94, 100, 104, 110) sts.
Work even until piece measures 12¼ (12¾, 13¼, 13¾, 14½) (14¼, 14¾, 14¼, 14¼)" [31 (32.5, 33.5, 35, 37) (36, 37.5, 36, 36) cm] from the beginning, ending with a WS row.
Place removable markers at beginning and end of last row worked to mark beginning of raglan shaping.

## SHAPE RAGLAN CAP

### SIZES 47, 48, 49, 50, AND 51 ONLY:

**Double Decrease Row (RS):** K1, k3tog, knit to last 4 sts, sssk, k1—4 sts decreased.
Repeat Double Decrease Row every RS row - (-, -, -, 0) (0, 1, 1, 2) more time(s) - (-, -, -, 84) (90, 92, 96, 98) sts remain.

## ALL SIZES:

**Decrease Row (RS):** K1, k2tog, knit to last 3 sts, ssk, k1—2 sts decreased.
Repeat Decrease Row every 4 rows 1 (1, 0, 0, 0) (0, 0, 0, 0) more time(s), then every RS row 29 (32, 36, 38, 39) (42, 43, 45, 46) more times—4 sts remain.
Purl 1 row.
**Next Row (RS):** Ssk, k2tog—2 sts remain.
BO sts.

## FINISHING

Block as desired.
With WSs of left Front and Back together (seam will be on the RS), with Back facing you, and working from right side edge to BO sts, use 3-Needle Bind-Off to BO first 42 (40, 39, 39, 39) (37, 36, 36, 35) sts. With Back still facing you, beginning at opposite side of BO sts, use 3-Needle Bind-Off to BO last 42 (40, 39, 39, 39) (37, 36, 36, 35) sts to left side edge.
Sew Sleeve seam from CO edge to markers at beginning of raglan cap. With RS of Back/Front facing, place removable markers 8¾ (9¾, 10½, 11, 11½) (12¼, 13, 13½, 14¼)" [22 (25, 26.5, 28, 29) (31, 33, 34.5, 36) cm] in from each 3-Needle Bind-Off seam, for armholes (see schematic); you should have 10" (25.5 cm) between markers for neck. Pin BO edge of Sleeve raglan cap at marker at neck edge and pin Sleeve underarm to bottom of armhole, just before 3-Needle Bind-Off seam; sew Sleeve in place.

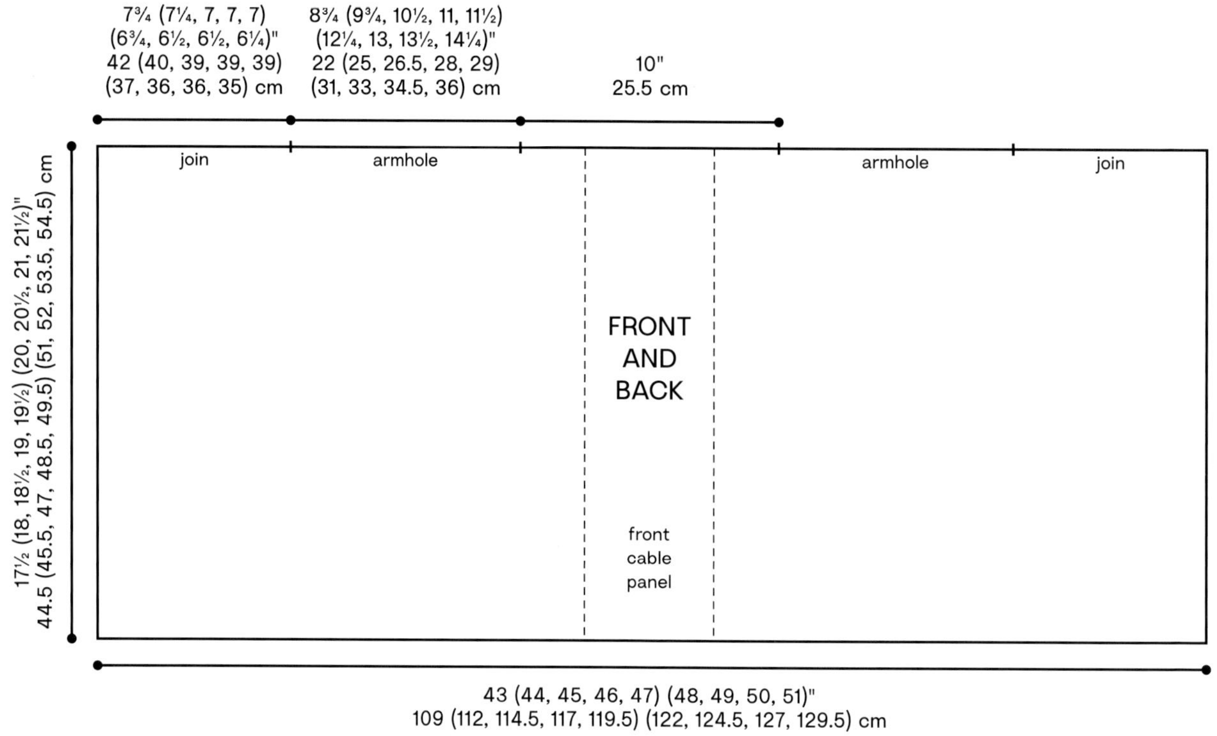

7¾ (7¼, 7, 7, 7)
(6¾, 6½, 6½, 6¼)"
42 (40, 39, 39, 39)
(37, 36, 36, 35) cm
8¾ (9¾, 10½, 11, 11½)
(12¼, 13, 13½, 14¼)"
22 (25, 26.5, 28, 29)
(31, 33, 34.5, 36) cm
10"
25.5 cm
join
armhole
armhole
join
17½ (18, 18½, 19, 19½) (20, 20½, 21, 21½)"
44.5 (45.5, 47, 48.5, 49.5) (51, 52, 53.5, 54.5) cm
FRONT AND BACK
front cable panel
43 (44, 45, 46, 47) (48, 49, 50, 51)"
109 (112, 114.5, 117, 119.5) (122, 124.5, 127, 129.5) cm


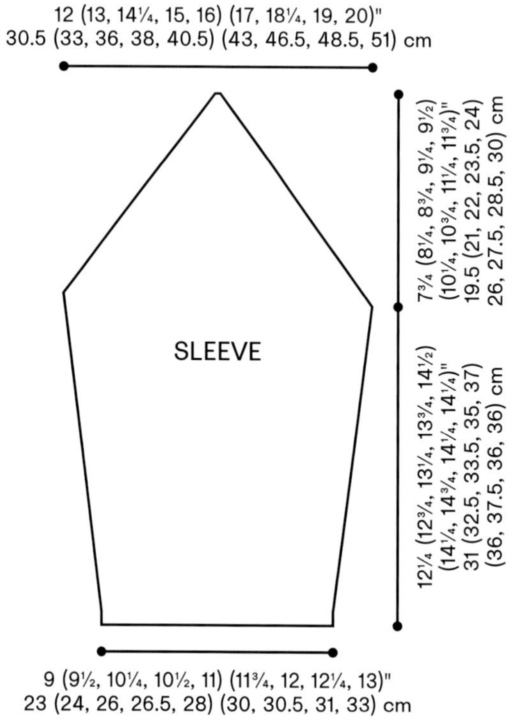

12 (13, 14¼, 15, 16) (17, 18¼, 19, 20)"
30.5 (33, 36, 38, 40.5) (43, 46.5, 48.5, 51) cm
7¾ (8¼, 8¾, 9¼, 9½)
(10¼, 10¾, 11¼, 11¾)"
19.5 (21, 22, 23.5, 24)
26, 27.5, 28.5, 30) cm
SLEEVE
12¼ (12¾, 13¼, 13¾, 14½)
(14¼, 14¾, 14¼, 14¼)"
31 (32.5, 33.5, 35, 37)
(36, 37.5, 36, 36) cm
9 (9½, 10¼, 10½, 11) (11¾, 12, 12¼, 13)"
23 (24, 26, 26.5, 28) (30, 30.5, 31, 33) cm

# DESIGN YOUR OWN

## DESIGNING AFLOAT

This is another instance of seeing an unusual idea years ago, experimenting with the thought at the time, then revisiting the idea and refining later. I told a similar story about Centrale, the pullover with shoulders folded down from the back (page 133).The sweater that inspired the process this time had an oversized box for the body with straight sleeves sprouting from the top edge, where we would expect the shoulders to be, instead of from the side, where sleeves are normally. I first experimented

with a pullover similar to the one described. Then I made the leap that the same idea would work for a wider, more poncho-like shape and that raglan-shaped sleeves would work even better, since they would already be pointing outward, not upward. The portion of the rectangle beyond each sleeve folds down to become the side, while the excess folds of knit fabric fall from each shoulder forming elongated points at the bottom edge. If you'd like to convert Afloat into a vest, leave out the sleeves and connect the front to the back with a short seam on either side of the neck.

## MAKE A FABRIC MODEL

When an idea is too different or new to you to visualize easily and a paper model doesn't give you any idea of the drape of knitted fabric, a model made from purchased knit fabric can be a great design aid. I usually search in the sale corner of the fabric store for jersey knits and fleece to have on hand, each simulating a different weight and stretch of hand-knit fabric. Stable textured or cabled knits act much like heavier poly fleece when it comes to stiffness, while a drapey knit, like in Centrale, requires a specialty fabric like slinky rayon knit to come close to its slippery and stretchy qualities. A lighter fleece works well if you are designing with fingering- or sport-weight yarns. Once you have your idea worked out as far as you can go with a schematic and a paper model, make a full-size model in your chosen fabric. It's usually a good idea to cut out pieces a bit larger rather than smaller than your first guess. You can always trim the pieces down to size—adding is more difficult. Here's a trick I learned from a student: Duct tape is your friend! Pinning floppy fabric can be difficult. Taping the pieces together with duct tape works really well. Try your test garment on your dress form, a friend, or yourself and evaluate what you see. Where do you need less length or width? How is the neckline working? Does it look how you imagined? Does it look better than you imagined? Try to think creatively about simple changes that might make the idea better. Should you let go of one of your original parameters? For instance, would cutting off the corners help the design, even though the pieces would no longer be rectangular? Pare the changes down to shapes or angles that are easy to knit.

# Tilt

The bulk of this skirt is just a big rectangle. The addition of a ribbed yoke, shaped with a few short rows, transforms the rectangle into a skirt with an outpouring of folds and an asymmetrical hem. Place the folds to one side or center front or even center back to suit your personality.

**FINISHED MEASUREMENTS**

30 (34, 38, 42, 46) (50, 54, 58, 62)" [76 (86.5, 96.5, 106.5, 117) (127, 137, 147.5, 157.5) cm] hip circumference

26¼" [66.5 cm] long at center back

*Note: Skirt will stretch in length when worn.*

**YARN**

Hinterland Dusk [70% Canadian rambouillet/30% Canadian alpaca; 395 yards (361 m)/3.95 ounces (112 g)]: 5 (5, 6, 7, 7) (8, 8, 9, 9) skeins Truffle

**NEEDLES**

One 24" (60 cm) or longer circular needle, size US 4 (3.5 mm)

One 24" (60 cm) or longer circular needle, size US 2 (2.75 mm)

Change needle size if necessary to obtain correct gauge.

**NOTIONS**

Stitch markers

Removable stitch markers

¾–1¾ yards (70–170 cm) of 1" (2.5 cm) firm waistband elastic (to fit waist measurement + 2"/5 cm)

Sewing needle and thread

**GAUGE**

24 sts and 34 rows = 4" (10 cm) in St st using larger needle

26 sts and 38 rows = 4" (10 cm) in Box Pattern using larger needle

## PATTERN STITCHES

### BOX PATTERN (SEE CHART)

(multiple of 13 sts + 2; 10-row repeat)
**Rows 1 and 3 (RS):** P2, *k1-tbl, p9, k1-tbl, p2; repeat from * to end.
**Row 2 and all WS Rows:** P2, *p1-tbl, k1, p7, k1, p1-tbl, p2; repeat from * to end.
**Rows 5, 7, and 9:** P2, *k1-tbl, p1, k7, p1, k1-tbl, p2; repeat from * to end.
**Row 10:** Repeat Row 2.
Repeat Rows 1–10 for pattern.

### 2×2 RIB

(multiple of 4 sts; 1-rnd repeat)
**All Rnds:** *K2, p2; repeat from * to end.

## PATTERN NOTES

The skirt is worked flat in one piece, then folded lengthwise and two sides are sewn together for half of the length, leaving an opening from which yoke sts are picked up. The yoke is shaped with short rows, then joined and worked in the round to the end. The bound-off edge is folded over elastic for the waistband, then sewn in place.
If you wish to adjust the center back length of the skirt, you may cast on more or fewer stitches in multiples of 13. Each 13-stitch repeat measures approximately 2" (5 cm). Be sure to purchase additional yarn if you increase the length of the skirt.

## SKIRT

Using larger needle and Long-Tail Cast-On (see Special Techniques, page 221), CO 145 sts. Do not join.
Purl 1 row.
Begin Box Pattern (working pattern from text or chart); work even until piece measures approximately 60½ (68½, 76, 84½, 92) (100½, 108½, 116, 124½)" [153.5 (174, 193, 214.5, 233.5) (255.5, 275.5, 294.5, 316) cm] from the beginning, ending with Row 2 of pattern.
BO all sts in pattern.
Wet-block to measurements.
Place removable markers along one long edge, 15¼ (17¼, 19, 21¼, 23) (25¼, 27¼, 29, 31¼)" [38.5 (44, 48.5, 54, 58.5) (64, 69, 73.5, 79.5)] in from CO and BO edges. Fold piece in half lengthwise and sew marked side edges together from CO/BO edge to markers.

## YOKE

With RS facing, using smaller needle and beginning at top of seam, pick up and knit 180 (204, 228, 252, 276) (300, 324, 348, 372) sts around opening (approximately 2 sts for every 3 rows). Join for working in the rnd; pm for beginning of rnd.

## SHAPE YOKE

*Note: Yoke is shaped using German Short Rows (see Special Techniques, page 221).*

**Short Row 1 (RS):** K2, p2, k2, turn;

**Short Row 2:** DS, p1, [k2, p2] twice, k2, turn;

**Short Row 3:** DS, work in 2×2 Rib as established to DS from previous RS row, close DS, p2, k2, p2, turn;

**Short Row 4:** DS, work in 2×2 Rib as established to DS from previous WS row, close DS, p2, k2, p2, turn;

**Short Row 5:** DS, work in 2×2 Rib as established to DS from previous RS row, close DS, k2, p2, k2, turn;

**Short Row 6:** DS, work in 2×2 Rib as established to DS from previous WS row, close DS, k2, p2, k2, turn;

Repeat Short Rows 3–6 seven more times.

**Next Row (RS):** DS, work in 2×2 Rib as established to DS from previous RS row, close DS, continue in 2×2 Rib to end. Work even until piece measures 3" (7.5 cm) at shortest point, closing final DS on first round.

BO all sts in pattern.

## FINISHING

Block pieces as desired. Using sewing needle and thread, sew ends of waistband elastic together, overlapping them by 2" (5 cm). Fold BO edge of Yoke to WS over elastic and sew to WS, being careful not to let sts show on RS and not to catch elastic in seam.

## Box Pattern

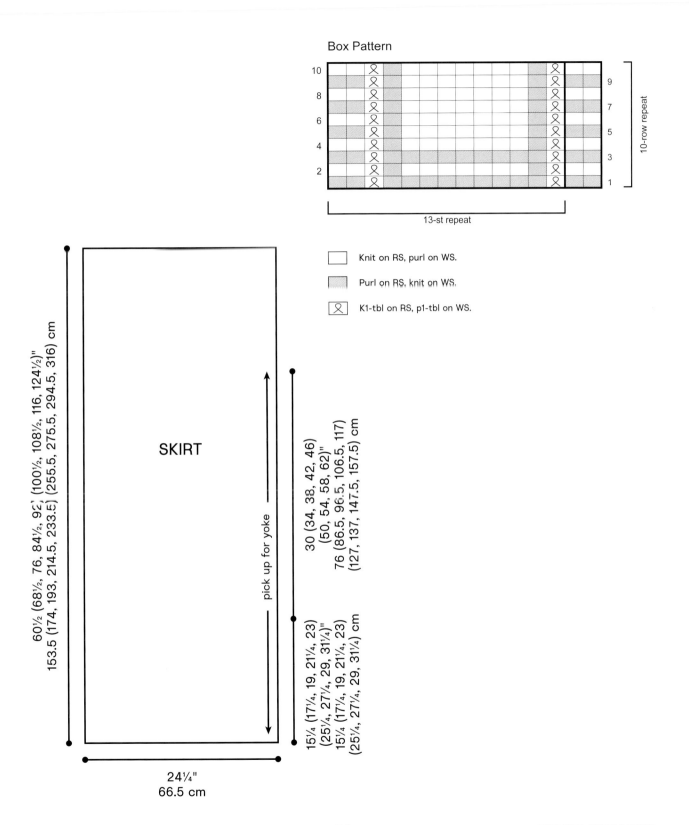

10-row repeat

13-st repeat

☐ Knit on RS, purl on WS.

▨ Purl on RS, knit on WS.

⊗ K1-tbl on RS, p1-tbl on WS.

SKIRT

60½ (68½, 76, 84½, 92) (100½, 108½, 116, 124½)"
153.5 (174, 193, 214.5, 233.5) (255.5, 275.5, 294.5, 316) cm

30 (34, 38, 42, 46) (50, 54, 58, 62)"
76 (86.5, 96.5, 106.5, 117) (127, 137, 147.5, 157.5) cm

pick up for yoke

15¼ (17¼, 19, 21¼, 23) (25¼, 27¼, 29, 31¼)"
15¼ (17¼, 19, 21¼, 23) (25¼, 27¼, 29, 31¼) cm

24¼"
66.5 cm

# DESIGN YOUR OWN

### DESIGNING TILT

Two different skirts inspired Tilt. One was in a photo, and the model wearing it was caught by the camera with her knit skirt flying off to the side, revealing its rectangular shape. Her waist was covered by a matching sweater, so I couldn't tell how the meeting of skirt and waistband was handled. The second was a skirt I had long admired. It was made of woven plaid, with an off-center yoke dipping down on one side, and below that an outpouring of folds ended in a pointed, asymmetrical hem. I connected the dots. These two skirts seemed quite different at first glance, but they were, in fact, very similar. The greater part of each was simply a long rectangle, folded around to meet three quarters of the way across the front, ends left to dangle. My skirt, Tilt, would be a long rectangle with an asymmetrical yoke. I set to work on a fleece model to help determine the length and width of the big rectangle. The width of the rectangle plus the yoke depth would become the length of most of the skirt, except where the folds extended downward. I cut a piece of fleece a few inches wider than the skirt length I thought I wanted and as long as the hip measurement plus 40" (100 cm) (20"/50 cm extra for each end). I picked 20" (50 cm) because that was approximately the length of the skirt below the yoke, and I wanted the extension to be at hem depth when it fell downward, for modesty. I wrapped my fleece model around the dress form to adjust the measurements. I had hoped I could skip shaping the yoke, but the fleece model on my dress form told me that the folds were heavy and would naturally pull the top of the skirt downward at their apex. It seemed best to conform the yoke to the dip created by the weight of the fabric.

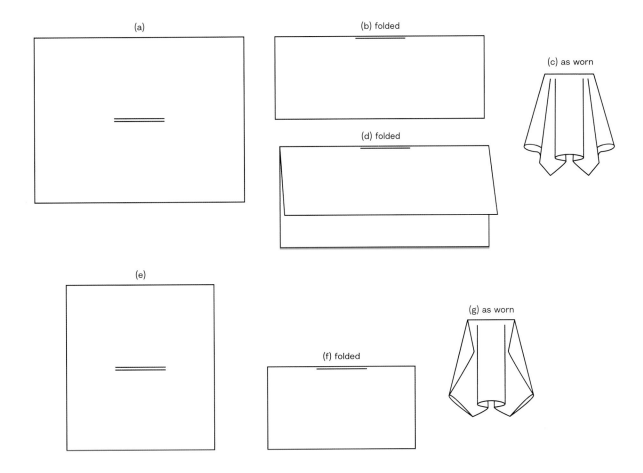

(a)

(b) folded

(c) as worn

(d) folded

(e)

(g) as worn

(f) folded

## SKIRT VARIATIONS

I've been collecting photos of interesting skirts for quite a while, and I've come to be able to recognize when a skirt is basically a draped rectangle. If you see cascading folds, each coming from a point and ending in a point, that's a telltale sign of simple rectangular construction. Tilt is a long rectangle folded in half, with all its excess fabric falling to one side of the front. I've also seen examples of rectangularly constructed skirts with the extra yardage distributed evenly at each hip. In these cases, the waist opening can be a slit in the middle of the rectangle.

I recommend starting with the opening matching your high hip measurement. You can add a ribbed band to bring the skirt to waist level and tighten the opening, but the opening needs to be large enough to pull over your head or up past your hips.

Within this idea, here are a few variations:

1. Begin with a rectangle that extends the same amount to each side of the slit as it does down to the center front hem and the center back hem (a & b). Your skirt will be about the same length on the sides, front, and back, while it dips down in four places, where the corners of the rectangle extend lower (c).

2. Starting with the same rectangle, move the waist slit closer to the front hem for a skirt that is longer in back and shorter in front (d).

3. Begin with a rectangle that is less wide, extending less to each side than it does to the center front and back (e & f). In this case, you will want to have side seams, or be working with a tube, unless you are going for a lot of leg exposure.

Consider knitting a skirt like this in the round. If you have a seam, place it in the center back so it doesn't affect the draping on one side and not the other.

# Outward

This quirky asymmetrical poncho stays on without twisting about because of its side seams. In a rectangle knit from front to back, bamboo-inspired cables flow across a field of twisted rib. There is no shaping into the cable pattern; instead, the diagonal lines of increases and decreases are worked into a much easier-to-knit panel of twisted rib. The same panel becomes a collar in the front, folding down at a pleasing angle.

## FINISHED MEASUREMENTS

*Note: Garment fits like a poncho, so conventional ease measurements don't apply. Choose your size based on the width between the base of both armholes (see schematic). I recommend a measurement that is 4–9" (10–23 cm) wider than half your chest measurement. The model has a chest measurement of 38" (96.5 cm), half of which is 19" (48.5 cm). She is wearing the first size with a measurement of 24" (61 cm) between armholes, which is 6" (15 cm) more than half her chest measurement.*

24 (29, 34)" [61 (73.5, 86.5) cm], base of armhole to base of armhole

28½ (33¾, 40½)" [72.5 (85.5, 103) cm] from neckline to longest point

## YARN

mYak Baby Yak Medium [100% baby yak; 125 yards (117 m)/1.76 ounces (50 g)]: 10 (14, 19) skeins Dusky Pink

## NEEDLES

One 29" (70 cm) or longer circular needle, size US 6 (4 mm)

Change needle size if necessary to obtain correct gauge.

## NOTIONS

Stitch markers

Removable stitch markers

Cable needle

## GAUGE

22 sts and 30 rows = 4" (10 cm) in St st

28 sts and 30 rows = 4" (10 cm) in Bamboo Cable Pattern

24 sts and 30 rows = 4" (10 cm) in Twisted Rib

## PATTERN STITCHES

### BAMBOO CABLE PATTERN (SEE CHART)

(multiple of 54 sts + 3)

**Row 1 (RS):** P3, *p1, k1-tbl, p2, k1-tbl, k3, p1, k1-tbl, [p2, k1-tbl] 3 times, p1, k3, p3, k3, p1, k1-tbl, [p2, k1-tbl] 3 times, p1, k3, p1, k1-tbl, p2, k1-tbl, p4; repeat from * to end.

**Row 2:** K3, *k1, p1-tbl, k2, p1-tbl, k1, p3, k1, p1-tbl, [k2, p1-tbl] 3 times, k1, p3, k3, p3, k1, p1-tbl, [k2, p1-tbl] 3 times, k1, p3, k1, p1-tbl, k2, p1-tbl, k4; repeat from * to end.

**Rows 3 and 4:** Repeat Rows 1 and 2.

**Row 5:** P3, *p1, k1-tbl, p1, 3/3 RC, p1, k1-tbl, [p2, k1-tbl] twice, p1, 3/3 RC, p3, 3/3 LC, p1, k1-tbl, [p2, k1-tbl] twice, p1, 3/3 LC, p1, k1-tbl, p4; repeat from * to end.

**Row 6:** K3, *k1, p1-tbl, k1, p6, k1, p1-tbl, [k2, p1-tbl] twice, k1, p6, k3, p6, k1, p1-tbl, [k2, p1-tbl] twice, k1, p6, k1, p1-tbl, k4; repeat from * to end.

**Row 7:** P3, *p1, k1-tbl, p1, k6, p1, k1-tbl, [p2, k1-tbl] twice, p1, k6, p3, k6, p1, k1-tbl, [p2, k1-tbl] twice, p1, k6, p1, k1-tbl, p4; repeat from * to end.

**Row 8:** Repeat Row 6.

**Row 9:** P3, *p1, k1-tbl, p1, 3/3 RPC, p1, k1-tbl, [p2, k1-tbl] twice, p1, 3/3 RPC, p3, 3/3 LPC, p1, k1-tbl, [p2, k1-tbl] twice, p1, 3/3 LPC, p1, k1-tbl, p4; repeat from * to end.

**Row 10:** K3, *k1, p1-tbl, k1, p3, k1, p1-tbl, [k2, p1-tbl] 3 times, k1, p3, k1, p1-tbl, k5, p1-tbl, k1, p3, k1, p1-tbl, [k2, p1-tbl] 3 times, k1, p3, k1, p1-tbl, k4; repeat from * to end.

**Row 11:** P3, *p1, k1-tbl, p1, k3, p1, k1-tbl, [p2, k1-tbl] 3 times, p1, k3, p1, k1-tbl, p5, k1-tbl, p1, k3, p1, k1-tbl, [p2, k1-tbl] 3 times, p1, k3, p1, k1-tbl, p4; repeat from * to end.

**Rows 12–15:** Repeat Rows 10 and 11 twice.

**Row 16:** Repeat Row 10.

**Row 17:** P3, *3/3 RC, p1, k1-tbl, [p2, k1-tbl] twice, p1, 3/3 RC, p1, k1-tbl, p5, k1-tbl, p1, 3/3 LC, p1, k1-tbl, [p2, k1-tbl] twice, p1, 3/3 LC, p3; repeat from * to end.

**Row 18:** K3, *p6, k1, p1-tbl, [k2, p1] twice, k1, p6, k1, p1-tbl, k5, p1-tbl, k1, p6, k1, p1-tbl, [k2, p1-tbl] twice, k1, p6, k3; repeat from * to end.

**Row 19:** P3, *k6, p1, k1-tbl, [p2, k1-tbl] twice, p1, k6, p1, k1-tbl, p5, k1-tbl, p1, k6, p1, k1-tbl, [p2, k1-tbl] twice, p1, k6, p3; repeat from * to end.

**Row 20:** Repeat Row 18.

**Row 21:** P3, *3/3 RPC, p1, k1-tbl, [p2, k1-tbl] twice, p1, 3/3 RPC, p1, k1-tbl, p5, k1-tbl, p1, 3/3 LPC, p1, k1-tbl, [p2, k1-tbl] twice, p1, 3/3 LPC, p3; repeat from * to end.

**Row 22:** K3, p3, k1, p1-tbl, [k2, p1-tbl] 3 times, k1, p3, k1, p1-tbl, k2, p1-tbl, k5, p1-tbl, k2, p1-tbl, k1, p3, k1, p1-tbl, [k2, p1-tbl] 3 times, k1, p3, k3; repeat from * to end.

**Row 23:** P3, *k3, p1, k1-tbl, [p2, k1-tbl] 3 times, p1, k3, p1, k1-tbl, p2, k1-tbl, p5, k1-tbl, p2, k1-tbl, p1, k3, p1, k1-tbl, [p2, k1-tbl] 3 times, p1, k3, p3; repeat from * to end.

**Rows 24–27:** Repeat Rows 22 and 23 twice.

**Row 28:** Repeat Row 22.

**Row 29:** P3, *k3, p1, k1-tbl, [p2, k1-tbl] twice, p1, 3/3 RC, p1, k1-tbl, p2, k1-tbl, p5, k1-tbl, p2, k1-tbl, p1, 3/3 LC, p1, k1-tbl, [p2, k1-tbl] twice, p1, k3, p3; repeat from * to end.

**Row 30:** K3, *k1, p1-tbl, [k2, p1-tbl] 3 times, k1, p6, k1, p1-tbl, k2, p1-tbl, k5, p1-tbl, k2, p1-tbl, k1, p6, k1, p1-tbl, [k2, p1-tbl] 3 times, k4; repeat from * to end.

**Row 31:** P3, *p1, k1-tbl, [p2, k1-tbl] 3 times, p1, k6, p1, k1-tbl, p2, k1-tbl, p5, k1-tbl, p2, k1-tbl, p1, k6, p1, k1-tbl, [p2, k1-tbl] 3 times, p4; repeat from * to end.

**Row 32:** Repeat Row 30.

**Row 33:** P3, *p1, k1-tbl, [p2, k1-tbl] 3 times, p1, 3/3 RPC, p1, k1-tbl, p2, k1-tbl, p5, k1-tbl, p2, k1-tbl, p1, 3/3 LPC, p1, k1-tbl, [p2, k1-tbl] 3 times, p4; repeat from * to end.

**Row 34:** K3, *k1, p1-tbl, [k2, p1-tbl] 3 times, k1, p3, k1, p1-tbl, [k2, p1-tbl] twice, k5, p1-tbl, [k2, p1-tbl] twice, k1, p3, k1, p1-tbl, [k2, p1-tbl] 3 times, k4; repeat from * to end.

**Row 35:** P3, *p1, k1-tbl, [p2, k1-tbl] 3 times, p1, k3, p1, k1-tbl, [p2, k1-tbl] twice, p5, k1-tbl, [p2, k1-tbl] twice, k3, p1, k1-tbl, [p2, k1-tbl] 3 times, p4; repeat from * to end.

**Rows 36–39:** Repeat Rows 34 and 35 twice.

**Row 40:** Repeat Row 34.

**Row 41:** P3, *p1, k1-tbl, [p2, k1-tbl] twice, p1, 3/3 RC, p1, k1-tbl, [p2, k1-tbl] twice, p5, k1-tbl, [p2, k1-tbl] twice, p1, 3/3 LC, p1, k1-tbl, [p2, k1-tbl] twice, p4; repeat from * to end.

**Row 42:** K3, *k1, p1-tbl, [k2, p1-tbl] twice, k1, p6, k1, p1-tbl, [k2, p1-tbl] twice, k5, p1-tbl, [k2, p1-tbl] twice, k1, p6, k1, p1-tbl, [k2, p1-tbl] twice, k4; repeat from * to end.

**Row 43:** P3, *p1, k1-tbl, [p2, k1-tbl] twice, p1, k6, p1, k1-tbl, [p2, k1-tbl] twice, p5, k1-tbl, [p2, k1-tbl] twice, p1, k6, p1, k1-tbl, [p2, k1-tbl] twice, p4; repeat from * to end.

**Row 44:** Repeat Row 42.

**Row 45:** P3, *p1, k1-tbl, [p2, k1-tbl] twice, p1, 3/3 RPC, p1, k1-tbl, [p2, k1-tbl] twice, p5, k1-tbl, [p2, k1-tbl] twice, p1, 3/3 LPC, p1, k1-tbl, [p2, k1-tbl] twice, p4; repeat from * to end.

**Row 46:** K3, *k1, p1-tbl, [k2, p1-tbl] twice, k1, p3, k1, p1-tbl, [k2, p1-tbl] 3 times, k5, p1-tbl, [k2, p1-tbl] 3 times, k1, p3, k1, p1-tbl, [k2, p1-tbl] twice, k4; repeat from * to end.

**Row 47:** P3, *p1, k1-tbl, [p2, k1-tbl] twice, p1, k3, p1, k1-tbl, [p2, k1-tbl] 3 times, p5, k1-tbl, [p2, k1-tbl] 3 times, p1, k3, p1, k1-tbl, [p2, k1-tbl] twice, p4; repeat from * to end.

**Rows 48–51:** Repeat Rows 46 and 47.

**Row 52:** Repeat Row 46.

**Row 53:** P3, *p1, k1-tbl, p2, k1-tbl, p1, 3/3 RC, p1, k1-tbl, [p2, k1-tbl] 3 times, p5, k1-tbl, [p2, k1-tbl] 3 times, p1, k1-tbl, p2, k1-tbl, p4; repeat from * to end.

**Row 54:** K3, *k1, p1-tbl, k2, p1-tbl, k1, p6, k1, p1-tbl, [k2, p1-tbl] 3 times, k5, p1-tbl, [k2, p1-tbl] 3 times, k1, p6, k1, p1-tbl, k2, p1-tbl, k4; repeat from * to end.

**Row 55:** P3, *p1, k1-tbl, p2, k1-tbl, p1, k6, p1, k1-tbl, [p2, k1-tbl] 3 times, p5, k1-tbl, [p2, k1] 3 times, p1, k6, p1, k1-tbl, p2, k1-tbl, p4; repeat from * to end.

**Row 56:** Repeat Row 54.

**Row 57:** P3, *p1, k1-tbl, p2, k1-tbl, p1, 3/3 RPC, p1, k1-tbl, [p2, k1-tbl] twice, p1, k3, p3, k3, p1, k1-tbl, [p2, k1-tbl] twice, p1, 3/3 LPC, p1, k1-tbl, p2, k1-tbl, p4; repeat from * to end.

**Row 58:** K3, *k1, p1-tbl, k2, p1-tbl, k1, p3, k1, p1-tbl, [k2, p1-tbl] 3 times, k1, p3, k3, p3, k1, p1-tbl, [k2, p1-tbl] 3 times, k1, p3, k1, p1-tbl, k2, p1-tbl, k4; repeat from * to end.

**Row 59:** P3, *p1, k1-tbl, p2, k1-tbl, p1, k3, p1, k1-tbl, [p2, k1-tbl] 3 times, p1, k3, p3, k3, p1, k1-tbl, [p2, k1-tbl] 3 times, p1, k3, p1, k1-tbl, p2, k1-tbl, p4; repeat from * to end.

**Row 60:** Repeat Row 58.

Repeat Rows 1–60 for pattern.

## TWISTED RIB

(odd number of sts; 2-row repeat)

**Row 1 (RS):** K1-tbl, *p1-tbl, k1-tbl; repeat from * to end.

**Row 2:** P1-tbl, *k1-tbl, p1-tbl; repeat from *to end.

Repeat Rows 1 and 2 for pattern.

## PATTERN NOTES

The Front and Back are worked flat in one piece, beginning at the lower edge of the Front and ending at the lower edge of the Back. Short seams are sewn for the left shoulder and side seams. The collar folds down in the Front.

## FRONT

Using Long-Tail Cast-On (see Special Techniques, page 221), CO 129 (151, 183) sts.

### SIZES 24 AND 34 ONLY:

**Row 1 (RS):** K1, work Twisted Rib over 7 sts, pm, work Bamboo Cable Pattern to last 10 sts, pm, work 9 sts in Twisted Rib, k1.

### SIZE 29 ONLY:

**Row 1 (RS):** K1, work Twisted Rib over 7 sts, pm, continue in Twisted Rib (beginning with p1-tbl) for 12 more sts, pm, work Bamboo Cable Pattern to last 10 sts, pm, work 9 sts in Twisted Rib, k1.

### ALL SIZES:

### INCREASE SECTION

**Row 2 (WS):** K1, work in patterns as established to last st, k1.

**Row 3:** Work to marker, M1L, sm, work to end—1 st increased.

**Row 4:** Work to second (third, second) marker, sm, p1-tbl, work to end.

**Row 5:** K1, work Twisted Rib over 7 sts, M1PL, k1-tbl, sm, work to end—1 st increased.

**Row 6:** Work to second (third, second) marker, sm, work in Twisted Rib to last st, k1.

**Row 7:** K1, work Twisted Rib over 7 sts, M1L, p1-tbl, k1-tbl, sm, work to end—1 st increased.

**Row 8:** Work to second (third, second) marker, sm, p1-tbl, k1-tbl, p1-tbl, work to end.

**Row 9:** K1, work Twisted Rib over 7 sts, M1PL, work to end—1 st increased.

**Row 10:** Work to second (third, second) marker, sm, k1-tbl, work in Twisted Rib to last st, k1.

**Row 11:** K1, work Twisted Rib over 7 sts, M1L, work to end—1 st increased.

**Row 12:** Work to second (third, second) marker, sm, p1-tbl, work to end.

Bamboo Cable Pattern

54-st repeat; worked 2 (2, 3) times

| | |
|---|---|
| ⧅ | 3/3 LC |
| ⧄ | 3/3 RC |
| ⧅ | 3/3 LPC |
| ⧄ | 3/3 RPC |

Knit on RS, purl on WS.

Purl on RS, knit on WS.

K1-tbl on RS, p1-tbl on WS.

**Row 13:** K1, work Twisted Rib over 7 sts, M1PL, work to end—1 st increased.
**Row 14:** Work to second (third, second) marker, k1-tbl, work to end.
Repeat Rows 11–14 fourteen (19, 23) more times—165 (195, 235) sts.
Place removable marker at right edge.
*End Increase Section.*
Work even until piece measures 23 (28½, 33½)" [58.5 (72.5, 85) cm] from the beginning, ending with a WS row.
**Next Row (RS):** BO 36 (44, 52) sts in pattern, work to end—129 (151, 183) sts remain.

## BACK

Work Increase Section as for Front—165 (195, 235) sts.
Work even until piece measures 13¾ (16½, 19¼)" [35 (42, 49) cm] from collar BO, ending with a WS row.

## DECREASE SECTION

**Row 1 (RS):** K1, work 6 sts, k2tog-tbl, work to end—1 st decreased.
Repeat Decrease Row every RS row 35 (43, 51) more times—129 (151, 183) sts remain.
Work 1 row even.
BO all sts purlwise.

## FINISHING

Block to measurements.
Place removable markers at letters as indicated in schematic; sew seams A-B, C-D, and E-F.

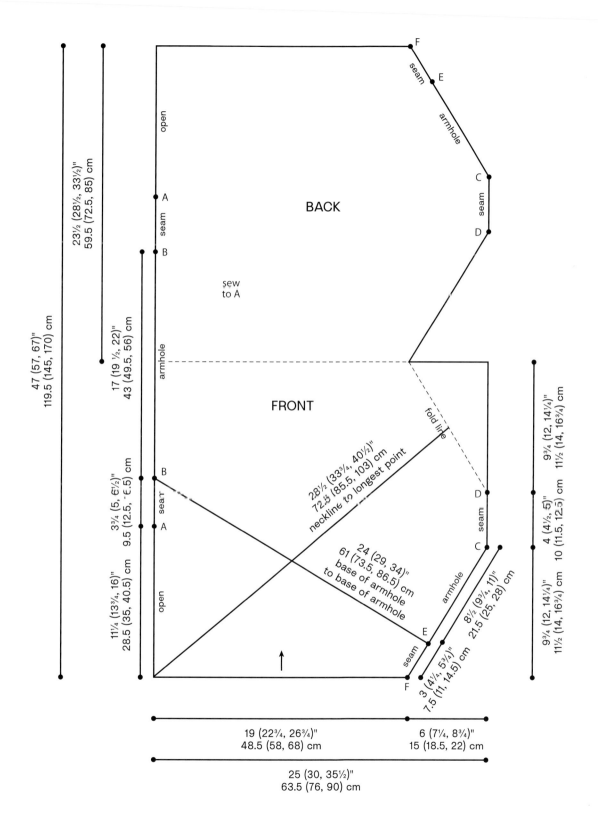

47 (57, 67)"
119.5 (145, 170) cm

23½ (28½, 33½)"
59.5 (72.5, 85) cm

17 (19 ½, 22)"
43 (49.5, 56) cm

F

seam

E

armhole

C

seam

D

BACK

open

A

seam

B

sew
to A

armhole

fold line

FRONT

28½ (33¾, 40½)"
72.5 (85.5, 103) cm
neckline to longest point

9¾ (12, 14¼)"
11½ (14, 16¾) cm

3¾ (5, 6½)"
9.5 (12.5, 16.5) cm

B

seam

A

open

24 (29, 34)"
61 (73.5, 86.5) cm
base of armhole
to base of armhole

D

seam

C

armhole

4 (4½, 5)"
10 (11.5, 12.5) cm

11¼ (13¾, 16)"
28.5 (35, 40.5) cm

E

8½ (9¾, 11)"
21.5 (25, 28) cm

9¾ (12, 14¼)"
11½ (14, 16¾) cm

seam

F

3 (4¼, 5¾)"
7.5 (11, 14.5) cm

19 (22¾, 26¾)"
48.5 (58, 68) cm

6 (7¼, 8¾)"
15 (18.5, 22) cm

25 (30, 35½)"
63.5 (76, 90) cm

# DESIGN YOUR OWN

## EXPLORING FURTHER

Outward was designed with the premise that there would be no shaping in the cable panel. I was determined to keep this garment relatively easy to knit, and shaping into an unusual cable panel doesn't qualify as easy. What if the entire piece were knit in a stitch that was easy to keep track of, plus easy to increase and decrease in while keeping in pattern? Where else might the design process have taken it? I might have eliminated the pointed hem or carved away at the right armhole opening, like I did with the left opening. At that point, I might have wanted to put raglan sleeves into both armholes. One sleeve would be short and one long. I might have changed the width of the panel to refine my new decisions. My mind is racing now, because with some of my original restrictions lifted there are many new avenues to explore. That's exciting and, at the same time, a tad overwhelming—one reason parameters can be good.

## DESIGNING OUTWARD

The idea for Outward started as a rectangle, one that was long enough to go from the base of the front to the bottom of the back. That could be said for a lot of pullovers, but there has been a trend lately to make pullovers asymmetrical by placing neck and armholes in unexpected locations, and I wanted to explore the possibilities. Using the tilted sweaters I saw online as a base, I decided to place the neckline at one end of the "shoulder line." It seemed impossible to know how a tilted rectangle might fit, so I made a fleece model to help me with design decisions. Starting with a longish rectangle, I made a split

for the neck starting at the right-hand edge (left as worn). Draping my split rectangle on the dress form, I could see that the neck opening would work well if it were a diagonal, with the top corner of the front falling forward, becoming a collar. The back would have done the same, but I decided to lop off the corner in the back. When knitting, the lopping would be done with shaping. I also lopped off triangles to make the left armhole and side seam. Seaming (or taping) my model together at each side made it more of a pullover than a poncho, and meant that it would stay in place instead of rotating around as the wearer went about their day.

# Ladder

Rectangles and tilted squares are melded together in Ladder, forming pieces that become both the sleeve and upper body of this geometric bolero. Paired ridges of garter stitch adorn the center back panel, cuffs, and front bands, which wrap around the neck to become a collar as well. Knit in pieces and sewn, this is a good project to take on the road, when you only have room for small pieces. A word of warning: Because of the geometry of this design, as the waist and chest size increases, the length increases significantly. Check the finished length before you start so you are not surprised.

## FINISHED MEASUREMENTS

38 (42, 46, 50) (54, 58, 62)" [96.5 (106.5, 117, 127) (107, 117.5, 157.5) cm] waist

To fit chest sizes 30–32 (34–36, 38–40, 42–44, 46–48) (50–52, 54–56)" [76–81.5 (86.5–91.5, 96.5–101.5, 106.5–112, 117–122) (127–132, 137–142) cm]

*Note: This piece is intended to be worn with approximately 6–8" (15–20.8 cm) positive ease over chest measurement.*

## YARN

Hudson + West Weld [70% US merino/30% US Corriedale; 200 yards (183 m)/1¾ ounces (50 g)]: 6 (7, 8, 8) (9, 10, 11) skeins Lake

## NEEDLES

One pair straight needles, size US 3 (3.25 mm)

Change needle size if necessary to obtain correct gauge.

## NOTIONS

Stitch markers

Removable stitch markers

Stitch holder or waste yarn

## GAUGE

24 sts and 34 rows = 4" (10 cm) in St st

## PATTERN STITCH

### INTERRUPTED GARTER

(any number of sts; 6-row repeat)
**Rows 1 and 2:** Knit.
**Row 3 (RS):** Knit.
**Row 4:** Purl.
**Rows 5–8:** Knit.
Repeat Rows 3–8 for pattern.

## PATTERN NOTES

This cardigan is worked in pieces, then sewn together. The Center Back Panel, Front Bands, and Bottom Bands (which are worked sideways) are worked first. The Sleeves are picked up from Sleeve Cuffs (which are worked sideways) and worked to the beginning of the Upper Body, which forms the main front and back portion of the body of the cardigan. The Upper Body is shaped with increases, then side and shoulder decreases. After blocking, removable markers are placed to help with assembly. Refer to the Assembly Diagram when sewing the pieces together.

## CENTER BACK PANEL

Using Long-Tail Cast-On (see Special Techniques, page 221), CO 38 sts. Begin Interrupted Garter; work even until piece measures 16¾ (18¼, 19¾, 21¼) (22½, 24, 25¾)" [42.5 (46.5, 50, 54) (57, 61, 65.5) cm], ending with a WS row. BO all sts.

## GARTER EDGING

With RS of Center Back Panel facing, pick up and knit 99 (108, 117, 126) (134, 143, 153) sts along one edge of panel. Knit 5 rows.
BO all sts knitwise. Repeat for opposite edge.

## FRONT BANDS (MAKE 2)

Using Long-Tail Cast-On, CO 18 sts. Begin Interrupted Garter; work even until piece measures 19¾ (21¼, 22¾, 24¼) (25½, 27, 28¾)" [50 (54, 58, 61.5) (65, 68.5, 73) cm] from the beginning, ending with a WS row. Transfer sts to st holder or waste yarn and set aside.
Repeat for second Band, leaving sts on needle.
With WSs of Bands together (seam will be on the outside), join Bands using 3-Needle Bind-Off (see Special Techniques, page 222).

## GARTER EDGING

With RS of Bands facing, pick up and knit 234 (252, 270, 288) (303, 321, 342) sts along one side edge.
Knit 4 rows.
BO all sts purlwise. Place a removable marker on BO row; Upper Body will be sewn to this edge.
Pick up the same number of sts along second edge (this will be the center front edge).
Knit 4 rows.
BO all sts knitwise.

## BOTTOM BANDS (MAKE 2)

Using Long-Tail Cast-On, CO 38 (38, 38, 38) (38, 32, 32) sts.
**Setup Row (RS):** Work Interrupted Garter for 5 sts, work in St st to last 5 sts, work in Interrupted Garter to end.
Work even in pattern as established until piece measures 13 (15, 17, 19) (21, 23, 25)" [33 (38, 43, 48.5) (53.5, 58.5, 63.5) cm], ending with a WS row.
BO all sts knitwise.

## SLEEVE CUFF

Using Long-Tail Cast-On, CO 18 sts.
Begin Interrupted Garter; work even until piece measures 8½ (9, 10, 10¼) (11½, 12, 12½)" [21.5 (23, 25.5, 26) (29, 30.5, 32) cm] from the beginning, ending with a WS row. BO all sts.

## GARTER EDGING

With RS of Cuff facing, pick up and knit 52 (54, 60, 62) (70, 72, 76) sts along edge of Cuff.
Knit 4 rows.
BO all sts knitwise.

## SLEEVE/UPPER BODY (MAKE 2)

With RS of Cuff facing, pick up and knit 52 (54, 60, 62) (70, 72, 76) sts along opposite edge of Cuff.
Knit 5 rows.
Change to St st; work 2 rows even.

## SIZES 50, 54, 58, AND 62 ONLY:
## SHAPE SLEEVE

**Sleeve Increase Row (RS):** K1, M1R, knit to last st, M1L, k1—2 sts increased.
Repeat Sleeve Increase Row every - (-, -, 22) (42, 4, 2) rows - (-, -, 2, 1, 7, 5) more time(s), then every - (-, -, -) (-, -, 4) rows - (-, -, -) (-, -, 3) more times— - (-, -, 68) (74, 88, 94) sts.

## ALL SIZES

Work even until piece measures 9 (8¼, 7½, 7¼) (7, 5¼, 4½)" [23 (21, 19, 18.5) (18, 13.5, 11.5) cm] from pick-up row, ending with a WS row. Place removable marker at both ends of last row.

## SHAPE UPPER BODY

**Row 1 (RS):** K1, M1L, knit to last st, M1R, k1—2 sts increased.
**Row 2:** Purl.
**Row 3:** Repeat Row 1—2 sts increased.
**Row 4:** Purl.
**Row 5:** [K1, M1L] twice, knit to last 2 sts, [M1R, k1] twice—4 sts increased.
**Row 6:** Purl.
Repeat Rows 1–6 six (7, 8, 8) (8, 9, 9) more times, then repeat Rows 1 and 2 zero (0, 1, 1, 0 1, 1) time(s), then repeat Rows 5 and 6 two (3, 2, 3) (5, 4, 6) more times, placing marker after 58 (65,

71, 77) (83, 93, 100) sts on final WS row, for shoulder shaping—116 (130, 142, 154) (166, 186, 200) sts.

## SHAPE UPPER BODY AND SHOULDER

*Note: Upper Body and shoulder shaping will be worked at the same time; please read entire section through before beginning. Shoulder shaping will begin on row 17 (17, 23, 23) (27, 27, 27) of upper body shaping.*
**Body Single Decrease Row (RS):** K1, k2tog, knit to last 3 sts, ssk, k1—2 body sts decreased.
Purl 1 row.
Repeat the last 2 rows once more—2 body sts decreased.
**Body Double Decrease Row (RS):** [K1, k2tog] twice, knit to last 6 sts, [ssk, k1] twice—4 body sts decreased.
Purl 1 row.
Repeat the last 6 rows 7 (9, 11, 12) (13, 15, 18) more times, then repeat Body Single Decrease Row every RS row 4 (3, 1, 3) (1, 1, 0) more time(s), then repeat Body Double Decrease Row every RS row 0 (0, 0, 0) (2, 3, 1) more time(s).
AT THE SAME TIME, beginning on row 17 (17, 23, 23) (27, 27, 27) of Upper Body shaping, shape shoulder as follows:
**Shoulder Decrease Row (RS):**
Continuing to work Upper Body shaping as established, work to 3 sts before shoulder marker, ssk, k1, sm, k1, k2tog, work to end—2 sts decreased.
Repeat Shoulder Decrease Row every 2 (4, 4, 6) (6, 6, 8) rows 1 (6, 5, 10) (9, 2, 6) time(s), then every 4 (6, 6, 0) (8, 8, 10) rows 9 (4, 5, 0) (1, 8, 4) time(s)—22 sts remain when all shaping is complete.
**Next Row (RS):** [K1, k2tog] twice, k2, ssk, k2, k2tog, k2, [ssk, k1] twice—16 sts remain.
Purl 1 row.
**Next Row (RS):** K1, k3tog, k1, ssk, k2, k2tog, k1, sssk, k1—10 sts remain.
Purl 1 row.
**Next Row (RS):** K1, k2tog, ssk, k2tog, ssk, k1—6 sts remain.
Purl 1 row.
**Next Row (RS):** K1, k2tog, ssk, k1—4 sts remain.
BO all sts purlwise; place removable marker in center of BO sts.

## FINISHING

Wet-block all pieces and pin to dry, stretching shaped edges of Upper Body aggressively.
Refer to Assembly Diagram when sewing pieces together.
Fold Bottom Bands in half lengthwise and place removable marker at fold line along one long edge (A). Place removable marker 6 (6, 6, 6) (6, 5, 5)" [15 (15, 15, 15) (15, 12.5, 12.5) cm] up from CO edge on each Front Band (B). Place marker on previously marked edge. Place marker along same edge on each Front Band, 3" (7.5 cm) down from 3-Needle Bind-Off (C). Place removable markers 6 (6, 6, 6) (6, 5, 5)" [15 (15, 15, 15) (15, 12.5, 12.5) cm] up from CO edge on both sides of Center Back Band (D and E).
Sew one Upper Body/Sleeve to Left Front Band, sewing decrease edge of Upper Body/Sleeve (beginning at widest point of piece and ending at marker in center of BO row) between markers on Left Front Band (B and C), easing piece into seam if necessary.
Sew opposite decrease edge of Upper Body/Sleeve between marker D and BO edge on left side of Center Back Band. Repeat for second Upper Body/Sleeve and Right Front Band and right side of Center Back Band.
Sew CO edge of Bottom Band to remaining length of Left Front Band (from B to CO edge of Front Band), then sew top edge of Bottom Band from Front Band seam to increase edge of Upper Body/Sleeve (from B to A), ending at marker at Bottom Band fold, easing seam if necessary. *Note: For some sizes, you may have an inch (2.5 cm) or so between the fold in the Bottom Band and the marked top of the Sleeve. That is fine; it isn't necessary to stretch Bottom Band to meet Sleeve marker. Repeat for back of Bottom Band and opposite Upper Body/Sleeve increase edge.*
Sew free top edge of Front Bands to BO edge of Center Back Panel. Sew Sleeve seams, extending the seam along a portion of the increase edge of the Upper Body/Sleeve if necessary.

## Assembly Diagram

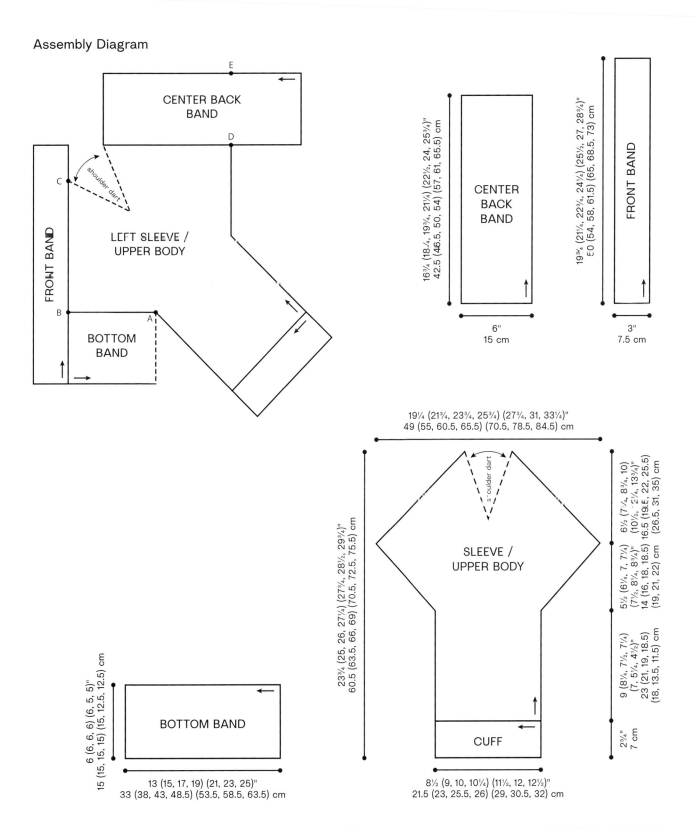

CENTER BACK BAND

E

D

C

shoulder dart

FRONT BAND

LEFT SLEEVE / UPPER BODY

B

A

BOTTOM BAND

CENTER
BACK
BAND

16¾ (18¼, 19¾, 21¼) (22½, 24, 25¾)"
42.5 (46.5, 50, 54) (57, 61, 65.5) cm

6"
15 cm

FRONT BAND

19¾ (21¼, 22¾, 24¼) (25½, 27, 28¾)"
50 (54, 58, 61.5) (65, 68.5, 73) cm

3"
7.5 cm

19¼ (21¾, 23¾, 25¾) (27¾, 31, 33¼)"
49 (55, 60.5, 65.5) (70.5, 78.5, 84.5) cm

shoulder dart

SLEEVE /
UPPER BODY

23¾ (25, 26, 27¼) (27¾, 28½, 29¾)"
60.5 (63.5, 66, 69) (70.5, 72.5, 75.5) cm

6½ (7¼, 8¾, 10)
(10½, 12¼, 13¾)"
16.5 (19.5, 22, 25.5)
(26.5, 31, 35) cm

5½ (6¼, 7, 7¼)
(7½, 8¼, 8¾)"
14 (16, 18, 18.5)
(19, 21, 22) cm

9 (8¼, 7½, 7¼)
(7, 5¼, 4½)"
23 (21, 19, 18.5)
(18, 13.5, 11.5) cm

CUFF

2¾"
7 cm

8½ (9, 10, 10¼) (11½, 12, 12½)"
21.5 (23, 25.5, 26) (29, 30.5, 32) cm

BOTTOM BAND

15 (15, 15, 15) (15, 12.5, 12.5) cm
6 (6, 6, 6) (6, 5, 5)"

13 (15, 17, 19) (21, 23, 25)"
33 (38, 43, 48.5) (53.5, 58.5, 63.5) cm

# DESIGN YOUR OWN

### DESIGNING LADDER

While not evident at first sight, the idea for this cardigan began as a rectangle pileup. First, a square, folded diagonally, forms the largest chunk of the front and back and at the same time, the top of the sleeve. A rectangle becomes the lower portion of the sleeve. To make these two elements work together, they weren't worked separately, I layered them, to make one piece, not literally, but in schematic form (see the schematic). The knitting starts at the bottom of the sleeve and is worked straight, forming the lower rectangle, until it's time to begin the rapid shaping as the bias-knit square emerges from the lower rectangle. This was an idea that needed to be worked out in the schematic stage and not entirely in my head. It wasn't until I was shifting shapes around on the computer screen that I even came up with the idea. I added the center back panel, front band, and lower rectangles to make up the rest of the cardigan. As a refinement, decreases are worked at the top of the bias square to create shoulder shaping.

### LIMITED BY GEOMETRY

Sometimes, the geometry of a more oddball construction means that not all of the wished-for sizes are possible. Below are diagrams of the nine sizes I was aiming for and how the pieces fit together. The large bias square naturally gets larger as the chest measurement increases, which means it also gets longer, along each side and from point to point as well. That means the sweater must get longer for each size by more than normal, so the look of the sweater changes quite a bit as the sizes get larger. The same is true for the sleeves. Human arms do not get much longer as chest size increases, which forces the lower sleeve to be shorter and shorter, completely changing the proportions of the cardigan (see diagrams at right). The extreme length needed for the largest sizes and the change of sleeve proportions led me to decide to offer the pattern in seven sizes, instead of the nine I had hoped for.

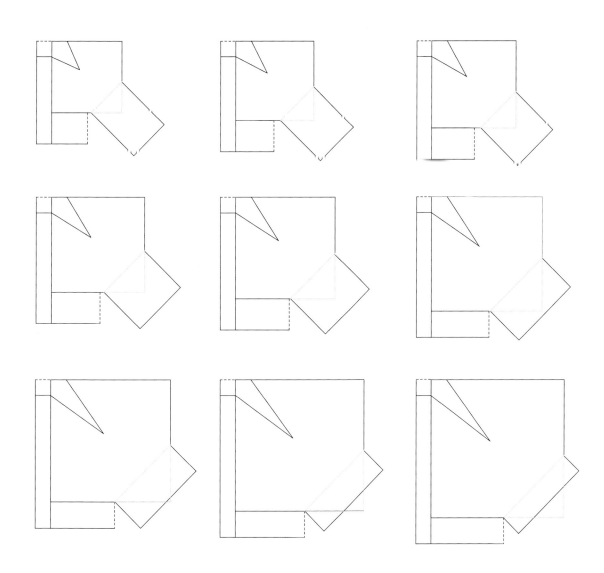

# CHAPTER 6
# HYBRID

Folds, tucks, and rectangular inserts enhance traditional garment shapes in this chapter. The techniques explored to shape rectangles earlier are now applied to familiar sweater shapes. Add a slit square to the bottom of a sleeve to make a fabulous flounce. Fold an extended hem upward forming an intriguing dimensional effect, or let pleats shape your next sweater.

# Skyward

This modest tank transforms from ordinary to sculptural when the front hem is folded up, secured to the center front seam, and left to drape as it will, forming dimensional swoops and folds while creating a pointed hemline. The back is left plain and simple. One strand of fine mohair with a strand of nubby silk creates a special fabric that is light as a feather and reduces curling at the edges, making the unfinished armholes and neck work like a dream.

## FINISHED MEASUREMENTS
32 (36½, 40, 44½, 48) (52½, 56, 60½, 64)" [81.5 (92.5, 101.5, 113, 122) (133.5, 142, 153.5, 162.5) cm] chest

*Note: This piece is intended to be worn with approximately 2–4" (5–10 cm) positive ease.*

## YARN
Shibui Lunar [60% extra fine merino/40% mulberry silk; 401 yards (365 m)/1.76 ounces (50 g)]: 2 (3, 3, 3, 3) (3, 4, 4, 4) skeins #2041 Pollen (A)

Shibui Silk Cloud [60% kid mohair/40% silk; 330 yards (300 m)/.88 ounces (25 g)]: 2 (3, 3, 3, 3) (3, 4, 4, 4) skeins #2012 Fjord (B)

## NEEDLES
One pair straight needles, size US 6 (4 mm)

Change needle size if necessary to obtain correct gauge.

## NOTIONS
Stitch markers

Removable stitch markers

## GAUGE
22 sts and 30 rows = 4" (10 cm) in St st with 1 strand each of A and B held together

## PATTERN NOTES

This top is worked in pieces from the bottom up, then sewn together. The Back is worked to be shorter than the Front, but the center Front is folded up so that it is the same length as the Back.

## BACK

Using 1 strand each of A and B held together and Long-Tail Cast-On (see Special Techniques, page 221), CO 88 (100, 110, 122, 132) (144, 154, 166, 176) sts. Begin garter st (knit every row); work even for 2" (5 cm), ending with a WS row. Change to St st; work even until piece measures 12 (12, 11¾, 11¾, 11¾) (12, 12¼, 12¾, 13)" [30.5 (30.5, 30, 30, 30) (30.5, 31, 32.5, 33) cm] from the beginning, ending with a WS row.

## SHAPE ARMHOLES

Using Sloped Bind-Off (see Special Techniques, page 222), BO 3 (4, 5, 6, 7) (8, 9, 10, 10) at beginning of next 2 rows, 3 sts at beginning of next 2 (2, 2, 4, 4) (4, 6, 6, 6) rows, then 2 sts at beginning of next 4 (4, 4, 4, 6) (6, 6, 6, 6) rows—68 (78, 86, 90, 94) (104, 106, 116, 126) sts remain.
**Decrease Row (RS):** K3, k2tog, knit to last 5 sts, ssk, k3—2 sts decreased. Repeat Decrease Row every RS row 2 (4, 5, 5, 6) (11, 9, 12, 15) more times—62 (68, 74, 78, 80) (80, 86, 90, 94) sts remain. Work even until armholes measure 5¾ (6¼, 6¾, 7, 7¼) (7¼, 7½, 7½, 7¾)" [14.5 (16, 17, 18, 18.5) (18.5, 19, 19, 19.5) cm], ending with a WS row.

## SHAPE NECK AND SHOULDERS

**Next Row (RS):** K19 (22, 22, 23, 24) (24, 25, 27, 29), join a second ball of yarn, knit to end.
Working both sides at the same time, BO 5 sts at each neck edge twice, then beginning on first RS row after initial neck BO, BO 5 (6, 6, 7, 7) (7, 8, 9, 10) sts at each armhole edge once, then 4 (6, 6, 6, 7) (7, 7, 8, 9) sts once.

## FRONT

Using 1 strand each of A and B held together and Long-Tail Cast-On, CO 116 (128, 138, 150, 160) (172, 182, 194, 204) sts. Begin garter st (knit every row); work even for 2" (5 cm), ending with a WS row. Change to St st; work even until piece measures 6" (15 cm) from the beginning, ending with a WS row.

## SHAPE BODY

**Body Decrease Row 1 (RS):** K3, k2tog, knit to last 5 sts, ssk, k3—2 sts decreased.
Repeat Body Decrease Row 1 every 6 rows 6 more times—102 (114, 124, 136, 146) (158, 168, 180, 190) sts remain.
Purl 1 row. Piece should measure approximately 11" (28 cm) from the beginning.

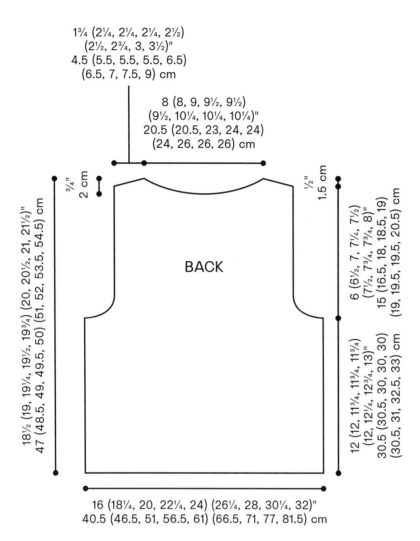

1¾ (2¼, 2¼, 2¼, 2½)
(2½, 2¾, 3, 3½)"
4.5 (5.5, 5.5, 5.5, 6.5)
(6.5, 7, 7.5, 9) cm

8 (8, 9, 9½, 9½)
(9½, 10¼, 10¼, 10¼)"
20.5 (20.5, 23, 24, 24)
(24, 26, 26, 26) cm

¾"
2 cm

½"
1.5 cm

18½ (19, 19¼, 19½, 19¾) (20, 20½, 21, 21½)"
47 (48.5, 49, 49.5, 50) (51, 52, 53.5, 54.5) cm

6 (6½, 7, 7¼, 7½)
(7½, 7¾, 7¾, 8)"
15 (16.5, 18, 18.5, 19)
(19, 19.5, 19.5, 20.5) cm

BACK

12 (12, 11¾, 11¾, 11¾)
(12, 12¼, 12¾, 13)"
30.5 (30.5, 30, 30, 30)
(30.5, 31, 32.5, 33) cm

16 (18¼, 20, 22¼, 24) (26¼, 28, 30¼, 32)"
40.5 (46.5, 51, 56.5, 61) (66.5, 71, 77, 81.5) cm

## BEGIN SPLIT

**Division Row (RS):** K51 (57, 62, 68, 73) (79, 84, 90, 95), join a second ball of yarn, knit to end.

Working both sides at the same time, work 3 rows even.

**Body Decrease Row 2 (RS):** K3, k2tog, knit to slit; on second side, knit to last 5 sts, ssk, k3—2 sts decreased.

Repeat Body Decrease Row 2 every 6 rows 6 times more—44 (50, 55, 61, 66) (72, 77, 83, 88) sts remain each side.

Work even until piece measures 12 (12, 11¾, 11¾, 11¾) (12, 12¼, 12¾, 13)" [30.5 (30.5, 30, 30, 30) (30.5, 31, 32.5, 33) cm] from the beginning, ending with a WS row.

## SHAPE ARMHOLES

Using Sloped Bind-Off, BO 3 (4, 5, 6, 7) (8, 9, 10, 10) at beginning of next 2 rows, 3 sts at beginning of next 2 (2, 2, 4, 4) (4, 6, 6, 6) rows, then 2 sts at beginning of next 4 (4, 4, 4, 6) (6, 6, 6, 6) rows—34 (39, 43, 45, 47) (52, 53, 58, 63) sts remain.

**Armhole Decrease Row (RS):** K3, k2tog, knit to last 5 sts, ssk, k3—2 sts decreased.

Repeat Armhole Decrease Row every RS row 2 (4, 5, 5, 6) (11, 9, 12, 15) more times—31 (34, 37, 39, 40) (40, 43, 45, 47) sts remain.

Work even until armholes measure 3½ (4, 4½, 4¾, 5) (4½, 4¾, 4¾, 5)" [9 (10, 11.5, 12, 12.5) (11.5, 12, 12, 12.5) cm], ending with a WS row.

## SHAPE NECK

Using Sloped Bind-Off, BO 5 (5, 5, 5, 6) (6, 6, 6, 6) sts at each neck edge once, 4 (4, 4, 4, 5) (5, 5, 5, 5) sts once, 3 sts 2 (2, 2, 3, 2) (2, 2, 2, 2) times, then 2 sts 2 (2, 3, 2, 3) (2, 3, 3, 3) times—12 (15, 16, 17, 17) (19, 20, 22, 24) sts remain each side.

Work even until armholes measure 6 (6½, 7, 7¼, 7½) (7½, 7¾, 7¾, 8)" [15 (16.5, 18, 18.5, 19) (19, 19.5, 19.5, 20.5) cm], ending with a WS row.

## SHAPE SHOULDERS

BO 5 (6, 6, 7, 7) (7, 8, 9, 10) sts at each armhole edge once, then 4 (6, 6, 6, 7) (7, 7, 8, 9) sts once.

Block as desired.
Sew shoulder, armhole and side seams, leaving bottom 6" (15 cm) of Front side edges unsewn. With WSs of center Front slit together, sew sides of slit (seam will be on the RS). Fold center point of CO edge of Front to RS and tack to base of slit seam (see photo).

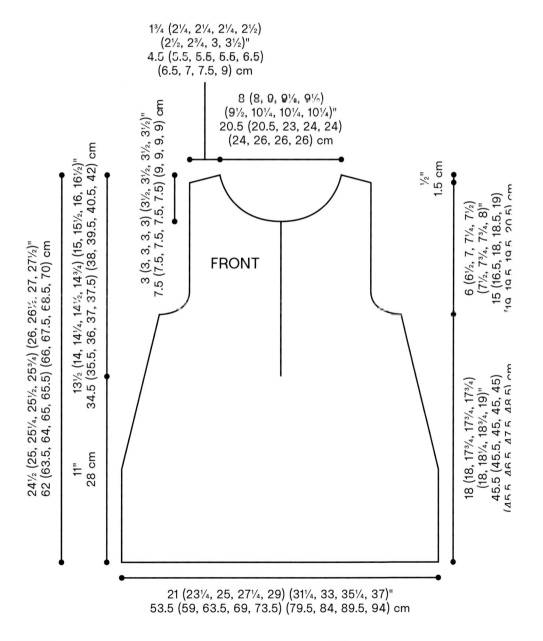

1¾ (2¼, 2¼, 2¼, 2½)
(2½, 2¾, 3, 3½)"
4.5 (5.5, 5.5, 5.5, 6.5)
(6.5, 7, 7.5, 9) cm

8 (8, 9, 9¼, 9½)
(9½, 10¼, 10¼, 10¼)"
20.5 (20.5, 23, 24, 24)
(24, 26, 26, 26) cm

3 (3, 3, 3, 3) (3½, 3½, 3½, 3½)"
7.5 (7.5, 7.5, 7.5, 7.5) (9, 9, 9, 9) cm

FRONT

24½ (25, 25¼, 25½, 25¾) (26, 26½, 27, 27½)"
62 (63.5, 64, 65, 65.5) (66, 67.5, 68.5, 70) cm

13½ (14, 14¼, 14½, 14¾) (15, 15½, 16, 16½)"
34.5 (35.5, 36, 37, 37.5) (38, 39.5, 40.5, 42) cm

11"
28 cm

½"
1.5 cm

6 (6½, 7, 7¼, 7½)
(7½, 7¾, 7¾, 8)"
15 (16.5, 18, 18.5, 19)
(19, 19.5, 20.5) cm

18 (18, 17¾, 17¾, 17¾)
(18, 18¼, 18¾, 19)"
45.5 (45.5, 45, 45, 45)
(45.5, 46.5, 47.5, 48.5) cm

21 (23¼, 25, 27¼, 29) (31¼, 33, 35¼, 37)"
53.5 (59, 63.5, 69, 73.5) (79.5, 84, 89.5, 94) cm

# DESIGN YOUR OWN

### DESIGNING SKYWARD

You've read it before in other patterns here. The idea for this knitted tank was sparked by garments I saw on Pinterest when I was researching concepts in preparation for writing this book. I had fun collecting related photos for several years before I actually got started. Many of the runway garments that caught my eye had interesting folds. Some, like this tank, had just one strategically tacked point, transforming the garment from plain to special. My goal became to take advantage of folding in the easiest possible way. I wanted to keep both the shape of the garment simple and minimize the folding required to get an interesting result. I felt a bit lost at first, not knowing where to begin. I started a bit aimlessly, with a paper model of the front of a tank top, and started folding. The paper helped me find the simple upward center fold and made me aware that I would need several inches of extra length in the front so the front length after folding would match the back. I needed to move on to a fabric model to know if there would be any interesting draping and if I would need to change the shape of the front to A-line instead of straight. My knit fabric model told me that the longer front, with an A-line shape, made nice draped forms. I also realized, when studying the folded tank on my dress form, that it would be a good idea to put a seam down the center front, extending to where the fold would be sewn down, for stability. Without the seam, the weight of the folded fabric would pull downward, stretching the tank out of shape and reducing the drama of the fold and its drapes.

### BIG FOLD VARIATIONS

Can you think of other ways to utilize big simple folds like the one in Skyward's front hem? A similar fold might be asymmetrical instead of centered. Would it still work to have a longer front and shorter back, or should extra length be added to the back as well? Think about an upward fold at one or both side seams. Where else could you place a big fold? I can picture an upward fold on a wide short sleeve, transforming it into a lovely cap sleeve. Something similar, but this time folding downward, might make a great collar or neckline treatment. Dream on and test your ideas with fabric models.

# Anne[2]

The focal point of this retro, 1940s-inspired top is the pleated sweetheart neckline, which is easily achieved with only a few hand-sewn stitches. Anne[2] is knit in two pieces, front and back, with shaped extensions forming subtle dolman sleeves. The cropped length, shaped sides, and deep ribbing at the hem all increase the retro effect.

**FINISHED MEASUREMENTS**
32 (36, 40, 44, 48) (52, 56, 60, 64)" [81.5 (91.5, 101.5, 112, 122) (132, 142, 152.5, 162.5) cm

*Note: This piece is intended to be worn with approximately 2" (5 cm) positive ease.*

**YARN**
Shibui Knits Pebble [48% recycled silk/36% fine merino/16% cashmere; 224 yards (205 m)/.88 ounces (25 g)]: 6 (7, 8, 9, 10) (11, 12, 13, 13) skeins #2194 Twilight

**NEEDLES**
One pair straight needles, size US 7 (4.5 mm)

One pair straight needles, size US 5 (3.75 mm)

Change needle size if necessary to obtain correct gauge.

**NOTIONS**
Stitch markers

Removable stitch markers

**GAUGE**
20 sts and 28 rows = 4" (10 cm) in St st using larger needles and 2 strands of yarn held together

## PATTERN STITCH

### 2×2 RIB

(multiple of 4 sts + 2; 2-row repeat)
**Setup Row (WS):** P2, *k2, p2; repeat from * to end.
**Row 1 (RS):** K2, *p2, k2; repeat from * to end.
**Row 2:** P2, *k2, p2; repeat from * to end.
Repeat Rows 1 and 2 for pattern.

## PATTERN NOTES

This top is worked in pieces from the bottom up, with stitches cast on for Sleeves, then sewn together. Stitches are bound off for the Front neck, then cast on again on the next row and worked to the shoulders. Once the piece is complete, stitches on either side of the Front neck are folded into pleats, then sewn to the bind-off ridge.

## BACK

Using smaller needles and 2 strands of yarn held together, CO 70 (82, 90, 102, 110) (122, 130, 142, 150) sts.
Begin 2×2 Rib; work even until piece measures 2¾" (7 cm) from the beginning, ending with a WS row.
Change to larger needles and St st; work 8 (10, 8, 10, 8) (10, 8, 10, 8) rows even.
Place markers 20 (23, 25, 28, 30) (33, 35, 38, 40) sts in from each edge.

## SHAPE BODY

**Body Increase Row (RS):** Knit to marker, sm, M1R, knit to marker, M1L, sm, knit to end—2 sts increased.
Repeat Increase Row every 8 (10, 8, 10, 8) (10, 8, 10, 8) rows 4 (3, 4, 3, 4) (3, 4, 3, 4) more times—80 (90, 100, 110, 120) (130, 140, 150, 160) sts.
Purl 1 row, removing markers.

## SHAPE UNDERARM GUSSET AND SLEEVES

**Underarm Increase Row (RS):** Knit 1, M1L, knit to last st, M1R, k1—2 sts increased.
Repeat Underarm Increase Row every RS row 7 more times—96 (106, 116, 126, 136) (146, 156, 166, 176) sts.
Purl 1 row.
Using Cable Cast-On (see Special Techniques, page 221), CO 6 (6, 7, 7, 8) (8, 9, 9, 10) sts at beginning of next 2 rows—108 (118, 130, 140, 152) (162, 174, 184, 196) sts.
Work even until piece measures 6¼ (6½, 7, 7¾, 8) (9, 9¾, 10, 10)" [16 (16.5, 18, 19.5, 20.5) (23, 25, 25.5, 25.5) cm] from Sleeve CO, ending with a WS row.

## SHAPE SHOULDERS

BO 4 (4, 4, 5, 5) (5, 6, 6, 7) sts at beginning of next 10 (20, 32, 10, 22) (32, 12, 22, 2) rows, then 3 (3, 0, 4, 4) (0, 5, 5, 6) sts at beginning of next 22 (12, 0, 22, 10) (0, 20, 10, 30) rows.
BO remaining 2 sts.

10¾ (11¾, 13, 14, 15¼) (16¼, 17½, 18½, 19½)"
27.5 (30, 33, 35.5, 38.5) (41.5, 44.5, 47, 49.5) cm

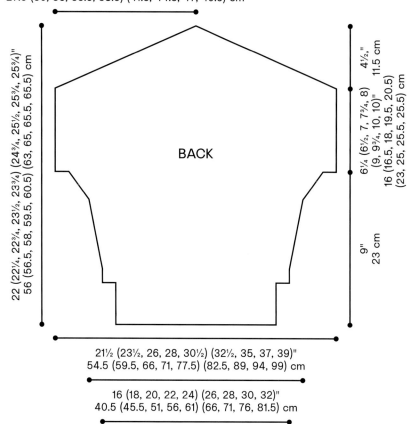

22 (22¼, 22¾, 23½, 23¾) (24¾, 25½, 25¾, 25¾)"
56 (56.5, 58, 59.5, 60.5) (63, 65, 65.5, 65.5) cm

4½"
11.5 cm

6¼ (6½, 7, 7¾, 8)
(9, 9¾, 10, 10)"
16 (16.5, 18, 19.5, 20.5)
(23, 25, 25.5, 25.5) cm

9"
23 cm

21½ (23½, 26, 28, 30½) (32½, 35, 37, 39)"
54.5 (59.5, 66, 71, 77.5) (82.5, 89, 94, 99) cm

16 (18, 20, 22, 24) (26, 28, 30, 32)"
40.5 (45.5, 51, 56, 61) (66, 71, 76, 81.5) cm

14 (16½, 18, 20½, 22) (24½, 26, 28½, 30)"
35.5 (42, 45.5, 52, 56) (62, 66, 72.5, 76) cm

## FRONT

Work as for Back until piece measures
2¼ (2½, 3, 3¼, 3½) (4½, 4¾, 5, 5)" [5.5
(6.5, 7.5, 8.5, 9) (11.5, 12, 12.5, 12.5) cm]
from Sleeve CO, ending with a WS
row—108 (118, 130, 140, 152) (162, 174, 184,
196) sts.

## SHAPE NECK

**Division Row (RS):** K19 (24, 30, 35, 41)
(44, 50, 55, 61), join a second ball of yarn,
BO 70 (70, 70, 70, 70) (74, 74, 74, 74) sts,
knit to end.

**CO Row (WS):** Working both sides at the
same time, purl to BO sts, turn to WS;
using Cable Cast-On, CO 35 (35, 35,
35, 35) (37, 37, 37, 37) sts, turn to RS;
on second side, using yarn attached to
second side and Cable Cast-On, CO 35
(35, 35, 35, 35) (37, 37, 37, 37) sts, purl
to end—54 (59, 65, 70, 76) (81, 87, 92, 98)
sts each side.

Work even until piece measures 6¼ (6½,
7, 7¾, 8) (9, 9¾, 10, 10)" [16 (16.5, 18, 19.5,
20.5) (23, 25, 25.5, 25.5) cm] from Sleeve
CO, ending with a WS row.

## SHAPE SHOULDERS

BO 4 (4, 4, 5, 5) (5, 6, 6, 7) sts at each
armhole edge 5 (10, 11, 5, 11) (11, 6, 11, 1)
time(s), then 3 (3, 2, 4, 2) (3, 5, 3, 6) sts
6 (1, 10, 6, 10) (4, 5, 4, 10) time(s), then 2
(2, 1, 2, 1) (2, 3, 2, 3) st(s) 5 (5, 1, 10, 1) (7,
4, 7, 9) times, then 1 (1, 0, 1, 0) (0, 2, 0, 2)
st(s) 6 (6, 0, 1, 0) (0, 7, 0, 2) time(s)—0 sts
remain each side.

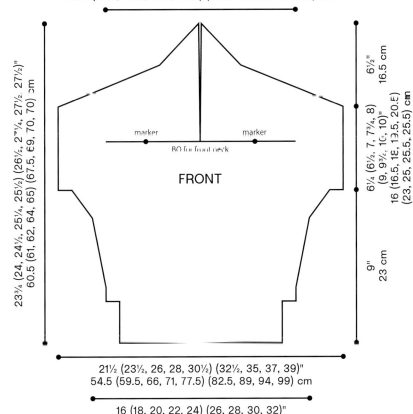

10¾ (11¾, 13, 14, 15¼) (16¼, 17½, 18½, 19½)"
27.5 (30, 33, 35.5, 38.5) (41.5, 44.5, 47, 49.5) cm

8 (8, 8, 8, 8) (9, 9, 9, 9)"
20½ (20½, 20½, 20½, 20½) (23, 23, 23, 23) cm

14 (14, 14, 14, 14) (14¾, 14¾, 14¾, 14¾)"
35.5 (35.5, 35.5, 35.5, 35.5) (37.5, 37.5, 37.5, 37.5) cm

23¾ (24, 24½, 25¼, 25½) (26½, 27¼, 27½, 27½)"
60.5 (61, 62, 64, 65) (67.5, 69, 70, 70) cm

marker — BO for front neck — marker

FRONT

6½" 16.5 cm

6¼ (6½, 7, 7¾, 8) (9, 9¾, 10, 10)"
16 (16.5, 18, 19.5, 20.5) (23, 25, 25.5, 25.5) cm

9" 23 cm

21½ (23½, 26, 28, 30½) (32½, 35, 37, 39)"
54.5 (59.5, 66, 71, 77.5) (82.5, 89, 94, 99) cm

16 (18, 20, 22, 24) (26, 28, 30, 32)"
40.5 (45.5, 51, 56, 61) (66, 71, 76, 81.5) cm

14 (16½, 18, 20½, 22) (24½, 26, 28½, 30)"
35.5 (42, 45.5, 52, 56) (62, 66, 72.5, 76) cm

## FINISHING

### NECK EDGING

With RS facing, using smaller needles and 2 strands of yarn held together, pick up and knit 74 (74, 74, 74, 74) (78, 78, 78, 78) sts across BO sts at base of neck opening. Begin 2×2 Rib; work 3 rows even. BO all sts in pattern. Sew side edges of rib to RS of Front.

Steam or wet-block pieces to measurements. Place removable marker at center of pick-up ridge for Front neck ribbing, then place one more marker 4 (4, 4, 4, 4) (4½, 4½, 4½, 4½)" [10 (10, 10, 10, 10) (11½, 11½, 11½, 11½) cm] to either side of center marker on pick-up ridge; remove center marker. Pin corner of CO edge of each side at markers. Make two left-facing pleats on right side of neck opening, each approximately 1" (2.5 cm) wide; pin layers together at CO edge. Sew pleated edge to pick-up ridge, beginning at marker and adjusting width of pleats if necessary to ease edge into seam. Repeat for left side of neck opening, making two right-facing pleats. Sew shoulder seams.

### ARMHOLE EDGING

With RS facing, using smaller needles and 2 strands of yarn held together, pick up and knit 66 (70, 74, 82, 86) (98, 106, 106, 106) sts along straight edge of Sleeve. Begin 2×2 Rib; work 3 rows even. BO all sts in pattern.
Sew side and sleeve seams.

# DESIGN YOUR OWN

## DESIGNING ANNE²

Most of the designing in this top is not new territory. The cropped length, extended dolmans, and sloped shoulder shaping are all elements I have worked with before and are shown easily on a typical schematic. The complications came in the neckline. How much width would each pleat take up? What shape would the neckline pieces need to be? First, I pleated my swatch to approximate the look I was going for and how much fabric each pleat took up. Then I took a good look at the schematic. In the vintage sketch that inspired me, there was a horizontal line that formed the bottom of the neck and on either side of the opening, served as a base for the attachment of the pleats. I could accomplish this by making a horizontal slit at the depth I wanted the neckline. I drew that as a horizontal line on the schematic. The simplest way to open up the neckline to make way for a head

is to split it down the middle, so I drew that line in, too. If I put the pleats in the bottom of each side of the neck, what would happen? How much width would I have left? Would I have to add more width to each side of the neck? Well, it turned out the width was already perfect. When knit and pleated, the neckline forms a diagonal line from the back of the neck to the bottom of the neckline. I left the neckline edges unfinished. The soft roll made a nice edge, and it is stretchy, which worked well as the once-vertical edge became a longer diagonal.

## SLIT AND PLEAT

As described above, Anne²'s focal point is the neckline, made by binding off to create a horizontal opening, pleating the knit fabric above it, then securing the pleats to the edge of the opening. This was my first foray into shaping a garment this way, which leads me

to wonder where else the technique might come in handy. Indulging in a little brainstorming, I can visualize doing something similar wherever I might want an isolated length of pleating—maybe on the side of a blousy hat, above the waistband of a feminine pullover, as an accent on sleeves, or placed near the top of a skirt. In all of these cases I wouldn't want to create an opening like Anne²'s neck opening. I wouldn't have fabric to pull to each side of an opening, so extra fabric would be needed to form the pleats. After binding off to create the slit, on the next row, I would immediately cast on not only the stitches needed to replace the bound-off stitches, but also enough additional stitches to form the pleating. The pleats could be sewn directly to the bound-off edge, forming a seam, or a finished edge like garter or ribbing could be added to disguise the base of the pleats, like at the lower edge of Anne²'s neckline.

# Ruche

A dramatic ruched sleeve is the focal point of this otherwise calm and refined pullover. The front and back both have a center panel, knit from bottom to top, with side panels picked up and worked outward. The sleeve is similarly constructed, with the ruched panel knit first then the side panels picked up in a way that forms loops in the side of the center panel. These loops are later reinforced with a few sewn stitches for maximum effect.

## FINISHED MEASUREMENTS
36½ (40½, 44½, 48, 52) (56, 60, 64, 68)" [92.5 (103, 113, 122, 132) (142, 152.5, 162.5, 172.5) cm] chest

Note: This piece is intended to be worn with approximately 6" (15 cm) positive ease.

## YARN
Brooklyn Tweed Dapple [60% merino wool/40% organic cotton; 165 yards (151 m)/1¾ ounces (50 g)]: 10 (11, 12, 13, 13) (14, 15, 16, 18) skeins #745 Seafoam

## NEEDLES
One pair straight needles, size US 6 (4 mm)

One 16" (40 cm) long circular needle, size US 4 (3.5 mm)

One pair straight needles, size US 4 (3.5 mm)

Change needle size if necessary to obtain correct gauge.

## NOTIONS
Stitch markers

Stitch holders or waste yarn

## GAUGE
22 sts and 32 rows = 4" (10 cm) in St st, using larger needles

## PATTERN STITCHES

### FLAT 2×2 RIB
(multiple of 4 sts + 2; 2-row repeat)
**Row 1 (WS):** P2, *k2, p2; repeat from * to end.
**Row 2:** K2, *p2, k2; repeat from * to end.
Repeat Rows 1 and 2 for pattern.

### CIRCULAR 2×2 RIB
(multiple of 4 sts; 1-rnd repeat)
**All Rnds:** *K2, p2; repeat from * to end.

### RUCHING PATTERN
(any number of sts; 12-row repeat)
**Row 1 (RS):** Knit.
**Row 2:** Purl.
**Rows 3 and 4:** Repeat Rows 1 and 2.
**Row 5:** P3, knit to last 3 sts, p3.
**Row 6:** K3, purl to last 3 sts, k3.
**Rows 7–10:** Repeat Rows 5 and 6 twice.
**Row 11:** Knit.
**Row 12:** Purl.
Repeat Rows 1–12 for pattern.

## PATTERN NOTES
The Back and Front are each worked in four sections. The Center Panel is worked from the bottom up, then each Side Panel is picked up from the Center Panel and worked outward to the armhole edge. The Bottom Rib is added last. The Sleeves are worked in five segments The Center Panel is worked from the bottom up, then each Side Panel is picked up and worked outward to the side edges. The top of the Sleeve is worked to the end of the cap from a combination of picked-up stitches and live stitches from the Center Panel. The sleeve cuff is added last. The shoulder seams are sewn together and the Sleeves are set in, then the side seams of the Back, Front, and Sleeves are joined using the 3-Needle Bind-Off (see Special Techniques, page 222).

## CENTER BACK PANEL
Using larger needles and Long-Tail Cast-On (see Special Techniques, page 221), CO 50 (56, 56, 60, 60) (60, 66, 66, 66) sts.
Begin St st; work even until piece measures 20½ (21, 21¼, 21½, 21¾) (22, 22½, 23, 23½)" [52 (53.5, 54, 54.5, 55) (56, 57, 58.5, 59.5) cm] from the beginning, ending with a WS row.

### SHAPE NECK
**Next Row (RS):** K18 (21, 21, 21, 21) (21, 21, 21, 21), join a second ball of yarn, BO center 14 (14, 14, 18, 18) (18, 24, 24, 24) sts, knit to end—18 (21, 21, 21, 21) (21, 21, 21, 21) sts remain each side.
Working both sides at the same time, BO 5 sts at each neck edge 3 times—3 (6, 6, 6, 6) (6, 6, 6, 6) sts remain each side.
Purl 1 row.
BO remaining sts.

## LEFT BACK PANEL
With RS of Center Back Panel facing, using larger needles, pick up and knit 118 (121, 122, 124, 125) (127, 129, 132, 135) sts along left edge of Center Back Panel.
Purl 1 row.

### SHAPE SHOULDER
**Shoulder Decrease Row (RS):** K2, k2tog, knit to end—1 st decreased.
Repeat Shoulder Decrease Row every other row 6 (6, 4, 4, 3) (3, 3, 1, 0) more time(s), then every 4 rows 0 (0, 2, 2, 3) (3, 3, 5, 5) times, then every 6 rows 0 (0, 0, 0, 0) (0, 0, 0, 1) time(s)—111 (114, 115, 117, 118) (120, 122, 125, 128) sts remain.
Purl 1 row.

## SHAPE ARMHOLE

Bind off at beginning of RS rows 34 (36, 36, 36, 34) (30, 30, 30, 30) sts once, then 2 sts 3 (3, 4, 5, 6) (8, 7, 7, 7) times—71 (72, 71, 71, 72) (74, 78, 81, 84) sts remain. Purl 1 row.

**Armhole Decrease Row (RS):** K1, k2tog, knit to end—1 st decreased.

Repeat Armhole Decrease Row every RS row 0 (1, 1, 1, 2) (3, 5, 6, 7) more time(s)—70 (70, 69, 69, 69) (70, 72, 74, 76) sts remain.

Work even until piece measures 4½ (5, 6, 6½, 7½) (8½, 9, 10, 11)" [11.5 (12.5, 15, 16.5, 19) (21.5, 23, 25.5, 28) cm] from pick-up row, ending with a WS row. Cut yarn, transfer sts to st holder or waste yarn, and set aside.

## RIGHT BACK PANEL

With RS of Center Back Panel facing, using larger needles, pick up and knit 118 (121, 122, 124, 125) (127, 129, 132, 135) sts along right edge of Center Back Panel. Purl 1 row.

### SHAPE SHOULDER

**Shoulder Decrease Row (RS):** Knit to last 4 sts, ssk, k2—1 st decreased.

Repeat Shoulder Decrease Row every other row 6 (6, 4, 4, 3) (3, 3, 1, 0) more time(s), then every 4 rows 0 (0, 2, 2, 3) (3, 3, 5, 5) times, then every 6 rows 0 (0, 0, 0, 0) (0, 0, 0, 1) time(s)—111 (114, 115, 117, 118) (120, 122, 125, 128) sts remain.

### SHAPE ARMHOLE

Bind off at beginning of WS rows 34 (36, 36, 36, 34) (30, 30, 30, 30) sts once, then 2 sts 3 (3, 4, 5, 6) (8, 7, 7, 7) times—71 (72, 71, 71, 72) (74, 78, 81, 84) sts remain.

**Armhole Decrease Row (RS):** Knit to last 3 sts, ssk, k1—1 st decreased.

Repeat Armhole Decrease Row every RS row 0 (1, 1, 1, 2) (3, 5, 6, 7) more time(s)—70 (70, 69, 69, 69) (70, 72, 74, 76) sts remain.

Work even until piece measures 4½ (5, 6, 6½, 7½) (8½, 9, 10, 11)" [11 (12.5, 15, 16.5, 19) (21.5, 23, 25.5, 28) cm] from pick-up row, ending with a WS row. Cut yarn, transfer sts to st holder or waste yarn, and set aside.

## BACK BOTTOM RIB

With RS of Back facing, using smaller needles, pick up and knit 110 (122, 134, 146, 158) (170, 182, 194, 206) sts along bottom edge.
Begin Flat 2×2 Rib; work even for 2" (5 cm), ending with a WS row.
BO all sts in pattern.

## CENTER FRONT PANEL

Work as for Center Back Panel until piece measures 18½ (19, 19¼, 19, 19¼) (19½, 19½, 20, 20½)" [47 (48.5, 49, 48.5, 49) (49.5, 49.5, 51, 52) cm] from the beginning, ending with a WS row.

### SHAPE NECK

**Next Row (RS):** K20 (23, 23, 23, 23) (23, 23, 23, 23), join a second ball of yarn, BO center 10 (10, 10, 14, 14) (14, 20, 20, 20) sts, work to end—20 (23, 23, 23, 23) (23, 23, 23, 23) sts remain each side.

Working both sides at the same time, BO 4 sts at each neck edge once, 3 sts twice, then 2 sts twice—6 (9, 9, 9, 9) (9, 9, 9, 9) sts remain each side.

**Decrease Row (RS):** Knit to 3 sts before neck, ssk, k1; k1, k2tog, knit to end—1 st decreased each side.

Repeat Decrease Row every RS row 2 more times—3 (6, 6, 6, 6) (6, 6, 6, 6) sts remain each side.

Work even until piece measures same as for Center Back Panel, ending with a WS row.
BO remaining sts.

## RIGHT FRONT PANEL

Work as for Left Back Panel.

## LEFT FRONT PANEL

Work as for Right Back Panel.

## FRONT BOTTOM RIB

Work as for Back Bottom Rib.

## CENTER SLEEVE PANEL

Using larger needles and Long-Tail Cast-On, CO 46 (49, 51, 53, 55) (56, 59, 62, 65) sts.
Purl 1 row.
Begin Ruching Pattern; work Rows 1–12 a total of 20 (21, 22, 23, 23) (23, 23, 23, 24) times, then work Rows 1 and

2 once more; piece should measure approximately 30¼ (31¾, 33¼, 34¾, 34¾) (34¾, 34¾, 34¾, 36¼)" [77 (80.5, 84.5, 88.5, 88.5) (88.5, 88.5, 88.5, 92) cm]. Cut yarn, transfer sts to st holder or waste yarn, and set aside.

## LEFT SLEEVE PANEL

*Note: You will pick up a total of 4 sts from the edge sts in each 12-row repeat of the Ruching Pattern, picking up sts from the rows where the edge sts are worked in St st and skipping the rows where the edge sts are worked in Rev St st (purl). This will reduce the length of the Center Sleeve Panel by approximately one half.*

With RS of Center Sleeve Panel facing, using larger needles, pick up and knit sts along left edge of Center Sleeve Panel as follows:

Beginning at top of Center Sleeve Panel, below held sts, and picking up between the first and second st of the row, pick up and knit 3 sts in the first 4-row section (rows with a knit edge st), *skip next 6-row section (rows with a purl edge st), pick up and knit 4 sts in next 6-row section (rows with a knit st at the edge); repeat from * to last St st section of Ruching Pattern, pick up and knit 3 sts to end—82 (86, 90, 94, 94) (94, 94, 94, 98) sts.

Begin St st; work even for 1" (2.5 cm), ending with a WS row.

### SHAPE SIDE PANEL

*Note: Side panel is shaped using German Short Rows (see Special Techniques, page 221).*

**Short Row 1 (RS):** Knit to last 6 (6, 5, 5, 5) (4, 4, 4, 4) sts, turn;

**Short Row 2 (WS):** DS, purl to end.

**Short Row 3:** Knit to 6 (6, 5, 5, 5) (4, 4, 4, 4) sts before DS from previous RS row, turn;

**Short Row 4:** DS, purl to end.

Repeat Short Rows 3 and 4 nine (9, 6, 8, 12) (16, 17, 17, 17) more times.

### SIZES 44½, 48, 52, 56, 60, 64, AND 68 ONLY:

**Short Row 5:** Knit to - (-, 6, 6, 6) (5, 5, 5, 5) sts before DS from previous RS row, turn;

**Short Row 6:** DS, purl to end.
Repeat Short Rows 5 and 6 - (-, 4, 3, 0) (0, 0, 0, 0) more times.

## ALL SIZES

**Short Row 7 (RS):** Knit to end, closing each DS as you come to it.
Cut yarn, transfer sts to st holder or waste yarn, and set aside.

## RIGHT SLEEVE PANEL

With RS of Center Sleeve Panel facing, using larger needles, pick up and knit sts along right edge of Center Sleeve Panel as follows:
Beginning at bottom of Center Sleeve panel, and picking up between the first and second st of the row, pick up and knit 3 sts in the first 4 row section (rows with a knit edge st), *skip next 6-row section (rows with a purl edge st), pick up and knit 4 sts in next 6-row section (rows with a knit st at the edge); repeat from * to last St st section of Ruching Pattern, pick up and knit 3 sts to end—82 (86, 90, 94, 94) (94, 94, 94, 98) sts.
Begin St st; work even for 1" (2.5 cm), ending with a RS row.

## SHAPE SIDE PANEL

**Short Row 1 (WS):** Purl to last 6 (6, 5, 5, 5) (4, 4, 4, 4) sts, turn;
**Short Row 2 (RS):** DS, knit to end
**Short Row 3:** Purl to 6 (6, 5, 5, 5) (4, 4, 4, 4) sts before DS from previous WS row, turn;
**Short Row 4:** DS, knit to end.
Repeat Short Rows 3 and 4 nine (9, 6, 8, 12) (16, 17, 17, 17) more times.

## SIZES 44½, 48, 52, 56, 60, 64, AND 68 ONLY:

**Short Row 5:** Purl to - (-, 6, 6, 6) (5, 5, 5, 5) sts before DS from previous WS row, turn;
**Short Row 6:** DS, knit to end.
Repeat Short Rows 5 and 6 - (-, 4, 3, 0) (0, 0, 0, 0) more times.

## ALL SIZES

**Short Row 7 (WS):** Purl to end, closing each DS as you come to it.
Cut yarn, transfer sts to st holder or waste yarn, and set aside.

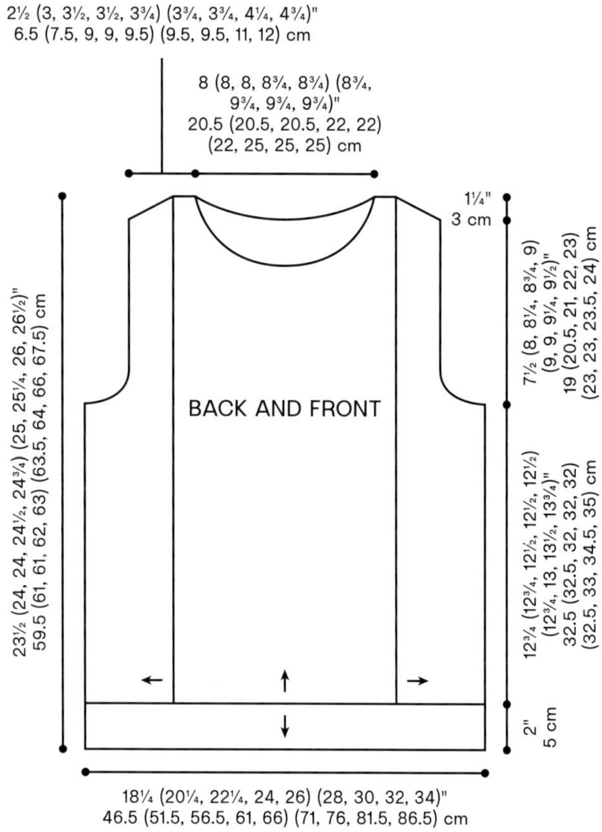
2½ (3, 3½, 3½, 3¾) (3¾, 3¾, 4¼, 4¾)"
6.5 (7.5, 9, 9, 9.5) (9.5, 9.5, 11, 12) cm
8 (8, 8, 8¾, 8¾) (8¾, 9¾, 9¾, 9¾)"
20.5 (20.5, 20.5, 22, 22) (22, 25, 25, 25) cm
1¼"
3 cm
7½ (8, 8¼, 8¾, 9) (9, 9, 9¼, 9½)"
19 (20.5, 21, 22, 23) (23, 23, 23.5, 24) cm
12¾ (12¾, 12½, 12½, 12½) (12¾, 13, 13½, 13¾)"
32.5 (32.5, 32, 32, 32) (32.5, 33, 34.5, 35) cm
2"
5 cm
23½ (24, 24, 24½, 24¾) (25, 25¼, 26, 26½)"
59.5 (61, 61, 62, 63) (63.5, 64, 66, 67.5) cm
BACK AND FRONT
18¼ (20¼, 22¼, 24, 26) (28, 30, 32, 34)"
46.5 (51.5, 56.5, 61, 66) (71, 76, 81.5, 86.5) cm

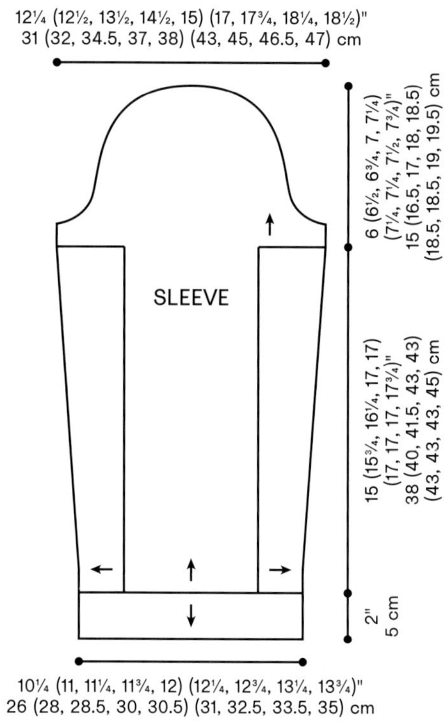
12¼ (12½, 13½, 14½, 15) (17, 17¾, 18¼, 18½)"
31 (32, 34.5, 37, 38) (43, 45, 46.5, 47) cm
6 (6½, 6¾, 7, 7¼) (7¼, 7¼, 7½, 7¾)"
15 (16.5, 17, 18, 18.5) (18.5, 18.5, 19, 19.5) cm
SLEEVE
15 (15¾, 16¼, 17, 17) (17, 17, 17, 17¾)"
38 (40, 41.5, 43, 43) (43, 43, 43, 45) cm
2"
5 cm
10¼ (11, 11¼, 11¾, 12) (12¼, 12¾, 13¼, 13¾)"
26 (28, 28.5, 30, 30.5) (31, 32.5, 33.5, 35) cm

## TOP OF SLEEVE

With RS of Right Sleeve Panel facing, using larger needles, pick up and knit 18 (18, 20, 22, 23) (28, 29, 29, 29) sts along top edge of Right Sleeve Panel; working across sts from Center Sleeve Panel, *k1, k2tog; repeat from * to last 1 (1, 0, 2, 1) (2, 2, 2, 2) st(s) of Center Sleeve Panel, k1 (1, 0, 2, 1) (2, 2, 2, 2); pick up and knit 18 (18, 20, 22, 23) (28, 29, 29, 29) sts along top edge of Left Sleeve Panel–67 (69, 74, 80, 83) (94, 98, 100, 102) sts.

Begin St st; work 5 rows even.

### SHAPE CAP

BO 3 (3, 4, 6, 7) (9, 11, 12, 13) sts at beginning of next 2 rows, then 2 sts at beginning of next 2 (2, 2, 4, 4) (6, 6, 6, 6) rows–57 (59, 62, 60, 61) (64, 64, 64, 64) sts remain.

**Decrease Row (RS):** K1, k2tog, knit to last 3 sts, ssk, k1–2 sts decreased.

Repeat Decrease Row every RS row 5 (5, 6, 5, 4) (7, 6, 5, 4) more times, then every 4 rows 2 (3, 3, 4, 5) (2, 2, 3, 5) times, then every RS row 6 (6, 6, 4, 4) (5, 6, 6, 4) times–29 (29, 30, 32, 33) (34, 34, 34, 36) sts remain.

BO 2 sts at beginning of next 2 rows, then 3 sts at beginning of next 2 rows. BO remaining 19 (19, 20, 22, 23) (24, 24, 24, 26) sts.

## SLEEVE CUFF

With RS of Sleeve facing, using smaller needles, pick up and knit 42 (46, 50, 54, 54) (58, 62, 62, 66) sts along bottom edge.

Begin Flat 2×2 Rib; work even for 2" (5 cm).

BO all sts in pattern.

## FINISHING

Block as desired.

Sew shoulder seams. Sew in Sleeves.

With RSs of Front and Back together, beginning at armhole, join side sts using 3-Needle Bind-Off, then sew side edges of Ribbing. Repeat for Sleeve seams.

### NECKBAND

With RS facing, using circular needle and beginning at center Back, pick up and knit 20 (22, 23, 24, 24) (25, 25, 25, 26) sts to left shoulder, 56 (56, 58, 60, 64) (62, 62, 66, 64) sts to right shoulder, then 20 (22, 23, 24, 24) (25, 25, 25, 26) sts to center Back–96 (100, 104, 108, 112) (112, 112, 116, 116) sts. Join for working in the rnd; pm for beginning of rnd.

Begin Circular 2×2 Rib; work even for 1" (2.5 cm). BO all sts in pattern.

To accentuate Sleeve ruching, with RS facing, using tapestry needle and yarn, pinch one protruding loop of ruching and tack through both layers about ¼" (6 mm) in from seam. Weave yarn along seam to next loop and tack that loop. Continue in this manner until all loops on first side are tacked. Repeat for opposite side.

# DESIGN YOUR OWN

## DESIGNING RUCHE

Resplendently puckered sleeves saved to my Pinterest boards spurred me to want to figure out how to translate the concept into hand knitting. Keen on the idea of using some sort of knit-in guides to make picking up stitches an easier task, I envisioned the center ruched panel worked from bottom to top, with a few stitches at each end alternating a half inch or so of stockinette, then reverse stockinette. The sides of the sleeves would be picked up and worked outward, with stitches picked up in the stockinette segments while skipping over the reverse stockinette. In my test swatch the skipped sections stood up nicely in a loop and looked like ruching. The side panels would be worked in stockinette stitch and shaped with short rows to make the sleeve go from narrow at the wrist to loose-fitting at the bicep. There was enough going on in this sleeve that I didn't want the ruching to complicate the sleeve cap. It was easier for me to figure out how to write the sleeve if, starting just below the armhole, the top of the sleeve was picked up and worked upward, with a few stitches decreased above the ruched panel. I had added extra width to the panel for fullness. With the puzzle of the ruched sleeve figured out, I could think about the body of the sweater. Wanting to echo the sleeve construction, I decided there would be a center panel knit from bottom to top, with side panels picked up and worked outward. Everything was going fine until the sample, beautifully knit by someone else, was returned to me and I could see that the ruching was not the striking feature I had hoped for. The loops formed between the picked-up stitches didn't stand up as dramatically as they did in my small swatch. They needed some help. I reached for yarn and a tapestry needle and sewed a few big stitches into the base of each loop, using one continuous piece of yarn as I put a tack into each loop down each side of the center panel. These simple sewn stitches made all the difference, creating the dimensional ruching I desired.

## ADD RUCHING

An alternative idea for making ruching, one that I haven't tested, would be to tuck as you go, the way the tucks are created for Hussar (page 71) and Pinion (page 77). Use the same alternation of stockinette and reverse stockinette on the edges of a ruched panel and connect the bottom of the reverse section to the top while working the first stockinette stitch row.

Where else can you picture adding ruching? My instinct is to use it sparingly. Maybe the center panel of a sweater, and not the sleeve panel. How about where the skirt meets the yoke in a baby dress? Narrower panels would create a more distinct, while still soft, ridge, spanning from one side of the panel to the other. You might make a compelling cowl or enchanting fingerless mitts.

# Waterfall

At first glance, the arched and fluttering front of Waterfall appears more complicated than it really is—it's simply a rectangle, knit into an upside down V-shaped opening of an otherwise basic pullover. The corners of the rectangle create an interesting pointed hem, while excess fabric in the center sways gracefully, forming ephemeral folds that change as the wearer moves.

## FINISHED MEASUREMENTS
32 (36¼, 40, 44¼, 48) (52½, 56, 60½, 64)" [81.5 (92.5, 101.5, 113, 122) (133.5, 142, 153.5, 162.5) cm]

*Note: This piece is intended to be worn with approximately 2" (5 cm) positive ease.*

## YARN
The Fibre Co. Acadia [60% merino wool/20% baby alpaca/20% silk; 145 yards (133 m)/1¾ ounces (50 g)]: 8 (8, 9, 10, 10) (11, 12, 13, 14) hanks Driftwood

## NEEDLES
One 32" (80 cm) or longer circular needle, size US 5 (3.75 mm)

One 24" (60 cm) circular needle, size US 4 (3.5 mm)

Change needle size if necessary to obtain correct gauge.

## NOTIONS
Stitch marker

## GAUGE
22 sts and 32 rows = 4" (10 cm) in St st using larger needle

## PATTERN NOTES
This top is worked flat in pieces, then sewn together. The front insert is picked up from the Right and Left Fronts, joining them at the base of the neck.

## BACK
Using larger needle and Cable Cast-On (see Special Techniques, page 221), CO 88 (100, 110, 122, 132) (144, 154, 166, 176) sts.
Purl 1 row, knit 1 row.
Begin St st; work even until piece measures 10¼ (10¼, 10, 10, 10) (10¼, 10½, 10¾, 11)" [26 (26, 25.5, 25.5, 25.5) (26, 26.5, 27.5, 28) cm] from the beginning, ending with a WS row.

## SHAPE ARMHOLES
BO 6 sts at beginning of next 0 (0, 0, 0, 0) (2, 2, 2, 2) rows, 5 sts at beginning of next 0 (0, 0, 0, 2) (2, 2, 2, 2) rows, 4 sts at beginning of next 2 rows, 3 sts at beginning of next 2 rows, then 2 sts at beginning of next 2 (2, 4, 4, 4) (4, 6, 6, 8) rows—70 (82, 88, 100, 100) (100, 106, 118, 124) sts remain.

**Decrease Row (RS):** K1, k2tog, knit to last 3 sts, ssk, k1—2 sts decreased.
Repeat Decrease Row every RS row 1 (4, 4, 8, 7) (6, 7, 10, 10) more time(s)—66 (72, 78, 82, 84) (86, 90, 96, 102) sts remain.
Work even until armholes measure 7 (7½, 8, 8¼, 8½) (8½, 8¾, 9, 9¼)" [18 (19, 20.5, 21, 21.5) (21.5, 22, 23, 23.5) cm], ending with a WS row.

## SHAPE SHOULDERS AND NECK
*Note: Shoulder and neck shaping are worked at the same time; please read entire section through before beginning.*
**Next Row (RS):** BO 3 (4, 5, 5, 5) (5, 6, 6, 7) sts (1 st left on right needle), k23 (24, 26, 28, 28) (29, 30, 31, 33), join a second ball of yarn and BO the next 12 (14, 14, 14, 16) (16, 16, 20, 20) sts, knit to end. Working both sides at the same time, BO 3 (4, 5, 5, 5) (5, 6, 6, 7) sts at beginning of next row, then BO 3 (4, 4, 5, 5) (5, 6, 6, 7) sts at each armhole edge 3 (1, 3, 2, 2) (3, 1, 2, 1) time(s), then 0 (3, 0, 4, 4) (0, 5, 5, 6) sts at each armhole edge 0 (2, 0, 1, 1) (0, 2, 1, 2) time(s). AT THE SAME TIME, BO 5 sts at each neck edge 3 times.

## LEFT FRONT
Using larger needle and your preferred CO method, CO 3 sts.
Purl 1 row.

## SHAPE LOWER FRONT EDGE, ARMHOLE, NECK, AND SHOULDER
*Note: Lower Front edge, armhole, neck, and shoulder shaping are worked at the same time. Lower Front edge shaping begins first and continues through the beginning of armhole shaping. When Lower Front edge shaping is complete, neck shaping begins. Neck shaping continues through beginning of shoulder shaping for some sizes. Each shaping section is presented separately, but must be worked at the same time as the section following it; please read through to Shape Shoulder before beginning.*

## SHAPE LOWER FRONT EDGE

### SIZES 30 AND 34 ONLY:

**Increase Row (RS):** Working in St st, work to last st, M1R, k1—1 st increased.
Repeat Increase Row every RS row 36 (46, -, -, -) (-, -, -, -) more times, then every 4th row 4 (0, -, -, -) (-, -, -, -) times—44 (50, -, -, -) (-, -, -, -) sts.
Purl 1 row.
AT THE SAME TIME, when piece measures 10¼" (26 cm) from the beginning, ending with a WS row, begin armhole shaping (see Shape Armhole below).

### SIZES 38, 42, 46, 50, 54, 58, AND 62 ONLY:

**\*Single Increase Row (RS):** Working in St st, work to last st, M1R, k1—1 st increased.
Repeat Single Increase Row every RS Row - (-, 10, 6, 2) (1, 0, 0, 0) time(s).
Purl 1 row.
**Double Increase Row (RS):** Work to last 3 sts, M1R, k2, M1R, k1—2 sts increased.
Purl 1 row.
Repeat from \* - (-, 3, 5, 11) (16, 21, 25, 27) more times— - (-, 55, 57, 63) (71, 69, 81, 87) sts.
Repeat Single Increase Row every RS row - (-, 0, 4, 3) (1, 8, 2, 1) more time(s)— - (-, 55, 61, 72) (72, 77, 83, 88) sts.
Purl 1 row.
AT THE SAME TIME, when piece measures - (-, 10, 10, 10) (10¼, 10½, 10¾, 11)" [26 (26, 25.5, 25.5, 25.5) (26, 26.5, 27.5, 28) cm] from the beginning, ending with a WS row, begin armhole shaping (see Shape Armhole below).

### ALL SIZES:

### SHAPE ARMHOLE

BO 6 sts at beginning of next 0 (0, 0, 0, 0) (1, 1, 1, 1) RS row(s), 5 sts at beginning of next 0 (0, 0, 0, 1) (1, 1, 1, 1) RS row(s), 4 sts at beginning of next RS row, 3 sts at beginning of next RS row, then 2 sts at beginning of next 1 (1, 2, 2, 2) (2, 3, 3, 4) RS row(s).
Purl 1 row.
**Armhole Decrease Row (RS):** K1, k2tog, work to end—1 st decreased.
Repeat Armhole Decrease Row every RS row 1 (4, 4, 8, 7) (6, 7, 10, 10) more time(s).
AT THE SAME TIME, when Lower Front edge shaping is complete, begin neck shaping as follows:

## SHAPE NECK

**Neck Decrease Row (RS):** Work to last 3 sts, ssk, k1—1 st decreased.
Repeat Neck Decrease Row every RS row 20 (21, 21, 21, 22) (22, 22, 24, 24) more times.
AT THE SAME TIME, when armhole measures 7 (7½, 8, 8¼, 8½) (8½, 8¾, 9, 9¼)" [18 (19, 20.5, 21, 21.5) (21.5, 22, 23, 23.5) cm], ending with a WS row, begin shoulder shaping, as follows:

## SHAPE SHOULDER

BO 3 (4, 5, 5, 5) (5, 6, 6, 7) sts at armhole edge 4 (2, 1, 3, 3) (4, 2, 3, 2) time(s), then 0 (3, 4, 4, 4) (0, 5, 5, 6) sts 0 (2, 3, 1, 1) (0, 2, 1, 2) time(s).

## RIGHT FRONT

Using larger needle and your preferred CO method, CO 3 sts.
Purl 1 row.

## SHAPE LOWER FRONT EDGE, ARMHOLE, NECK, AND SHOULDER

*Note: Lower Front edge, armhole, neck, and shoulder shaping are worked at the same time. Lower Front edge shaping begins first and continues through the beginning of armhole shaping. When Lower Front edge shaping is complete, neck shaping begins. Neck shaping continues through beginning of shoulder shaping for some sizes. Each shaping section is presented separately, but must be worked at the same time as the section following it; please read through to Shape Shoulder before beginning.*

## SHAPE LOWER FRONT EDGE

### SIZES 30 AND 34 ONLY:

**Increase Row (RS):** Working in St st, k1, M1L, work to end—1 st increased.
Repeat Increase Row every RS row 36 (46, -, -, -) (-, -, -, -) more times, then every 4th row 4 (0, -, -, -) (-, -, -, -) times—44 (50, -, -, -) (-, -, -, -) sts.
Purl 1 row.
AT THE SAME TIME, when piece measures 10¼" (26 cm) from the beginning, ending with a RS row, begin armhole shaping (see Shape Armhole below).

### SIZES 38, 42, 46, 50, 54, 58, AND 62 ONLY:

**\*Single Increase Row (RS):** Working in St st, k1, M1L, work to end—1 st increased.
Repeat Single Increase Row every RS Row - (-, 10, 6, 2) (1, 0, 0, 0) time(s).
Purl 1 row.
**Double Increase Row (RS):** K1, M1L, k2, M1L, work to end—2 sts increased.
Purl 1 row.
Repeat from \* - (-, 3, 5, 11) (16, 21, 25, 27) more times— - (-, 55, 57, 63) (71, 69, 81, 87) sts.
Repeat Single Increase Row every RS row - (-, 0, 4, 3) (1, 8, 2, 1) more time(s)— - (-, 55, 61, 72) (72, 77, 83, 88) sts.
Purl 1 row.
AT THE SAME TIME, when piece measures - (-, 10, 10, 10) (10¼, 10½, 10¾, 11)" [26 (26, 25.5, 25.5, 25.5) (26, 26.5, 27.5, 28) cm] from the beginning, ending with a RS row, begin armhole shaping (see Shape Armhole below).

### ALL SIZES:

### SHAPE ARMHOLE

BO 6 sts at beginning of next 0 (0, 0, 0, 0) (1, 1, 1, 1) WS row(s), 5 sts at beginning of next 0 (0, 0, 0, 1) (1, 1, 1, 1) WS row(s), 4 sts at beginning of next WS row, 3 sts at beginning of next WS row, then 2 sts at beginning of next 1 (1, 2, 2, 2) (2, 3, 3, 4) WS row(s).
**Armhole Decrease Row (RS):** K1, k2tog, work to end—1 st decreased.
Repeat Armhole Decrease Row every RS row 1 (4, 4, 8, 7) (6, 7, 10, 10) more time(s).
AT THE SAME TIME, when Lower Front edge shaping is complete, begin neck shaping as follows:

### SHAPE NECK

**Neck Decrease Row (RS):** K1, k2tog, work to end—1 st decreased.
Repeat Neck Decrease Row every RS row 20 (21, 21, 21, 22) (22, 22, 24, 24) more times.
AT THE SAME TIME, when armhole measures 7 (7½, 8, 8¼, 8½) (8½, 8¾, 9, 9¼)" [18 (19, 20.5, 21, 21.5) (21.5, 22, 23, 23.5) cm], ending with a RS row, begin shoulder shaping, as follows:

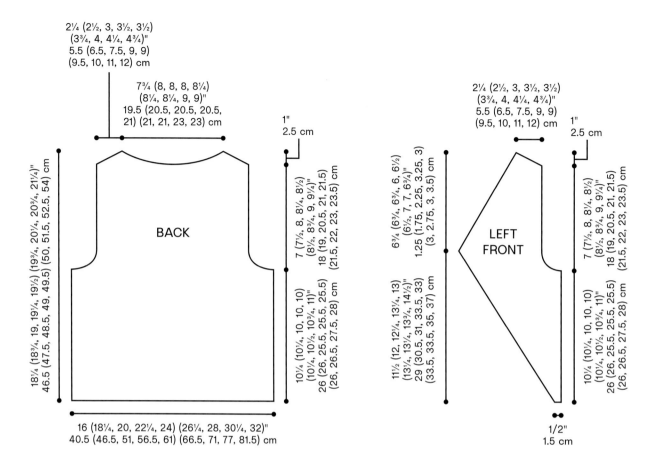

**SHAPE SHOULDER**

BO 3 (4, 5, 5) (5, 6, 6, 7) sts at armhole edge 4 (2, 1, 3, 3) (4, 2, 3, 2) time(s), then 0 (3, 4, 4, 4) (0, 5, 5, 6) sts 0 (2, 3, 1, 1) (0, 2, 1, 2) time(s).

**FRONT INSERT**

*Note: Front Insert is worked across both Right and Left Fronts, joining pieces at base of neck.*
With RS of Right and Left Fronts facing, using larger needle and beginning at bottom edge of Right Front, pick up and knit 77 (83, 87, 95, 97) (102, 106, 112, 119) sts along shaped edge to base of neck shaping, then beginning at base of Left Front neck shaping pick up and knit 77 (83, 87, 95, 97) (102, 106, 112, 119) sts along shaped lower edge of Left Front to bottom—154 (166, 174, 190, 194) (204, 212,

224, 238) sts. *Note: Pick up sts at a rate of approximately 11 sts for every 12 rows along shaped edge.*
**Row 1 (WS):** K1, purl to last st, k1.
**Row 2:** Knit.
Repeat Rows 1 and 2 until piece measures 8" (20.5 cm) from pick-up row, ending with a RS row.
BO all sts knitwise.

**SLEEVES**

Using larger needle and Cable Cast-On, CO 56 (58, 60, 62, 64) (66, 68, 72, 74) sts. Do not join.
Purl 1 row, knit 1 row.
Begin St st, beginning with a knit row; work even until piece measures 7" (18 cm) from the beginning, ending with a WS row.

**SHAPE SLEEVE**

**Increase Row (RS):** K2, M1L, knit to last 2 sts, M1R, k2–2 sts increased.
Repeat Increase Row every 24 (16, 12, 8, 6) (4, 4, 4, 4) rows 1 (1, 5, 4, 1) (8, 14, 11, 10) time(s), then every 26 (18, 0, 10, 8) (6, 6, 6, 6) rows 1 (2, 0, 3, 7) (5, 1, 3, 4) time(s)–62 (66, 72, 78, 82) (94, 100, 102, 104) sts.
Work even until piece measures 16¾ (17, 18, 18¼, 18¼) (18¼, 18¼, 18¼, 18½") [42.5 (43, 45.5, 46.5, 46.5) (46.5, 46.5, 46.5, 47) cm] from the beginning, ending with a WS row.

**SHAPE CAP**

BO 5 sts at beginning of next 0 (0, 0, 0, 0) (2, 2, 2, 2) rows, 4 sts at beginning of next 0 (0, 0, 0, 2) (2, 2, 2, 2) rows, 3 sts at beginning of next 2 rows, then 2 sts at

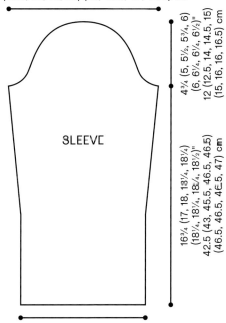

11¼ (12, 13, 14¼, 15) (17, 18¼, 18½, 19)"
28.5 (30.5, 33, 36, 38) (43, 46.5, 47, 48.5) cm

4¾ (5, 5½, 5¾, 6) (6, 6¼, 6¼, 6½)"
12 (12.5, 14, 14.5, 15) (15, 16, 16, 16.5) cm

SLEEVE

16¾ (17, 18, 18¼, 18¼) (18¼, 18¼, 18¾, 18½)"
42.5 (43, 45.5, 46.5, 46.5) (46.5, 46.5, 46.5, 47) cm

10¼ (10½, 11, 11¼, 11¾) (12, 12¼, 13, 13½)"
26 (26.5, 28, 28.5, 30) (30.5, 31, 33, 34.5) cm

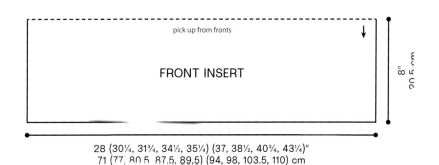

pick up from fronts

FRONT INSERT

8"
20.5 cm

28 (30¼, 31¾, 34½, 35¼) (37, 38½, 40¾, 43¼)"
71 (77, 80.5, 87.5, 89.5) (94, 98, 103.5, 110) cm

beginning of next 2 rows–52 (56, 62, 68, 64) (66, 72, 74, 76) sts remain.
**Decrease Row (RS):** K1, k2tog, knit to last 3 sts, ssk, k1–2 sts remain.
Repeat Decrease Row every RS row 2 (3, 5, 7, 4) (5, 7, 8, 8) more times, every 4 rows 5 (4, 3, 2, 5) (4, 3, 2, 2) times, then every RS row 2 (4, 6, 7, 5) (6, 7, 8, 9) times–32 (32, 32, 34, 34) (34, 36, 36, 36) sts remain.
BO 2 sts at beginning of next 2 rows, then 3 sts at beginning of next 2 rows.
BO remaining 22 (22, 22, 24, 24) (24, 26, 26, 26) sts.

## FINISHING

Block pieces as desired. Sew shoulder seams. Sew in sleeves; sew sleeve and side seams, leaving side edge of Front Inserts unsewn.

## NECKBAND

With RS facing, using smaller needle and beginning at base of Front neck, pick up and knit 43 (46, 46, 42, 45) (45, 48, 49, 47) sts to back neck edge, 45 (49, 49, 47, 51) (51, 51, 53, 55) sts along back neck edge, then 43 (46, 46, 42, 45) (45, 48, 49, 47) sts to center Front–137 (141, 141, 131, 141) (141, 147, 151, 149) sts. Do not join. Working back and forth in St st, work even for 1" (2.5 cm), ending with a WS row. BO all sts knitwise. *Note: Neckband will curl to the RS.*

# DESIGN YOUR OWN

### DESIGNING WATERFALL

I discovered the trick to Waterfall's cunning illusion a few years back. This isn't the first time I've taken advantage of the shape a rectangle becomes when set into an angled opening. I believe this is a trick worth repeating. While a soft, drapey knit rectangle added to the bottom of a straight edge is still nothing but a rectangle, one set into a tent shape folds over itself, mostly in the center, and begins to form rounded folds where gravity pulls it downward,

all giving the appearance of something more complicated. The exact angle doesn't matter much. Experiment with a large swatch pinned to your corkboard, shifting the angle until you start to see the draping you like.

### RECTANGULAR INSERTIONS

Consider a rectangular insertion when you want to create flowy areas and don't want to work hard to achieve the look. Here are three ways you might use a rectangular insertion:

1. Pick up and knit (or sew) a long rectangle up along the sides of a vertical slit for an easy ruffle.

2. Insert a rectangle into an upside-down V-shaped opening as in Waterfall. It doesn't have to be center front. What about on one side, or both sides, maybe replacing the center of a sleeve?

3. An arched opening can transform a rectangular insertion into an interesting godet, peplum, or bustle. Give it a try.

# Georgia

Two-color stripes of similar value and nearly opposite shades add a subtle color play to this cropped A-line jacket. In keeping with this book's philosophy of minimal finishing, the collar and neckband fold to the inside, forming a self facing. German short rows shape the collar perfectly to wrap around the neck, barely interrupting the strip pattern. A variation on seed stitch makes stripes less, well, stripy. The dramatic element of this jacket is provided by kicking off each sleeve with a large square that drapes naturally in curved folds when your arm is dropped at your side and shows its true shape more clearly when arms are raised—drama without melodrama.

## FINISHED MEASUREMENTS

32 (36, 40, 44, 48) (52, 56, 60, 64)" [81.5 (91.5, 101.5, 112, 122) (132, 142, 152.5, 162.5) cm] chest, with fronts overlapped

Note: This piece is intended to be worn with approximately 2–4" (5–10 cm) positive ease.

## YARN

Peace Fleece Worsted [75% Navajo Rambouillet and domestic fine wool/25% mohair; 200 yards (183 m)/4 ounces (113 g)]: 3 (3, 4, 4, 4) (5, 5, 5, 6) skeins each #736 Anna's Grasshopper (A) and #721 Mourning Dove (B)

## NEEDLES

One pair straight needles, size US 7 (4.5 mm)

Change needle size if necessary to obtain correct gauge.

## NOTIONS

Stitch markers

Removable stitch markers

Stitch holders

## GAUGE

16 sts and 30 rows = 4" (10 cm) in Seeded Stripe pattern

## PATTERN STITCH

### SEEDED STRIPE

(multiple of 2 sts + 6; 4-row repeat)
**Setup Row (WS):** With A, k3, *k1, p1; repeat from * to last 3 sts, k3.
**Row 1 (RS):** With B, knit.
**Row 2:** K3, *p1, k1; repeat from * to last 3 sts, k3.
**Row 3:** With A, knit.
**Row 4:** K3, *k1, p1; repeat from * to last 3 sts, k3.
Repeat Rows 1–4 for pattern.

## PATTERN NOTES

The Sleeve Flounces are worked first, then the Sleeves are picked up and worked from the Flounces. The Back and Fronts are worked separately with short-row shaping to shape the collar extensions, which are joined using 3-Needle Bind-Off (see Special Techniques, page 222).
When changing colors, do not cut yarn; carry color not in work loosely up edge.

## RIGHT SLEEVE FLOUNCE

Using A and Long-Tail Cast-On (see Special Techniques, page 221), CO 48 (50, 52, 54) (56, 56, 58, 60) sts.
Begin Seeded Stripe; work even until piece measures approximately 10" (25.5 cm) from the beginning, ending with a WS row.

## MAKE SLIT

**BO Row (RS):** BO 19 (20, 21, 23, 25) (26, 27, 29, 30) sts work to end—29 (30, 29, 29, 29) (30, 29, 29, 30) sts remain.
**CO Row (WS):** Work to end; using Cable Cast-On (see Special Techniques, page 221), CO 19 (20, 21, 23, 25) (26, 27, 29, 30) sts—48 (50, 50, 52, 54) (56, 56, 58, 60) sts.
Work even until piece measures approximately 10" (25.5 cm) from the slit, ending with a WS row.
BO all sts in pattern.

## LEFT SLEEVE FLOUNCE

Using A and Long-Tail Cast-On, CO 48 (50, 50, 52, 54) (56, 56, 58, 60) sts.
Begin Seeded Stripe; work even until piece measures approximately 10" (25.5 cm) from the beginning, ending with a RS row.

## MAKE SLIT

**BO Row (WS):** BO 19 (20, 21, 23, 25) (26, 27, 29, 30) sts, work to end—29 (30, 29, 29, 29) (30, 29, 29, 30) sts remain.
**CO Row (RS):** Work to end; using Cable Cast-On, CO 19 (20, 21, 23, 25) (26, 27, 29, 30) sts—48 (50, 50, 52, 54) (56, 56, 58, 60) sts.
Work even until piece measures approximately 10" (25.5 cm) from the slit, ending with a WS row.
BO all sts in pattern.

## LEFT SLEEVE

With RS of Left Sleeve Flounce facing, using A, and beginning at outside edge of Flounce, pick up and knit 20 (21, 22, 24, 26) (27, 28, 30, 31) sts along CO edge of Flounce slit, then 20 (21, 22, 24, 26) (27, 28, 30, 31) sts along BO edge of slit. Complete as for Right Sleeve.

## BACK

Using A and Long-Tail Cast-On, CO 80 (88, 96, 104, 112) (120, 128, 136, 144) sts. Begin Seeded Stripe; work even until piece measures approximately 2" (5 cm) from the beginning, ending with a WS row.

## SHAPE BODY

**Body Decrease Row (RS):** K3, k2tog, work to last 5 sts, ssk, k3—2 sts decreased.
Repeat Body Decrease Row every 8 rows 7 more times—64 (72, 80, 88, 96) (104, 112, 120, 128) sts remain.
Work even until piece measures 10¼ (10½, 10, 10, 10) (10, 10¼, 10½, 10¾)" [26 (26.5, 25.5, 25.5, 25.5) (25.5, 26, 26.5, 27.5) cm] from the beginning, ending with a WS row.

## SHAPE ARMHOLES

BO 2 (3, 4, 4, 6) (7, 7, 8, 9) sts at beginning of next 2 rows, then 2 sts at beginning of next 2 (2, 2, 4, 4) (6, 6, 6, 8) rows—56 (62, 68, 72, 76) (78, 86, 92, 94) sts remain.
**Armhole Decrease Row (RS):** K1, k2tog, work to last 3 sts, ssk, k1—2 sts decreased.
Repeat Armhole Decrease Row every RS row 3 (4, 5, 5, 7) (7, 9, 10, 9) more times—48 (52, 56, 60, 60) (62, 66, 70, 74) sts remain.
Work even until armholes measure 7¼ (7½, 8¼, 8½, 8¾) (9, 9¼, 9½, 9¾)" [18.5 (19, 21, 21.5, 22) (23, 23.5, 24, 25) cm], ending with a WS row.

## SHAPE SHOULDERS

BO 4 (4, 6, 6, 6) (5, 5, 7, 7) sts at beginning of next 2 rows, then 4 (5, 5, 5, 5) (6, 6, 6, 7) sts at beginning of next 4 rows.
BO remaining 24 (24, 24, 28, 28) (28, 32, 32, 32) sts.

## RIGHT SLEEVE

With RS of Right Sleeve Flounce facing, using A, and beginning at outside edge of Flounce, pick up and knit 20 (21, 22, 24, 26) (27, 28, 30, 31) sts along BO edge of Flounce slit, then 20 (21, 22, 24, 26) (27, 28, 30, 31) sts along CO edge of slit—40 (42, 44, 48, 52) (54, 56, 60, 62) sts. Place a removable marker on the RS to indicate that this is the Right Sleeve.
Begin Seeded Stripe; work 5 rows even.

### SHAPE SLEEVE

**Increase Row (RS):** K3, M1L, work to last 3 sts, M1R, k3—2 sts increased.
Repeat Increase Row every 6 (6, 4, 4, 6) (2, 2, 2, 4) rows 4 (4, 2, 5, 5) (1, 3, 1, 5) time(s), then every 0 (0, 6, 6, 0) (4, 4, 4, 6) rows 0 (0, 3, 1, 0) (7, 7, 8, 3) time(s)—50 (52, 56, 62, 64) (72, 78, 80, 80) sts.
Work even until piece measures 5 (5, 5½, 5½, 6) (6, 6½, 6½, 7)" [12.5 (12.5, 14, 14, 15) (15, 16.5, 16.5, 18) cm] from pick-up row, ending with a WS row.

### SHAPE CAP

BO 2 (3, 4, 4, 6) (7, 7, 8, 9) sts at beginning of next 2 rows, then 2 sts at beginning of next 2 (2, 2, 4, 4) (6, 6, 6, 8) rows—42 (42, 44, 46, 44) (46, 52, 52, 46) sts remain.
**Decrease Row (RS):** K1, k2tog, work to last 3 sts, ssk, k1—2 sts decreased.
Repeat Decrease Row every RS row 3 (3, 4, 4, 3) (4, 5, 5, 5) more times—34 (34, 34, 36, 36) (36, 40, 40, 34) sts remain.
Work 17 (17, 19, 17, 21) (19, 15, 17, 23) rows even.
Repeat Decrease Row every RS row 4 (4, 4, 4, 4) (4, 5, 5, 2) more times—26 (26, 26, 28, 28) (28, 30, 30, 30) sts remain.
BO 2 sts at beginning of next 2 rows, then 3 sts at beginning of next 2 rows.
BO remaining 16 (16, 16, 18, 18) (18, 20, 20, 20) sts.

## RIGHT FRONT

Using A and Long-Tail Cast-On, CO 56 (60, 64, 68, 72) (76, 80, 84, 88) sts. Begin Seeded Stripe; work even until piece measures 2" (5 cm) from the beginning, ending with a WS row.

### SHAPE BODY

**Body Decrease Row (RS):** Work to last 5 sts, ssk, k3—1 st decreased.
Repeat Body Decrease Row every 8 rows 7 more times—48 (52, 56, 60, 64) (68, 72, 76, 80) sts remain.
Work even until piece measures 10¼ (10½, 10, 10, 10) (10, 10¼, 10½, 10¾)" [26 (20.5, 25.5, 25.5, 25.5) (25.5, 26, 26.5, 27.5) cm] from the beginning, ending with a RS row.

### SHAPE ARMHOLE

BO 2 (3, 4, 4, 6) (7, 7, 8, 9) sts at armhole edge once, then 2 sts 1 (1, 1, 2, 2) (3, 3, 3, 4) time(s)—44 (47, 50, 52, 54) (55, 59, 62, 63) sts remain.
**Armhole Decrease Row (RS):** Work to last 3 sts, ssk, k1—1 st decreased.
Repeat Armhole Decrease Row every RS row 3 (4, 5, 5, 7) (7, 9, 10, 9) more times—40 (42, 44, 46, 46) (47, 49, 51, 53) sts remain.
Work even until armhole measures 7¼ (7½, 8¼, 8½, 8¾) (9, 9¼, 9½, 9¾)" [18.5 (19, 21, 21.5, 22) (23, 23.5, 24, 25) cm], ending with a RS row.

### SHAPE SHOULDER

BO 4 (4, 6, 6, 6) (5, 5, 7, 7) sts at armhole edge once, then 4 (5, 5, 5, 5) (6, 6, 6, 7) sts twice—28 (28, 28, 30, 30) (30, 32, 32, 32) sts remain.
Work even if necessary until you have completed Row 2 of pattern.

### SHAPE COLLAR EXTENSION

*Note: Collar Extension is shaped using German Short Rows (see Special Techniques, page 221). Close each DS as you come to it.*
**Short Row 1 (RS):** With A, k20 (20, 20, 22, 22) (22, 24, 24, 24), turn;
**Short Row 2 (WS):** DS, k11 (11, 11, 13, 13) (13, 15, 15, 15), turn;
**Short Row 3:** DS, work to end.
**Row 4:** *K1, p1; repeat from * to last 3 sts, k3.
**Row 5:** With B, knit.

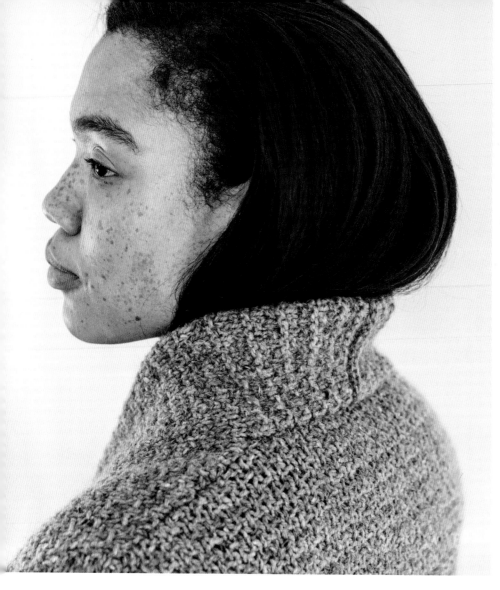

**Armhole Decrease Row (RS):** K3, k2tog, work to end—1 st decreased.
Repeat Armhole Decrease Row every RS row 3 (4, 5, 5, 7) (7, 9, 10, 9) more times—40 (42, 44, 46, 46) (47, 49, 51, 53) sts remain.
Work even until armhole measures 7¼ (7½, 8¼, 8½, 8¾) (9, 9¼, 9½, 9¾)" [18.5 (19, 21, 21.5, 22) (23, 23.5, 24, 25) cm], ending with a WS row.

### SHAPE SHOULDER

BO 4 (4, 6, 6, 6) (5, 5, 7, 7) sts at armhole edge once, then 4 (5, 5, 5, 5) (6, 6, 6, 7) sts twice—28 (28, 28, 30, 30) (30, 32, 32, 32) sts remain.
Work even if necessary until you have completed Row 2 of pattern.

### SHAPE COLLAR EXTENSION

*Note: Close each DS as you come to it.*
**Short Row 1 (RS):** With A, k20 (20, 20, 22, 22) (22, 24, 24, 24), turn;
**Short Row 2 (WS):** DS, k11 (11, 11, 13, 13) (13, 15, 15, 15), turn;
**Short Row 3:** DS, work to end.
**Row 4:** *K1, p1; repeat from * to last 3 sts, k3.
**Row 5:** With B, knit.
**Row 6:** *P1, k1; repeat from * to last 3 sts, k3.
Repeat Short Row 1–Row 6 four (4, 4, 5, 5) (5, 6, 6, 6) more times, then repeat Short Row 1–Row 5 once. Cut yarn, leaving a tail 3 times the width of your piece, and place sts on st holder.

### FINISHING

Block as desired.
With WSs of Right and Left Fronts together, join Collar Extensions using 3-Needle Bind-Off.
Sew shoulder seams. Sew edge of Collar to back neck edge. Fold Collar to WS and, using removable marker, pin Collar seam to center of back neck. Working from shoulder seam to shoulder seam, sew edge of Collar to WS of back neck. Fold Front edges to WS, 3½" (9 cm) in from edge, and steam to help set fold line. Sew in Sleeves, making sure to sew them into the correct armholes; sew side and Sleeve seams, sewing Sleeves all the way to bottom edge of Flounce.

**Row 6:** *P1, k1; repeat from * to last 3 sts, k3.
Repeat Short Row 1–Row 6 four (4, 4, 5, 5) (5, 6, 6, 6) more times, then repeat Short Row 1–Row 5 once. Cut yarn, leaving a tail 3 times the width of your piece, and place sts on st holder.

### LEFT FRONT

Using A and Long-Tail Cast-On, CO 56 (60, 64, 68, 72) (76, 80, 84, 88) sts.
Begin Seeded Stripe pattern; work even until piece measures approximately 2" (5 cm) from the beginning, ending with a WS row.

### SHAPE BODY

**Body Decrease Row (RS):** K3, k2tog, work to end—1 st decreased.
Repeat Body Decrease Row every 8 rows 7 more times—48 (52, 56, 60, 64) (68, 72, 76, 80) sts remain.
Work even until piece measures 10¼ (10½, 10, 10, 10) (10, 10¼, 10½, 10¾)" [26 (26.5, 25.5, 25.5, 25.5) (25.5, 26, 26.5, 27.5) cm] from the beginning, ending with a RS row.

### SHAPE ARMHOLE

BO 2 (3, 4, 4, 6) (7, 7, 8, 9) sts at armhole edge once, then 2 sts 1 (1, 1, 2, 2) (3, 3, 3, 4) time(s)—44 (47, 50, 52, 54) (55, 59, 62, 63) sts remain.

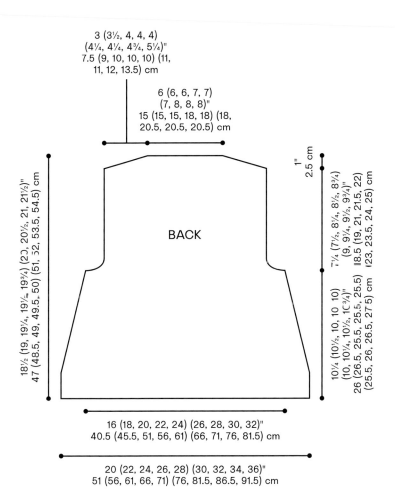

3 (3½, 4, 4, 4)
(4¼, 4¼, 4¾, 5¼)"
7.5 (9, 10, 10, 10) (11,
11, 12, 13.5) cm

6 (6, 6, 7, 7)
(7, 8, 8, 8)"
15 (15, 15, 18, 18) (18,
20.5, 20.5, 20.5) cm

BACK

1"
2.5 cm

7¼ (7½, 8¼, 8½, 8¾)"
(9, 9¼, 9½, 9¾)"
18.5 (19, 21, 21.5, 22)
(23, 23.5, 24, 25) cm

18½ (19, 19¼, 19½, 19¾) (20, 20½, 21, 21½)"
47 (48.5, 49, 49.5, 50) (51, 52, 53.5, 54.5) cm

10¼ (10½, 10, 10, 10)
(10, 10¼, 10½, 10¾)"
26 (26.5, 25, 25.5, 25.5)
(25.5, 26, 26.5, 27.5) cm

16 (18, 20, 22, 24) (26, 28, 30, 32)"
40.5 (45.5, 51, 56, 61) (66, 71, 76, 81.5) cm

20 (22, 24, 26, 28) (30, 32, 34, 36)"
51 (56, 61, 66, 71) (76, 81.5, 86.5, 91.5) cm

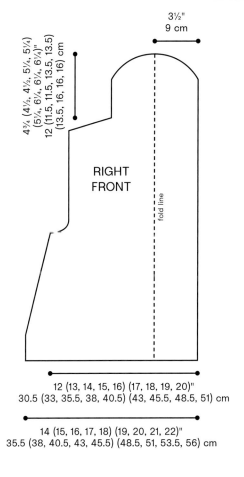

3½"
9 cm

4¾ (4½, 4½, 5¼, 5¼)
(5¼, 6¼, 6¼, 6¼)"
12 (11.5, 11.5, 13.5, 13.5)
(13.5, 16, 16, 16) cm

RIGHT
FRONT

fold line

12 (13, 14, 15, 16) (17, 18, 19, 20)"
30.5 (33, 35.5, 38, 40.5) (43, 45.5, 48.5, 51) cm

14 (15, 16, 17, 18) (19, 20, 21, 22)"
35.5 (38, 40.5, 43, 45.5) (48.5, 51, 53.5, 56) cm

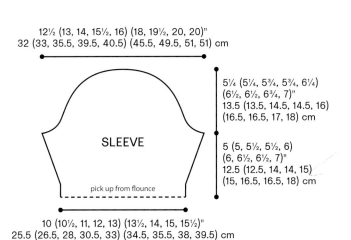

12½ (13, 14, 15½, 16) (18, 19½, 20, 20)"
32 (33, 35.5, 39.5, 40.5) (45.5, 49.5, 51, 51) cm

5¼ (5¼, 5¾, 5¾, 6¼)
(6½, 6½, 6¾, 7)"
13.5 (13.5, 14.5, 14.5, 16)
(16.5, 16.5, 17, 18) cm

SLEEVE

5 (5, 5½, 5½, 6)
(6, 6½, 6½, 7)"
12.5 (12.5, 14, 14, 15)
(15, 16.5, 16.5, 18) cm

pick up from flounce

10 (10½, 11, 12, 13) (13½, 14, 15, 15½)"
25.5 (26.5, 28, 30.5, 33) (34.5, 35.5, 38, 39.5) cm

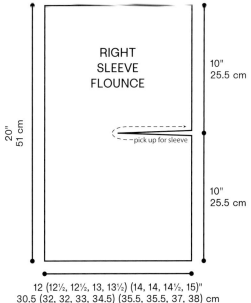

RIGHT
SLEEVE
FLOUNCE

10"
25.5 cm

pick up for sleeve

20"
51 cm

10"
25.5 cm

12 (12½, 12½, 13, 13½) (14, 14, 14½, 15)"
30.5 (32, 32, 33, 34.5) (35.5, 35.5, 37, 38) cm

## SQUARE WITH SLIT

## SLIT FOLDED OUTWARD

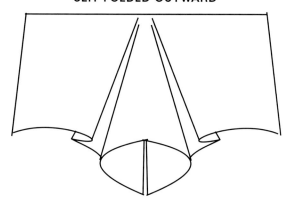

## HEXAGON WITH SLIT

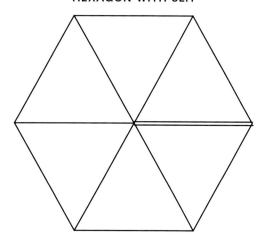

## SLIT FOLDED OUTWARD

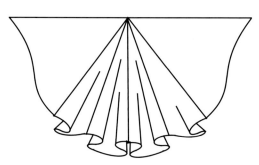

# DESIGN YOUR OWN

## DESIGNING GEORGIA

I knew from the outset that a fluttery box gracing the base of Georgia's sleeve would be the focal point of my design. Playing around with some fleece, I figured out that a split rectangle was the shape I needed. I had been studying photos of a ready-to-wear blouse and I thought that was the case, but I still needed to prove it to myself. The fleece also helped me determine what dimensions my split rectangle would be. The split needed to be half the width of the sleeve at its base so that when I picked up along the bound-off edge and continued along the cast-on edge, the total width would be correct for the bottom of the sleeve. I

guessed the rest of the dimensions by eyeing it. Holding the split open flat, as it would be when attached to the bottom of my sleeve, I held it up to an arm to see how long it draped and where, in relation to an arm, I needed to begin the rest of the sleeve. The remainder of the jacket would take a supporting role—I didn't want any other drama that might threaten to outshine the sleeves. The fronts fold inward to form their own facings. An extension of the fronts, the collar is shaped with subtle short rows to perfect the fit. The A-line shape is easy to wear, and the textured pattern stitch lies flat on its own, requiring no added finishing.

## SPLIT EXTENSIONS

The solid rectangle insertion in the center front of Waterfall (page 193) becomes interesting when set into a shaped opening, while a square, rectangle, or any polygon for that matter, split then splayed open, creates its own dramatic folds. Like the flounce of Georgia's sleeve, a split square could make a lovely shaped peplum in the back of a sweater, with the two sides of the split folded outward to become a horizontal line (opposite). Try the same with a hexagon knit back and forth, instead of in the round. Where else might you place these fluttery additions?

# Jabot

Semicircular flounces cascade down the center of this shawl like water down Multnomah Falls. Once destined to be worn over the shoulders, the repetition of folds proved so beguiling, the feature needed to be showcased up front, necessitating its transformation to a more capelet form. An abbreviated back and the fuller front are joined at the shoulders, allowing the tapered tails to curve into loose spirals from each shoulder.

**FINISHED MEASUREMENTS**
62" (157.5 cm) wide at widest point x 20½" (52 cm) long at longest point

**YARN**
Rauma Garn Alpakka Lin [48% baby alpaca/44% linen/8% wool; 191 yards (175 m)/1¾ ounces (50 g)]: 3 skeins #1386

*Note: Shawl uses nearly all of the third skein; you may wish to purchase an additional skein due to variations in individual gauge.*

**NEEDLES**
One 24" (60 cm) or longer circular needle, size US 6 (4 mm)

One 24" (60 cm) or longer circular needle, size US 8 (6 mm)

Change needle size if necessary to obtain correct gauge.

**NOTIONS**
Stitch markers

**GAUGE**
17 sts and 26 rows = 4" (10 cm) in St st

## PATTERN NOTES

This triangle shawl is worked from the long edge down. Stitches for the center Flounces are picked up from the slipped-stitch ribs in the center. The back is a plain, smaller triangle.
Unless otherwise indicated, slip all slipped sts purlwise wyib.

## FRONT

Using larger needle and Long-Tail Cast-On (see Special Techniques, page 221), CO 263 sts.
Change to smaller needle.
**Setup Row (WS):** P128 sts, pm, k2, p1, k1, p1, k2, pm, purl to end.

## SHAPE BODY

**Decrease Row:** K2, ssk, k2tog, knit to marker, sm, p2, slip 1, p2, slip 1, p2, knit to last 6 sts, ssk, k2tog, k2–4 sts decreased.
**Next Row:** Purl to marker, sm, k2, p1, k1, p1, k2, sm, purl to end.

Repeat last 2 rows 62 more times–15 sts remain.

## SHAPE POINT

**Row 1 (RS):** K2, ssk, k2tog, slip 1, p1, slip 1, ssk, k2tog, k2–11 sts remain.
**Row 2:** P5, k1, purl to end.
**Row 3:** K2, ssk, s2kp2, k2tog, k2–7 sts remain.
**Rows 4, 6, and 8:** Purl.
**Row 5:** K2, s2kp2, k2–5 sts remain.
**Row 7:** K1, s2kp2, k1–3 sts remain.
**Row 9:** S2kp2–1 st remains. Cut yarn and fasten off.

## LEFT FLOUNCE

Following diagrams, pick up and knit 1 st in each slipped st, picking up under both legs of st–63 sts.
Begin St st; work 2 rows even.
**Increase Row 1 (RS):** *K2, M1L; repeat from * to last 3 sts, k3–93 sts.
Work 5 rows even.
**Increase Row 2 (RS):** *K3, M1L; repeat from * to last 3 sts, k3–123 sts.
Work 5 rows even.
**Increase Row 3 (RS):** *K4, M1L; repeat from * to last 3 sts, k3–153 sts.
Work 5 rows even.
**Increase Row 4 (RS):** *K5, M1L; repeat from * to last 3 sts, k3–183 sts.
Work 5 rows even.
Using larger needle, BO all sts.

## RIGHT FLOUNCE

Following diagrams, pick up and knit 1 st in each slipped st, picking up under both legs of st–63 sts.
Begin St st; work 2 rows even.
**Increase Row 1 (RS):** K3, *M1R, k2; repeat from * to end–93 sts.
Work 5 rows even.
**Increase Row 2 (RS):** K3, *M1R, k3; repeat from * to end–123 sts.
Work 5 rows even.
**Increase Row 3 (RS):** K3, *M1R, k4; repeat from * to end–153 sts.
Work 5 rows even.
**Increase Row 4 (RS):** K3, *M1R, k5; repeat from * to end–183 sts.
Work 5 rows even.
Using larger needle, BO all sts.

## BACK

Using larger needle and Long-Tail Cast-On, CO 143 sts.
Change to smaller needle.
**Setup Row (WS):** Purl.

## SHAPE BODY

**Decrease Row (RS):** K2, ssk, k2tog, knit to last 6 sts, ssk, k2tog, k2–4 sts decreased.
**Next Row:** Purl.
Repeat the last 2 rows 31 more times–15 sts remain.

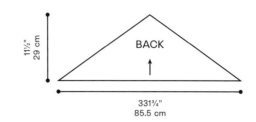

BACK

11½"
29 cm

33¾"
85.5 cm

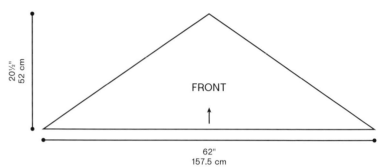

FRONT

20½"
52 cm

62"
157.5 cm

## SHAPE POINT

**Row 1 (RS):** K2, ssk, k2tog, k3, ssk, k2tog, k2—11 sts remain.

**Rows 2, 4, 6, and 8:** Purl.

**Row 3:** K2, ssk, s2kp2, k2tog, k2—7 sts remain.

**Row 5:** K2, s2kp2, k2—5 sts remain.

**Row 7:** K1, s2kp2, k1—3 sts remain.

**Row 9:** S2kp2—1 st remains. Cut yarn and fasten off.

## FINISHING

Steam or wet-block pieces, tugging at outer edges to stretch them out as much as possible. Sew Front to Back with a tack at each shoulder, 7" (18 cm) to either side of the center. Lay flat and arrange Flounces as shown in photos. Place a small tack at each place the Flounces meet to help keep the formation. Tack upper corners of Flounces to neckline.

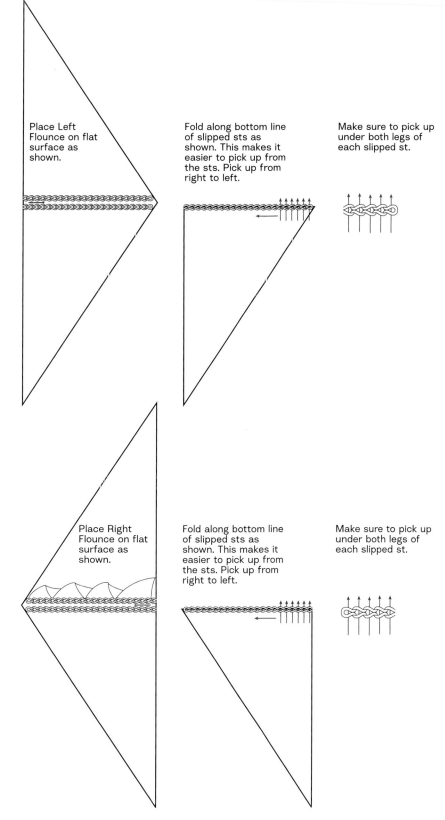

Place Left Flounce on flat surface as shown.

Fold along bottom line of slipped sts as shown. This makes it easier to pick up from the sts. Pick up from right to left.

Make sure to pick up under both legs of each slipped st.

Place Right Flounce on flat surface as shown.

Fold along bottom line of slipped sts as shown. This makes it easier to pick up from the sts. Pick up from right to left.

Make sure to pick up under both legs of each slipped st.

# DESIGN YOUR OWN

### DESIGNING JABOT

Veering the farthest from my original idea of designing with rectangles, Jabot contains no actual rectangles. Since semicircular strips make the best folded flounces, they became the shape of choice to continue my exploration of folds. Using the lessons I learned while designing pieces shown earlier in this book, knit-in slipped-stitch guidelines are worked as the front triangle is knit, becoming the foundation of the flounces. Stitches are picked up into each slipped stitch and then worked outward, with increases added every few rows to expand the flounce into the desired shape. A few well-placed sewing stitches ensure that the folds are secured in place and stay in their best formation. Originally, this piece was planned as a shawl to be worn like most others, either across the back or tied like a bandana. When the garment returned from my knitter, I realized my plan was flawed. The beauty of the folds seemed wasted on the back, and too much of the interest became obscured when tying the piece like a kerchief. Holding the be-ruffled triangle up to my own shoulders and chest in front of a mirror, it was clear that the folded ruffle, which resembles an eighteenth-century jabot, needed to be center front. I opted for an abbreviated back triangle sewn to the front at two shoulder points, making it possible to wear the result as a capelet.

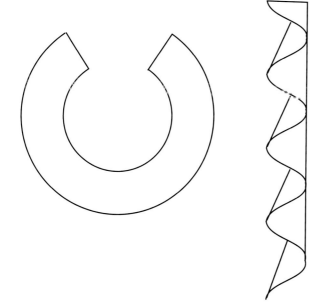

## FLOUNCES

To achieve the fullness needed for a flounce of deep undulating folds, the flounce needs to be constructed of a circular or a semicircular strip. If you were working with woven fabric, you'd cut strips in the shape of a circle or curved arch. While knitting, we can create the proper shape with increases. For Jabot, the first row of increases grows the number of stitches by half again. An inch later, the size increases by a third (a new stitch after every third stitch). In another inch, the increases are after every 4th stitch, an inch later, every 5th, and so on. When you think about it, it's like stacking bigger and bigger rectangles on top of each other, except the rectangles are all attached to each other and stretch to become a big arch. I didn't perform any fancy mathematics to figure out how to space the rows of increases. I did refer to a vintage book I love dearly, *Mary Thomas's Knitting Book*, for one of her circle-making formulas. I recommend looking at some of the other methods she uses to knit circles for more inspiration.

# Squash

The folded centerpiece of this top is inspired by the origami squash fold. The yoke starts out as a rectangle and is then transformed by decreases and short rows to fit beautifully on the shoulders and form an elegant V at the front neck and a shallow V at the back.

## FINISHED MEASUREMENTS

32 (36, 40, 44, 48) (52, 56, 60, 64)" [81.5 (91.5, 101.5, 112, 122) (132, 142, 152.5, 162.5) cm] chest

*Note: This piece is intended to be worn with approximately 2–4" (5–10 cm) positive ease.*

## YARN

Brooklyn Tweed Peerie [100% American merino wool; 210 yards (192 m)/1¾ ounces (50 g)] 5 (6, 6, 6, 7) (7, 8, 8, 9) skeins Morel

## NEEDLES

One pair straight needles, size US 3 (3.25 mm)

One circular needle, size US 3 (3.25 mm)

Change needle size if necessary to obtain correct gauge.

## NOTIONS

Stitch markers (including 1 in a unique color or style)

Removable stitch markers

## GAUGE

28 sts and 42 rows = 4" (10 cm) in St st, after blocking

## PATTERN STITCH

### 1×1 RIB

(any number of sts; 1-row repeat)
**Row 1 (RS):** *K1, p1; repeat from * to end, ending with k1 if an odd number of sts.

## PATTERN NOTES

The Back and Front of this top are both worked the same. They are worked flat from the bottom up, with a V-shaped divide in the center into which the Yoke and inserts will be sewn. The Yoke begins as two separate pieces that are joined at the center, then worked with short rows and decreases to shape the neck, shoulders, and center Back.

## BACK AND FRONT (BOTH ALIKE)

Using straight needles and Long-Tail Cast-On (see Special Techniques, page 221), CO 140 (154, 168, 182, 196) (210, 224, 238, 252) sts.
Knit 6 rows, purl 1 row.
Begin St st, beginning with a RS row; work even until piece measures 1" (2.5 cm) from the beginning.

## SHAPE BODY, CENTER CUTOUT, AND ARMHOLES

*Note: Body, Center Cutout, and Armhole shaping are worked at the same time. Body shaping begins first, then is completed after Center Cutout shaping begins. Center Cutout shaping continues while Armhole shaping is worked. Please read entire section through before beginning.*
**Body Decrease Row (RS):** K2, k2tog, knit to last 4 sts, ssk, k2—2 sts decreased.
Repeat Body Decrease Row every 8 rows 13 more times.
AT THE SAME TIME, when piece measures 7 (7, 7, 7½, 7½) (7½, 8, 8, 8)"

[18 (18, 18, 19, 19) (19, 20.5, 20.5, 20.5) cm] from the beginning, ending with a RS row, begin center cutout shaping. Place removable marker between 2 center sts.
**Division Row (WS):** Purl to marker, remove marker, join a second ball of yarn, purl to end.
Work both sides at the same time for remainder of piece.
**\*\*Center Cutout Single Decrease Row (RS):** Work to 3 sts before opening, ssk, k1; on second side, k1, k2tog, work to end—1 st decreased each side.
Purl 1 row.
Repeat last 2 rows once.
**Center Cutout Double Decrease Row (RS):** Work to 5 sts before opening, [ssk] twice, k1; on second side, k1, [k2tog] twice, work to end—2 st decreased each side.
Purl 1 row.
Repeat from \*\* 9 (11, 11, 11, 13) (13, 15, 15, 16) more times, then repeat Center Cutout Single Decrease Row every other row 4 (0, 0, 0, 2) (6, 1, 1, 4) more time(s).
AT THE SAME TIME, when piece measures 13 (13, 13, 13½, 13½) (13½, 14, 14, 14)" [33 (33, 33, 34.5, 34.5) (34.5, 35.5, 35.5, 35.5) cm] from the beginning, ending with a WS row, begin armhole shaping, as follows:
At each armhole edge, BO 4 (4, 4, 5, 6) (7, 7, 8, 9) sts once, 3 sts 2 (1, 1, 1, 1) (1, 1, 1, 1) time(s), 2 sts 0 (2, 4, 5, 4) (4, 5, 5, 4) times, then 1 st 0 (2, 2, 3, 7) (10, 11, 14, 18) times—2 sts remain when all shaping is complete. *Note: As you get close to the end of armhole shaping, you may find you don't have enough sts to work Center Cutout shaping exactly as given. If necessary, you may work single decreases at the Center Cutout instead of double decreases, or you may shift the decreases so that they are worked at the edge instead of 1 st in from the edge.*

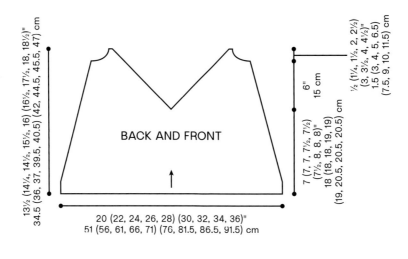

BACK AND FRONT

13½ (14¼, 14½, 15½, 16) (16½, 17½, 18, 18½)"
34.5 (36, 37, 39.5, 40.5) (42, 44.5, 45.5, 47) cm

20 (22, 24, 26, 28) (30, 32, 34, 36)"
51 (56, 61, 66, 71) (76, 81.5, 86.5, 91.5) cm

7 (7, 7, 7½, 7½)
(7½, 8, 8, 8)"
18 (18, 18, 19, 19)
(19, 20.5, 20.5, 20.5) cm

6"
15 cm

½ (1¼, 1½, 2, 2½)
(3, 3½, 4, 4½)"
1.5 (3, 4, 5, 6.5)
(7.5, 9, 10, 11.5) cm

YOKE

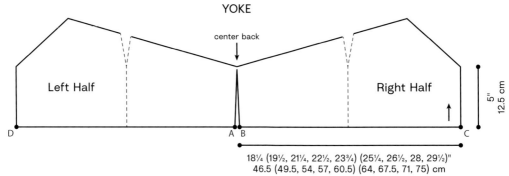

center back

Left Half

Right Half

5"
12.5 cm

D                                    A B                                    C

18¼ (19½, 21¼, 22½, 23¾) (25¼, 26½, 28, 29½)"
46.5 (49.5, 54, 57, 60.5) (64, 67.5, 71, 75) cm

## YOKE

### RIGHT HALF

Using straight needles and Long-Tail Cast-On, CO 128 (136, 148, 158, 166) (176, 186, 196, 206) sts.
Knit 2 rows, purl 1 row.
Begin St st, beginning with a RS row; work even until piece measures 5" (12.5 cm) from the beginning, ending with a WS row. Cut yarn and set aside, leaving sts on needle.

### LEFT HALF

Using circular needle, work as for Right Half. Do not cut yarn; leave sts on needle.

### JOIN HALVES

Place marker for shoulder shaping at center of each Half of Yoke [after 64 (68, 74, 79, 83) (88, 93, 98, 103) sts].

**Joining Row (RS):** Working across Left Half, knit to 5 sts before shoulder marker, ssk, k6 (slipping marker), k2tog, knit to last 2 sts of Left Half, k2tog, place unique marker for center Back; working across Right Half, ssk, knit to 5 sts before shoulder marker, ssk, k6 (slipping marker), k2tog, knit to end—250 (266, 290, 310, 326) (346, 366, 386, 406) sts.

### SHAPE SHOULDERS, CENTER BACK, AND CENTER FRONT

*Note: Center Front is shaped using German Short Rows (see Special Techniques, page 221).*
**Short Row 1 (WS):** Purl to last 4 sts, turn;
**Short Row 2 (RS):** DS, knit to 4 sts before center Back marker, ssk, k2tog, sm, ssk, k2tog, knit to last 4 sts, turn;
**Short Row 3:** Purl to 3 sts before DS from previous WS row, turn;

**Short Row 4:** DS, knit to 5 sts before shoulder marker, ssk, k6, k2tog, knit to 2 sts before center Back marker, k2tog, sm, ssk, knit to 5 sts before shoulder marker, ssk, k6, k2tog, knit to 3 sts before DS from previous RS row, turn;
**Short Row 5:** Purl to 3 sts before DS from previous WS row, turn;
**Short Row 6:** DS, knit to 4 sts before center Back marker, ssk, k2tog, sm, ssk, k2tog, knit to 3 sts before DS from previous RS row, turn;
**Short Row 7:** Purl to 3 sts before DS from previous WS row, turn;
Repeat Short Rows 4–7 until short rows interfere with shoulder shaping. At this point, discontinue working shoulder shaping and continue working center Back shaping and short rows as established. When short rows and center Back decreases cannot both be worked, on the following RS row, knit to end, closing each DS as you come to it.

Purl 1 row, closing each DS as you come to it.
Knit 3 rows.
BO all sts in 1×1 Rib.
Sew right and left edges together for 1½" (4 cm) from BO edge.

## SQUASH FOLD CENTER FRONT PANEL

With RS of Yoke facing, beginning at point A (see Schematic and Assembly Diagram), pick up and knit 35 sts from point A to center Front, 1 st in center Front seam, then 35 sts to point B—71 sts.
Begin St st; work even until piece measures 5" (12.5 cm) from pick-up row, ending with a WS row.
BO all sts.
Fold completed Center Front Panel in half widthwise so you have a 5" (12.5 cm) square. Using a tapestry needle and yarn, and working small running sts, hand sew layers together along a diagonal from outermost corner (opposite folded edge; shown in blue on Assembly Diagram) to center Front. Squash free flapping triangle along lines shown in red on Assembly Diagram (see detail photo) and steam press in place.

## CENTER BACK MITER

With RS of Yoke facing, pick up and knit 35 sts from point C (see Schematic and Assembly Diagram) to Center Back, then 35 sts to point D—70 sts.
Purl 1 row, placing marker between 2 center sts.
**Row 1 (RS):** Knit to 2 sts before marker, k2tog, sm, ssk, knit to end—2 sts decreased.
**Row 2:** Purl.
**Row 3:** Knit to 4 sts before marker, ssk, k2tog, sm, ssk, k2tog, knit to end—4 sts decreased.
**Row 4:** Purl.
Repeat Rows 1–4 ten times more—4 sts remain.
**Next Row (RS):** K2tog, ssk.
BO remaining 2 sts.

## FINISHING

Block pieces as desired. Sew side seams. Sew Yoke to Body.

## Assembly Diagram

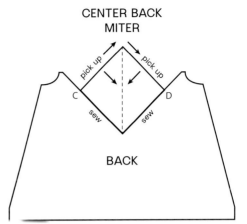

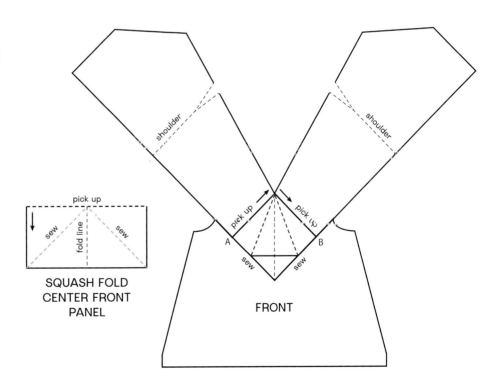

SQUASH FOLD CENTER FRONT PANEL

# DESIGN YOUR OWN

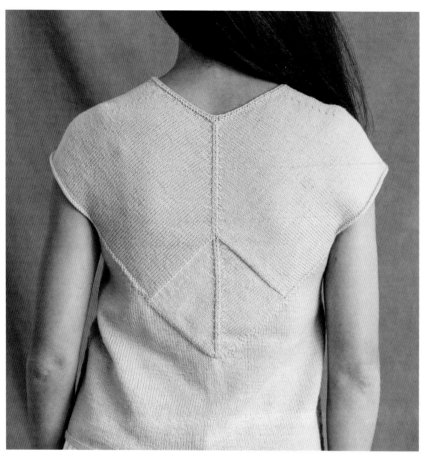

folded piece. I realized that just as the front piece was a tilted square, once folded, I was left with a tilted square to fill in at the center back. I thought about placing another folded piece in the center back, but it seemed a bit odd to me, and I thought it might be uncomfortable to have those multiple layers of knit on your center back when sitting back in a chair. I put a mitered square in its place. Of course, there were other options—aren't there always? One easier option would have been extending one of the long rectangles to fill the center space. At this point, I needed the help of a schematic to work out the remaining details. I make all of my schematics on my computer using the program EazyDraw. Any drawing program should do the trick. Good old paper, along with scissors and tape, can work, too, if you are persistent. I decided that the folded square should be 5 by 5" (12.5 by 12.5 cm). It had to be placed at a 45-degree angle in the center, and everything was built from there. After the schematic was built, with the neck and shoulders in place as I thought they should be, the tricky part was figuring out the easiest way to knit everything. In my drawing program, I grouped the part of the design in question—all of the yoke elements—and duplicated them so the original schematic stayed in place. I could then rotate the yoke to see how it might best be knit and clearly see what the dimension should be. I decided that casting on for the long side of the rectangle, then working straight for 5" (12.5 cm), was the easiest way to go before the shoulder, center back, and neck shaping began. Simplify as you go. I originally thought that the back neck might be straight across, until I realized that keeping the slope of the neck constant from the center front to the center back was much easier for everyone, and the back neck changed in a minor way.

## DESIGNING SQUASH

During the many years I dreamed about writing this book, I grabbed at every inspiration I saw, tearing pages from magazines, taking photos of store windows during my travels, and saving any folded garment I tripped across on Pinterest. The woven and sewn blouse that inspired Squash had a center element that looked very much like folded paper. That was the element I needed to reproduce in knit. Perusing books on origami, the Japanese art of paper folding, I discovered that the fold was a common one and even had a name:

the squash fold, called that because after folding diagonals together, the remaining flap is squashed down to make the flattened cone shape. Playing around with paper, I discovered that I needed a rectangle twice as long as it was high to achieve the squash fold I desired. Once that major detail was under control, the next step was figuring out how to complete the yoke. My aim was to keep the garment as simple as possible. Wrapping a rectangle around each shoulder would be a good start. With the help of my paper model (for more on paper models, see page 143) I figured out where the shoulder-wrapping rectangle needed to attach to the front

## FOLDED ADDITIONS

Once you get an idea—from an existing garment, paper fold you've seen, or who know where—you have to figure out how to achieve the fold, or at least something reminiscent of the inspiration. Even though it's rather scary to not know whether an idea will work, this is my favorite part. Begin with paper. It doesn't have to be life size or even to scale (yet). Start folding and learning, and don't let failures be a deterrent. You may start with a square and realize that you needed a longer rectangle. Trying is the only way to learn. You may find yourself coming up with different ideas based on the folds you've tried, even if they have little resemblance to your goal. Make notes and keep the folded bits! Referring to a book on origami may be a big help achieving the look you want. I'd recommend studying beginner guides. You'll want to start with the basics to really get your head into thinking about folding. I cannot claim to be a folding expert. I've made flapping paper cranes, and those boxes you inflate with your breath, since I was a kid, and I haven't progressed past those. Still, what is possible fascinates me. Pulling back from your explorations, think about how you are going to describe the maneuvers if you are going to share your finished idea with other knitters. It never hurts to simplify, even if the design is only for yourself.

# ABBREVIATIONS

**BO:** Bind off

**CO:** Cast on

**Dpn:** Double-pointed needle(s)

**K1-f/b:** Knit into the front loop and back loop of the same stitch to increase 1 stitch.

**K1-tbl:** Knit 1 stitch through the back loop.

**K2tog:** Knit 2 stitches together.

**K3tog:** Knit 3 stitches together.

**K:** Knit

**M1 or M1L (make 1-left slanting):** With the tip of the left-hand needle inserted from front to back, lift the strand between the 2 needles onto the left-hand needle; knit the strand through the back loop to increase 1 stitch.

**M1P or M1PR (make 1 purlwise-right slanting):** With the tip of the left-hand needle inserted from back to front, lift the strand between the 2 needles onto the left-hand needle; purl the strand through the front loop to increase 1 stitch.

**M1PL (make 1 purlwise-left slanting):** With the tip of the left-hand needle inserted from front to back, lift the strand between the 2 needles onto the left-hand needle; purl the strand through the back loop to increase 1 stitch.

**M1R (make 1-right slanting):** With the tip of the left-hand needle inserted from back to front, lift the strand between the 2 needles onto the left-hand needle; knit the strand through the front loop to increase 1 stitch.

**P1-f/b:** Purl into the front loop and back loop of the same stitch to increase 1 stitch.

**P1-tbl:** Purl 1 stitch through the back loop.

**P2tog:** Purl 2 stitches together.

**Pm:** Place marker

**P:** Purl

**Rnd(s):** Round(s)

**RS(s):** Right side(s)

**S2kp2:** Slip the next 2 stitches together to the right-hand needle as if to knit 2 together, k1, pass the 2 slipped stitches over.

**S3k2p3:** Slip the next 3 stitches together to the right-hand needle as if to knit 3 together, k2tog, pass the 3 slipped stitches over.

**Sm:** Slip marker

**Ssk (slip, slip, knit):** Slip the next 2 stitches to the right-hand needle one at a time as if to knit; return them to the left-hand needle one at a time in their new orientation; knit them together through the back loops.

**Sssk:** Same as ssk, but worked on the next 3 stitches.

**Ssp (slip, slip, purl):** Slip the next 2 stitches to the right-hand needle one at a time as if to knit; return them to the left-hand needle one at a time in their new orientation; purl them together through the back loops.

**St(s):** Stitch(es)

**Tbl:** Through the back loop(s)

**WS(s):** Wrong side(s)

**Wyib:** With yarn in back

**Wyif:** With yarn in front

**Yf:** Yarn front

**Yo:** Yarnover

# SPECIAL TECHNIQUES

### CABLE CAST-ON

Make a loop (using a slipknot) with the working yarn and place it on the left-hand needle (first stitch CO), knit into slipknot, draw up a loop but do not drop stitch from left-hand needle; place new loop on left-hand needle; *insert the tip of the right hand needle into the space between the last 2 stitches on the left-hand needle and draw up a loop; place the loop on the left-hand needle. Repeat from * for remaining stitches to be CO, or for casting on at the end of a row in progress.

### GERMAN SHORT ROWS

Work to specified turning point, then turn work. Slip 1 stitch purlwise to right-hand needle with yarn in front. Pull yarn over top of needle to back, creating a double stitch (DS) on the right-hand needle. If the next stitch to be worked is a knit stitch, leave yarn at back, and keep yarn tight when working the first stitch to ensure the double stitch stays in place. If the next stitch to be worked is a purl stitch, bring yarn to the front, ready to work the next stitch.

When short rows are completed, or when working progressively longer short rows, knit or purl the two legs (the one created by taking the yarn over the needle and the original slipped stitch) of the double stitch together. When counting stitches, always count the double stitch as a single stitch.

### GRAFTING LIVE STITCHES TO A CAST-ON EDGE

Using a blunt tapestry needle, thread a length of yarn approximately 4 times the length of the section to be joined. The front is the side closest to you and the back is the side farthest from you. Hold the live stitches in front with the needle tips pointing to the right; you will begin grafting the live stitches with the stitches on the front needle. Bring the cast-on edge up behind the live stitches, being careful not to twist the piece. You will begin grafting the cast-on stitches with the back side of the cast-on edge. Working from right to left, insert the tapestry needle into the first stitch on the front needle as if to purl, pull the yarn through, leaving the stitch on the needle; insert the tapestry needle purlwise under both legs of the first cast-on stitch on the back side of the cast-on edge, pull the yarn through; *insert the tapestry needle into the first stitch on the front needle as if to knit, pull the yarn through, remove the stitch from the needle; insert the tapestry needle into the next stitch on the front needle as if to purl, pull the yarn through, leaving the stitch on the needle; insert the tapestry needle under both legs of the next cast-on stitch on the back side of the cast-on edge as if to purl, pull the yarn through. Repeat from *, working 3 or 4 stitches at a time, then go back and adjust the tension to match the pieces being joined. When 1 live stitch remains, cut yarn and pass through the last live stitch and cast-on stitch to fasten off.

### LONG-TAIL CAST-ON

Leaving tail with about 1" (2.5 cm) of yarn for each stitch to be cast-on, make a slipknot in the yarn and place it on the right-hand needle, with the tail to the front and the working end to the back. Insert the thumb and forefinger of your left hand between the strands of yarn so that the working end is around your forefinger and the tail end is around your thumb, "slingshot" fashion; *insert the tip of the right-hand needle into the front loop on the thumb, hook the strand of yarn coming from the forefinger from back to front, and draw it through the loop on your thumb; remove your thumb from the loop and pull on the working yarn to tighten the new stitch on the right-hand needle; return your thumb and forefinger to their original positions, and repeat from * for remaining stitches to be CO.

### MATTRESS STITCH

Lay two pieces of fabric side by side, with RSs facing up. *Bring threaded needle under 2 strands of yarn near edge of first piece of fabric. Bring needle under 2 corresponding strands of yarn on second piece of fabric. Repeat from *, reinserting needle into the fabric at the point from which the needle last exited the fabric.

### PROVISIONAL (CROCHET CHAIN) CAST-ON

Using a crochet hook and smooth yarn (crochet cotton or ravel cord used for machine knitting), work a crochet chain with a few more chains than the number of stitches needed; fasten off. If desired, tie a knot on the fastened-off end to mark the end that you will be unraveling from later. Turn the chain over; with a needle 1 size smaller than required for the piece and working yarn, starting a few chains in from the beginning of the chain, pick up and knit one stitch in each bump at the back of the chain, leaving any extra chains at the end unworked.

Change to needle size required for project on first row.

When ready to work the live stitches, unravel the chain by loosening the fastened-off end and unzipping the chain, placing the live stitches on a spare needle.

### SLOPED BIND-OFF

To eliminate the stair-step look of standard bind-offs along a neck, armhole, or shoulder edge, work the sloped bind-off as follows: Bind off the first row in the usual manner. On the following row, work to the last stitch, slip the last stitch purlwise, turn. Slip the first 2 stitches purlwise, then pass the first slipped stitch over the last stitch to bind off the first stitch. Continue binding off the rest of the stitches in the usual manner.

### 3-NEEDLE BIND-OFF

Place the stitches to be joined onto two same-size needles; hold the pieces to be joined with the right or wrong sides facing each other, as directed in the pattern, and the needles parallel, both pointing to the right. Holding both needles in your left hand, using working yarn and a third needle the same size or one size larger, insert third needle into first stitch on front needle, then into first stitch on back needle; knit these two stitches together; *knit next stitch from each needle together (two stitches on right-hand needle); pass first stitch over second stitch to BO one st. Repeat from * until one stitch remains on third needle; cut yarn and fasten off.

# RESOURCES

**Ancient Arts**
ancientartsfibre.com

**Augustbird**
etsy.com/shop/augustbird

**Berroco**
berroco.com

**Blue Sky Fibers**
blueskyfibers.com

**Brooklyn Tweed**
brooklyntweed.com

**Dandelions and Daisies Fiber Arts**
dandelionsand
daisiesfiberarts.com

**The Fibre Co.**
thefibreco.com

**Halcyon Yarn**
halcyonyarn.com

**Handspun Hope**
handspunhope.org

**Hinterland**
hinterlandfarm.ca

**Harrisville Designs**
harrisville.com

**Hudson + West**
hudsonandwestco.com

**Jagger Spun**
jaggeryarn.com

**Jill Draper Makes Stuff**
jilldraper.com

**Julie Asselin**
julie-asselin.com

**mYak**
myak.it

**Neighborhood Fiber Co.**
neighborhoodfiberco.com

**Peace Fleece**
peacefleece.com

**Purl Soho**
purlsoho.com

**Quince & Co.**
quinceandco.com

**Rauma Garn**
raumagarn.no

**Rowan**
knitrowan.com

**Seacolors**
getwool.com

**Shibui Knits**
shibuiknits.com

**Spincycle Yarns**
spincycleyarns.com

**Sugar Bush Yarns**
sugarbushyarns.com

**DURING THE WRITING** of this book, I relied on sample knitters not only to knit the garments but to patiently and intelligently catch any problems with my original instructions as well. Thanks for your invaluable help: Nancy Brown, Janet D'Alesandre, Lynn Marlow, Patricia McMullen, Cindy Prevett, Elke Probst, and Martha Wissing. I am also grateful for the talents brought to this book by Caroline Goddard's photography and Emily Nora O'Neil's styling. They are a talented team, bringing their intelligence, knowledge, and a like-minded aesthetic to this project. My gratitude and thanks also go to models Alexis Manson, Lisa Goddard, and, playing a dual role, Emily Nora O'Neil.

This book would not be possible without the efforts and technical editing talents of Sue McCain, whom I have had the pleasure to work with starting with my first book, *Knitting Nature*. Thanks also to my editor, Shawna Mullen, who shares my geeky and unusual fascination with coelacanths.

Thanks again to my design mentor, Margery Winter, who taught me invaluable lessons about thinking differently—about thinking outside of the box.

Special thanks to my husband, John Ranta, for his constant, daily support, through good times and through the pandemic times in which this book was written.

Editor: Shawna Mullen
Designer: Heesang Lee
Managing Editor: Lisa Silverman
Production Manager: Kathleen Gaffney

Library of Congress Control Number: 2021932514

ISBN: 978-1-4197-4968-1
eISBN: 978-1-64700-046-2

Printed and bound in China
10 9 8 7 6 5 4 3 2 1

Abrams books are available at special discounts when
purchased in quantity for premiums and promotions as well as
fundraising or educational use. Special editions can also be
created to specification. For details, contact specialsales
@abramsbooks.com or the address below.

Abrams® is a registered trademark of Harry N. Abrams, Inc.

ABRAMS The Art of Books
195 Broadway, New York, NY 10007
abramsbooks.com